Apache Tomcat 7 Essentials

Learn Apache Tomcat 7 step-by-step through a practical approach, achieving a wide vision of enterprise middleware along with building your own middleware servers, and administrating 24x7x365

Tanuj Khare

open source*

community experience distilled

BIRMINGHAM - MUMBAI

Apache Tomcat 7 Essentials

First published: March 2012

Production Reference: 1160312

Published by Packt Publishing Ltd.
Livery Place
35 Livery Street
Birmingham B3 2PB, UK..

ISBN 978-1-84951-662-4

www.packtpub.com

Cover Image by Vinayak Chittar (vinayak.chittar@gmail.com)

Credits

Author
Tanuj Khare

Reviewers
Zeeshan Chawdhary
Ty Lim
Vidyasagar N V

Acquisition Editor
Usha Iyer

Lead Technical Editor
Susmita Panda

Technical Editor
Unnati Shah

Copy Editor
Laxmi Subramanian

Project Coordinator
Vishal Bodwani

Proofreader
Linda Morris

Indexer
Rekha Nair

Graphics
Valentina D'Silva
Manu Joseph

Production Coordinator
Alwin Roy

Cover Work
Alwin Roy

About the Author

Tanuj Khare has been a professional in IT for over six years. He is involved in process improvements using the ITIL framework and techniques such as Lean Six Sigma. He is MCSA and ITIL certified, and has expertise in handling critical production server issues. He also has a track record of dealing with many complex problems. His quick resolution to issues faced in the production environment has helped his team and clients in a big way.

Tanuj has **Subject Matter Expertise (SME)** in Tomcat, WebLogic, and JBoss server administration. His experience includes working with large-enterprise web hosting environments for J2EE containers with small teams, and his quick turnaround time gave on-time delivery. Apart from this, his technical expertise in Root Cause Analysis, Problem Management, Migration of enterprise applications, and upgrade of web application servers are commendable. Up to now, he has migrated more than 100 enterprise applications and upgraded J2EE web applications. He has also managed environments with over 1000 middleware instances.

Apart from work life, Tanuj enjoys playing Table Tennis and exploring new technologies. He is a good dancer. This is his first book.

Acknowledgement

I would like to express my gratitude to all the people who have helped me to make this book better. I thank Ranveer Chandel, who has helped me to provide high technical standards for this book.

I would like to thank Archana Kannoujia, who has patiently helped me to improve my writing style.

I would like to thank Mitesh Parikh and Giri Moturi for their support.

I would like to thank Usha Iyer, Vishal Bodwani, Susmita Panda, and everyone else at Packt Publishing for all their hard work to get this book published. A special thanks to Unnati Shah for her hard work and dedication to get this book published.

I would like to thank Ty Lim, Vidyasagar N V, and Zeeshan Chawdhury for providing their valuable guidance and support that helped me achieve the high technical standards.

And finally, I'd like to thank all my colleagues and friends, with whom I've worked throughout my career, for contributing to my professional development.

About the Reviewers

Zeeshan Chawdhary is the CTO of Wcities Inc., a location-based travel content provider, running technical operations from their Technical Headquarters in Mumbai.

He is a do-it-all and code-in-any-language guy, having worked with various technologies from 3D gaming to consumer websites, from iPhone apps to serving over 30 million hits over the Cloud.

He is currently writing two real-world-use books with Packt Publishing which are, *iPhone Location Aware Applications by Example - Beginners Guide* and *Windows Phone 7.5 - Building Location Aware Applications.*

He can be reached at `imzeeshan` on Twitter. He currently blogs at `http://justgeeks.in`.

I would like to thank the great people at Packt for letting me review this book. Special thanks to Vishal Bodwani, Susmita Panda, Leena Purkait, Amey Kanse, Alina Lewis, and a special mention for Mary Nadar, for having introduced me to the Packt family.

Ty Lim has been in the IT industry for over 15 years. He has worked for several startup companies in the mid 1990s and found himself working at several major corporations after his stint in Silicon Valley. He has worked in the following industries: Software Development, Consulting, Healthcare, Telecommunications, and Finance. He has experience in utilizing JBoss, Tomcat, and WebSphere middleware technologies. He holds a Bachelor of Science degree in Computer Science from the University of the Pacific, and is currently pursuing a Master of Science degree in CIS from Boston University.

He has also worked on *IBM WebSphere Application Server v7.0 Security, Packt Publishing*.

I would like to thank all my friends and family for their continued support. I am truly blessed to have such great support. It is because of all of you that I consider myself a very happy man.

Vidyasagar N V was interested in Computer Science since his early age. Some of his serious work in computers and computer networks began during his high school days. Later, he went to the prestigious institute of technology, Banaras Hindu University for his B.Tech. He has been working as a Software Developer, Data Expert, developing and building scalable systems since then. He has worked with a variety of 2nd, 3rd, and 4th generation languages. He has also worked with Flat files, Indexed files, Hierarchical databases, Network databases, Relational databases, NoSQL databases, Hadoop, and related technologies.

Currently, he is working as a Senior Developer at Ziva Software Pvt. Ltd, developing a big data-based structured data extraction technique from the Web and local information. He enjoys producing high-quality software, web-based solutions, and designing secure and scalable data systems.

He has also worked on *PHP and MongoDB Web Development Beginner's Guide, Packt Publishing.*

He can be reached at `vidyasagar1729@gmail.com`.

I thank the almighty for giving me such a blessed life and thank my parents, Mr. N. Srinivasa Rao and Mrs. Latha Rao, and my family who supported and backed me throughout my life. I thank my friends and all those people who donated their time, effort, and expertise by participating in open source software projects. Also, thanks to Packt Publishing for selecting me as one of the technical reviewers for this wonderful book. It is my honor to be a part of this book.

www.PacktPub.com

Support files, eBooks, discount offers and more

You might want to visit www.PacktPub.com for support files and downloads related to your book.

Did you know that Packt offers eBook versions of every book published, with PDF and ePub files available? You can upgrade to the eBook version at www.PacktPub.com and as a print book customer, you are entitled to a discount on the eBook copy. Get in touch with us at service@packtpub.com for more details.

At www.PacktPub.com, you can also read a collection of free technical articles, sign up for a range of free newsletters and receive exclusive discounts and offers on Packt books and eBooks.

http://PacktLib.PacktPub.com

Do you need instant solutions to your IT questions? PacktLib is Packt's online digital book library. Here, you can access, read and search across Packt's entire library of books.

Why Subscribe?

- Fully searchable across every book published by Packt
- Copy and paste, print and bookmark content
- On demand and accessible via web browser

Free Access for Packt account holders

If you have an account with Packt at www.PacktPub.com, you can use this to access PacktLib today and view nine entirely free books. Simply use your login credentials for immediate access.

I would like to dedicate this book to my mom, Mrs. Shashi Khare and dad, Mr. Rajkumar Khare, for standing beside me during the writing of this book.

Without their support and encouragement, completing this book would have been a much more difficult task.

Table of Contents

Preface   **1**

Chapter 1: Installation of Tomcat 7   **7**

  History of Tomcat   **8**

    Tomcat support matrix   8

    Features and enhancements of Apache Tomcat 7   10

      Web application memory leak detection and prevention   10

      Servlet 3.0   10

      Improved logging   11

      Aliases   11

  Installation of Tomcat 7   **12**

    How to download the Tomcat software   12

      Binary package   13

      RPM/exe   14

      Source   14

    Prerequisites for the Tomcat 7 installation   14

      Installation of Java   15

      Configuration of OS environment variables   21

    Installation of Apache Tomcat 7   27

      Installation on a Windows environment   27

      Installation on a Linux environment   31

    Startup and shutdown of Tomcat services   32

      Services in Windows   32

      Services in Linux   33

      Startup script   35

      Shutdown script   35

    Verification of Tomcat status   36

  Common problems and troubleshooting in installation   **37**

    Error: Permission denied for the Java binary   37

    Error: Tomcat is not able to find JAVA_HOME   38

    Error: Error in the logs showing port already in use   38

  Summary   **38**

Chapter 2: Configuration and Deployment	**39**
Configuration files and their usage	**39**
Configuration of Tomcat 7	**41**
DataSource configuration	42
JDBC	44
JNDI	44
DataSource	44
Comparison of the datasource for common databases	**49**
Tomcat Manager configuration	50
Enabling the Tomcat Manager	51
Context path	55
Enabling the context path	56
Deployment in Tomcat 7	**59**
Structure of the WebArchive	59
Archive Files	60
Types of deployment	**62**
Ways of application deployment in Tomcat 7	63
Common issues in deployment, configuration, and their troubleshooting	**65**
Summary	**67**
Chapter 3: Performance Tuning	**69**
Performance tuning for Tomcat 7	**69**
Why we need performance tuning?	70
How to start performance tuning	**71**
Tomcat components tuning	**73**
Types of connectors for Tomcat 7	73
Java HTTP Connector	74
Java AJP Connector	74
APR (AJP/HTTP) Connector	74
Thread optimization for Tomcat 7	75
Shared thread pool (shared executor)	75
Dedicated thread pool	76
Shared thread pool versus dedicated thread pool	76
maxThreads	76
maxKeepAlive	77
JVM tuning	**77**
Why do we need to tune the JDK for Tomcat?	78
JMAP (Memory Map)	79
How to increase the heap size in Tomcat 7	81
Garbage collection	82
JVM options	84
Standard options	84
Non-standard options	85
Parameters displayed in the logs for GC	87

SurvivorRatio	87
OS tuning	**88**
Summary	**89**
Chapter 4: Integration of Tomcat with the Apache Web Server	**91**
User request flow (web/application level)	**91**
Why the Apache HTTP server	**92**
Installation of the Apache HTTP	**93**
Apache HTTP installation on Windows	94
How to monitor the Apache service	99
Installation of Apache HTTP on Linux (non-DOS environment)	100
Apache Portable Runtime	103
Apache Jserv protocol	**109**
Installation and configuration of mod_jk	109
Installation of mod_jk	110
Configuration of mod_jk in Apache	112
mod_proxy configuration	116
Comparison between mod_jk and mod_proxy	117
IIS integration with Tomcat 7	**117**
Prerequisites	117
Steps for installation	118
Common issues and troubleshooting for integration	**121**
Summary	**123**
Chapter 5: Securing Tomcat 7	**125**
Tomcat Manager	**125**
Tomcat security permissions	**126**
catalina.properties	126
catalina.policy	127
System Code permissions	127
Catalina Code permissions (Tomcat core permission)	128
Web application permissions	129
tomcat-users.xml	131
server.xml	131
Enabling Tomcat Manager	**132**
How to enable the Tomcat Manager	132
Securing Tomcat 7 for production	**132**
Tomcat settings	133
Connector Port	133
Slimming of Tomcat application	134
Disable hot deployment	135
Non-Tomcat settings	135
Service as a separate user	135
Firewall	136
Password	137

SSL configuration on Tomcat 7	**139**
Types of SSL certificates	139
Process of installing SSL	139
Summary	**143**
Chapter 6: Logging in Tomcat 7	**145**
JULI	**145**
Loggers, appenders, and layouts	**147**
Types of logging in Tomcat 7	**148**
Application log	149
Server log	149
Console log	149
Access log	151
Host manager	152
Types of log levels in Tomcat 7	**153**
Log4j	**155**
Log level for log4j	155
How to use log4j	156
Log level mapping	157
Values for Tomcat 7	**157**
Log analysis	**159**
Helpful commands for log analysis	160
Summary	**161**
Chapter 7: Troubleshooting in Tomcat	**163**
Common problem areas for web administrators	**164**
How to troubleshoot a problem	**165**
Slowness issue in applications	165
How to solve slowness issues in Tomcat 7	166
Troubleshooting at the database level	171
How to obtain a thread dump in Tomcat 7	**174**
Thread dump using Kill command	174
Thread dump using jstack	175
How to analyze the thread dump for Tomcat instance	176
Thread dump analysis using Samurai	177
Thread dump analysis using the Thread Dump Analyzer	178
Errors and their solutions	182
JVM (memory) issues	183
Database-related issues	185
Web server benchmarking	**188**
ApacheBench	188
JMeter	189
Summary	**189**

Chapter 8: Monitoring and Management of Tomcat 7   191
Different ways of monitoring   192
Monitoring setup for a web application and database server   193
Tomcat Manager in Tomcat 7   194
Monitoring in Tomcat 7   196
  Summary of the Server Status of Tomcat 7   196
    Complete Server Status of Tomcat 7   198
JConsole configuration on Tomcat 7   201
  Remote JMX enabling   202
  How to connect to the JConsole   203
  Different tabs for the JConsole and their features   205
    Memory overview   205
    Threads overview   206
    VM Summary and Overview   207
    MBeans   209
Summary   213

Chapter 9: Clustering in Tomcat 7   215
What is a cluster?   216
  Benefits of clustering   216
  Disadvantages of clustering   217
Clustering architecture   217
  Vertical clustering   218
    Advantages of vertical clustering   218
    Disadvantages of vertical clustering   219
  Horizontal clustering   219
    Advantages of horizontal clustering   220
    Disadvantages of horizontal clustering   220
Vertical clustering in Apache Tomcat 7   220
  Installation of the Tomcat instance   221
  Configuration of a vertical cluster   221
    Configuration of instance 1   222
    Configuration of instance 2   224
  Apache web server configuration for vertical clustering   228
Horizontal clustering in Apache Tomcat 7   229
  Installation of the Tomcat instance   230
  Configuration of the cluster   230
    Configuration of instance 1   230
    Configuration of instance 2   233
  Apache web server configuration for horizontal clustering   235
Testing of the clustered instance   237
Monitoring of Tomcat clustering   238
Summary   239

Chapter 10: Tomcat Upgrade	**241**
Different types of environment	**241**
Development environment	242
Quality Assurance environment	242
Staging environment	242
Production environment	242
Life cycle of the upgrade	**242**
Tomcat upgrade from 6 to 7	**244**
Prerequisites for Tomcat 7	245
Installation of Tomcat 7 for the upgrade	245
Configuration of Tomcat 7	246
JVM configuration	247
Database connection settings	248
Application migration	249
Alias configuration	250
ITIL process implementation	**250**
Availability management	250
Capacity management	251
Service Transition	251
Summary	**252**
Chapter 11: Advanced Configuration for Apache Tomcat 7	**253**
Virtual hosting	**254**
Name-based virtual hosting	254
IP-based virtual hosting	255
Virtual hosting in Tomcat 7	**256**
Hostname aliases	**258**
Multiple applications hosting on a single Tomcat 7 instance	**258**
Multiple Tomcat environments—Development/QA/Stage/Production	**259**
Tuning cache	**260**
Optimization of Tomcat 7	**261**
Running Tomcat 7 as a non privileged user	261
Summary	**262**
Index	**263**

Preface

This book will help you resolve these issues and boost your confidence in handling Apache Tomcat 7 administration using the tips, tricks, and best practices used by various industry experts to maintain their middleware infrastructure. The best thing that the author did while designing the content is a practical solution, with a detailed description of why we are doing this solution.

Apache Tomcat (or Jakarta Tomcat, or simply Tomcat) is an open source servlet container developed by The Apache Software Foundation. The latest major stable release, Apache Tomcat version 7, implements the Servlet 3 and JavaServer Pages 2 specifications from the Java Community Process. It includes many additional features that make it a useful platform for developing and deploying web applications and web services.

Apache Tomcat 7 Essentials follows a practical approach to explain installing, configuring, and maintaining Tomcat. It helps you to understand the middleware architecture to host multiple websites and also provides the confidence to implement middleware support. It imparts to you the capacity to resolve migration issues and also provides regular maintenance solutions. This is the first, and only, book to cover upgrading to Tomcat 7 from the previous versions.

The journey of the reader starts at the beginner's level and ends at the expert level. The content is designed in such a way that it balances the theory and practical approach for understanding concepts related to handling middleware and web issues.

In this book, you will go through a three-phase life cycle. The first cycle consists of the installation, configuration of Tomcat 7 on different OSes, other configurations related to the JDBC, port, deployment, and so on.

The second phase deals with the building of an enterprise application setup and high availability architectures (clustering and load balancing). The third and critical phase will teach you to handle critical issues, performance tuning, and the best practices for various environments such as Dev/QA/Stage/Production.

This book gives you a wider vision of using Tomcat 7 in web technologies and the skill to optimize its performance using Apache Tomcat 7.

What this book covers

Chapter 1, Installation of Tomcat, covers the Apache Tomcat history and the new features introduced in Tomcat 7. The step-by-step installation of Tomcat 7 on Windows and Linux operating systems and common problems that may arise during the installation and their possible solutions are also discussed.

Chapter 2, Configuration and Deployment, covers the configuration of Tomcat including the DataSource configuration for different databases such as Oracle, MySQL, and PostgreSQL, and Context Path creation using an application. Various ways to perform deployment including deployment using Tomcat Manager for a sample application and troubleshooting common issues are also discussed.

Chapter 3, Performance Tuning, explains the different ways of performance improvement and techniques in Apache Tomcat 7. Step-by-step configurations for Connectors, JVM performance tuning, and OS parameter optimization are also covered.

Chapter 4, Integration of Tomcat with the Apache Web Server, explains the integration of Apache/IIS with Tomcat 7, integration of various components such as mod_jk, mod_proxy, and real-time issues which may arise during integration, along with their solutions.

Chapter 5, Securing Tomcat 7, explains the various policies of Tomcat 7 and its functionalities such as the Catalina policy and System level policy. Measures to enable security and their benefits such as SSL, best practices used in real-time industries to secure Tomcat 7 in the production environment, by doing the configuration change and SSL implementation are also covered.

Chapter 6, Logging in Tomcat 7, explains the different methods of enabling logs in Tomcat 7—log4j and JULI. Also, the best practices used for log analysis, tips, and tricks are discussed.

Chapter 7, Troubleshooting in Tomcat, covers different issues faced by the application/web administrators in a real-time environment, how to avoid these issues in the production environment using different techniques with errors and their solutions, thread dump analysis and tools used for thread dump analysis, memory issues, steps for troubleshooting real-time problems, and web server benchmarking.

Chapter 8, Monitoring and Management of Tomcat 7, explains various processes of monitoring in Tomcat 7, components using Tomcat Manager and JConsole, such as different ways of monitoring, how monitoring is done in Tomcat 7, JConsole, and how it is used.

Chapter 9, Clustering in Tomcat 7, explains clustering of Tomcat 7 and its implementation technique. Topics included are clustering architecture, horizontal and vertical clusters and their benefits, implementation of horizontal and vertical clustering on Tomcat 7, and verification of clusters.

Chapter 10, Tomcat Upgrade, explains various strategies used in the upgrade from Tomcat 6 to Tomcat 7 and the various steps followed during the upgrade process such as the life cycle of the upgrade, upgrade configuration of Tomcat 7, DataSource configuration, and discussions on various ITIL processes used during upgrade.

Chapter 11, Advanced Configuration for Apache Tomcat 7, explains the advanced configuration of Tomcat 7 and its optimization parameters. Key points covered in the environment are virtual hosting, features of Development/QA/Stage/Production, Tomcat as a service, and running Tomcat as a non privileged user.

What you need for this book

To understand the contents of this book, you should have a basic knowledge of Windows or Linux operating systems and it is an added advantage if you have some knowledge in Java.

Who this book is for

If you are a J2EE Administrator, Migration Administrator, Technical Architect, or Project Manager for a web hosting domain, and are interested in Apache Tomcat 7, then this book is for you. If you are responsible for the installation, configuration, and management of Tomcat 7, then this book will be of help to you too.

Conventions

In this book, you will find a number of styles of text that distinguish between different kinds of information. Here are some examples of these styles, and an explanation of their meaning.

Code words in text are shown as follows: "Due to Tomcat 7's support for web fragments, developers now don't need to implement the specific library configurations for their application web.xml."

A block of code is set as follows:

```
# .bash_profile
# Get the aliases and functions
if [ -f ~/.bashrc ];then
        . ~/.bashrc
fi
# User specific environment and start-up programs
JAVA_HOME=/opt/jdk1.6.0_24
PATH=$JAVA_HOME/bin:$PATH:$HOME/bin
export PATH JAVA_HOME
unset USERNAME
```

When we wish to draw your attention to a particular part of a code block, the relevant lines or items are set in bold:

```
<Executor name="tomcatThreadPool"
   namePrefix="catalina-exec-"
   maxThreads="150"
   minSpareThreads="4"/>
```

Any command-line input or output is written as follows:

```
[root@localhost opt]# cksum apache-tomcat-7.0.12.zip
```

New terms and **important words** are shown in bold. Words that you see on the screen, in menus or dialog boxes for example, appear in the text like this: "The previous screenshot shows the packages which are available in md5, and by clicking on **md5** on the website, we can compare the checksum generated in our system with the value given on the site."

Warnings or important notes appear in a box like this.

 Tips and tricks appear like this.

Reader feedback

Feedback from our readers is always welcome. Let us know what you think about this book—what you liked or may have disliked. Reader feedback is important for us to develop titles that you really get the most out of.

To send us general feedback, simply send an e-mail to feedback@packtpub.com, and mention the book title through the subject of your message.

If there is a topic that you have expertise in and you are interested in either writing or contributing to a book, see our author guide on www.packtpub.com/authors.

Customer support

Now that you are the proud owner of a Packt book, we have a number of things to help you to get the most from your purchase.

Downloading the example code

You can download the example code files for all Packt books you have purchased from your account at http://www.packtpub.com. If you purchased this book elsewhere, you can visit http://www.packtpub.com/support and register to have the files e-mailed directly to you.

Errata

Although we have taken every care to ensure the accuracy of our content, mistakes do happen. If you find a mistake in one of our books—maybe a mistake in the text or the code—we would be grateful if you would report this to us. By doing so, you can save other readers from frustration and help us improve subsequent versions of this book. If you find any errata, please report them by visiting http://www.packtpub.com/support, selecting your book, clicking on the **errata submission form** link, and entering the details of your errata. Once your errata are verified, your submission will be accepted and the errata will be uploaded to our website, or added to any list of existing errata, under the Errata section of that title.

Piracy

Piracy of copyright material on the Internet is an ongoing problem across all media. At Packt, we take the protection of our copyright and licenses very seriously. If you come across any illegal copies of our works, in any form, on the Internet, please provide us with the location address or website name immediately so that we can pursue a remedy.

Please contact us at copyright@packtpub.com with a link to the suspected pirated material.

We appreciate your help in protecting our authors, and our ability to bring you valuable content.

Questions

You can contact us at questions@packtpub.com if you are having a problem with any aspect of the book, and we will do our best to address it.

1
Installation of Tomcat 7

Apache Tomcat is an open source Java-based web and servlet container, which is used to host Java-based applications. It was first developed for Jakarta Tomcat. Due to an increase in demand, it was later hosted as a separate project called Apache Tomcat, which is supported by The Apache Software Foundation. It was initially developed by James Duncan Davidson, a software architect at Sun Microsystems. He later helped make this project open source and played a key role in donating this project from Sun Microsystems to The Apache Software Foundation. Tomcat implements the **Java Servlet** and the **JavaServer Pages (JSP)** specifications from Sun Microsystems, and provides a "pure Java" HTTP web server environment for Java code to run.

Apache Tomcat version 7.0 implements the Servlet 3.0 and Java Server Pages 2.2 specifications from the Java Community Process. It includes many additional features that makes it a useful platform for developing and deploying web applications and web services.

In this chapter, we will discuss the following topics:

- Introduction to Tomcat 7
- Features of Tomcat 7
- Installation of Tomcat
    - Prerequisites for Tomcat 7 installation
    - Installation on Linux and Windows operating systems
- Common areas of troubleshooting during installation

History of Tomcat

Tomcat was first introduced to the open source group in 1999 and its first version was released with 3.0.x version. Since then, it has been greatly supported by the open source community and widely accepted in the IT industry. In the current scenario, Tomcat is running in production environments, as well as being used for mission-critical projects in various industries. The following mentioned details give us a quick history of the versions.

Over the 12 years of of its successful journey, Tomcat has reached various states and given the IT industry various releases. Tomcat road maps outlined with their stable releases are mentioned as follows:

Version	Release Date	Description
3.0.x. (initial release)	1999	Merger of donated Sun Java Web Server code and ASF, and implements Servlet 2.2 and JSP 1.1 specifications.
3.3.2	March 9, 2004	Latest 3.x release.
4.1.40	June 25, 2009	Latest 4.x release.
5.5.32	February 1, 2011	Latest 5.x release.
6.0.32	February 3, 2011	Latest 6.x release.
7.0.0 beta	June 29, 2010	First Apache Tomcat release to support Servlet 3.0, JSP 2.2, and EL 2.2 specifications.
7.0.11	March 11, 2011	Fourth stable version.
7.0.12	April 6, 2011	Current stable version.

For more information on version changes, release, and comparison, visit
`http://en.wikipedia.org/wiki/Apache_Tomcat` and `http://wiki.apache.org/tomcat/FrontPage`.

Tomcat support matrix

Apache Tomcat can be classified based on different components, such as the JDK version, enhancement, stability, and so on. Let's take a real time example, where you want to take a decision on which Apache Tomcat version to deploy for an application. For example, if an application is using Servlet 2.4 and JSP 2.0, then we should always go for the 5.x version. In reality, it's a difficult job to find out which version of Tomcat we should use to utilize the system resource properly.

Normally, these tasks would be done by the company's technical architect, and they are solely responsible for the technical specifications used in any product. Based on the features of Tomcat, let us quickly go through the comparison of Tomcat with different versions:

Features	7.x	6.x	5.x	4.x	3.x
Version specifications	Servlet 3.0, JSP 2.2, EL 2.2	Servlet 2.5, JSP 2.1	Servlet 2.4, JSP 2.0	Servlet 2.3, JSP 1.2	Servlet 2.2, JSP 1.1
Stable:	Yes	Yes	Yes	Yes	Yes
Enhancements	Yes	Yes	Unlikely	Highly unlikely	Highly unlikely
Bug Fixes	Yes	Yes	Yes	Highly unlikely	Highly unlikely
Security Fixes	Yes	Yes	Yes	Highly unlikely	Highly unlikely
Releases	Yes	Yes	Yes	Highly unlikely	Highly unlikely
Release Manager	Mark Thomas (markt)	Jean-Frederic Clere (jfclere)	Filip Hanik (fhanik)	Mark Thomas (markt)	Bill Barker (billbarker)
Process	CTR	RTC	RTC	CTR	CTR
Listed on download pages	Yes	Yes	Yes	No	No
JDK version	1.6	1.5	1.4	1.3	1.1

In the previous table, highly unlikely means that the user using the previous version necessarily needs to have the upgraded higher version to support the new improved features. It also involves security fixes for the current version.

Features and enhancements of Apache Tomcat 7

In the previous section, we discussed the various support matrices for Tomcat versions, we are now aware of the support specifications (JDK support, EJB, and Servlet) for Tomcat. Let's try to understand, and quickly review the new features/enhancements for Tomcat 7.

Apache Tomcat 7.x was released with some key improvements over Tomcat 6.x and real time implementation of Servlet 3.0, JSP 2.2, and EL 2.2 specifications. Apart from these, it also solves some major issues from previous releases.

Web application memory leak detection and prevention

Tomcat had a chronological problem of memory leaks in 4.x/5.x versions. While reloading the applications in the entire life cycle of Tomcat, OutOfMemoryError exceptions were generated. Tomcat has put an exceptional effort in tracking down the bugs and issues related to memory, in order to avoid memory leaks.

Servlet 3.0

Tomcat 7 offers great support for Servlet 3.0. Servlet 3.0 helps developers to code very easily and also provides significant support for asynchronous programming techniques. The types of support provided are:

- **Asynchronous Support**: Servlet 3.0's asynchronous support has been fully integrated into Tomcat 7. The biggest advantage of asynchronous programming is that the server doesn't have to wait for the response from the resources. For example, if you have 2000 concurrent users using an application, then we cannot allocate 2000 connections to the database and make the connection idle untill we get the response. By using asynchronous programming, your application can handle other user requests while this particular user is waiting for the response from the resources, such as DB, NAS, and so on.

- **Dynamic Configuration**: It is again, a very vital feature of Servlet 3.0. Due to Tomcat 7's support for web fragments, developers now don't need to implement the specific library configurations for their application web.xml. This means, you can integrate the library reference in web.xml.

- **Annotation-based Configuration**: With the additional support for Servlet 3.0 in Tomcat 7, developers can include decorative programming styles. The biggest advantage of implementing decorator is you can configure rewrite rules in the application servlet classes instead of web servers. Hence, you reduce the dependency on web servers. It also eliminates the need for deployment descriptors.

Improved logging

Tomcat 7 includes two new features for logging, in order to provide a good understanding to the users for log analysis:

- **Asynchronous file handler**: The asynchronous handler allows Tomcat to write logs to the disk by a dedicated thread, so that logging operations do not cause any delay in processing threads.
- **Single line log formatter**: The single line formatter writes logs in a single line, which is a better feature for administrators.

Aliases

This is the best feature for an administrator. It provides the administrator with the freedom to eliminate the dependency of another web server to host multiple websites. In addition to this, you can host the entire static content (image/JavaScript in a single package).

Important points to remember about Tomcat 7 features

Apache Tomcat 7 can be run through JRE 1.6 or later. It means that we don't have to install the complete **Java Development Kit (JDK)**. This will be really helpful in space crunch issues and the slimming of Java will utilize less memory. But, it is also recommended from the administrator's point of view, to install the complete Java Development Kit as it provides other utilities (jmap, jstack) which are very helpful to administrators. This has an inbuilt eclipse **JIT** (Just in Time) compiler.

Apache Tomcat 7 resolves class loading conflict issues, such as ClassCastExceptions. ClassCastExceptions mean that there is an issue with class while loading in runtime.

Installation of Tomcat 7

In the previous section, we have discussed the new enhancements in Apache Tomcat 7. Now, it's time to move on to the Tomcat installation.

How to download the Tomcat software

Perform the following steps to download the software:

- Before we start the installation of Apache Tomcat 7 software, the first thing that comes to mind is where can you download the software from and also how much does the license cost? By default, Apache comes with Apache License, Version 2.0 ,which is compatible to GPL (General Public License). In simple terms, it is free of cost! For more information on licenses, you can visit `http://www.apache.org/licenses/`. Now, the second problem is how to download the software.

- It is always recommended to download the software from its official site, `http://tomcat.apache.org/download-70.cgi`. By default, on `http://tomcat.apache.org/`, we get the latest stable version of Tomcat package and we have to download the package based on the operating system, where we want to install it.

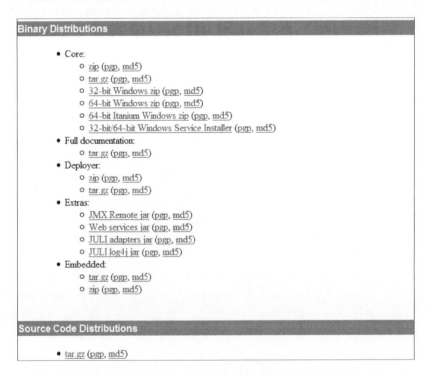

Once the download is complete, then you have to do the integrity check for the downloaded software using the MD5 checksum.

> MD5 Message-Digest Algorithm is a widely used cryptographic hash function that produces a 128-bit (16 byte) hash value.

Following is the process to perform the integrity check using the MD5 checksum:

1. Download the MD5 checksum from the website `apache.org`. The MD5 check sum is integrated with every package we download. The previous screenshot shows the packages which are available in MD5, and by clicking on **md5** on the website, we can compare the checksum generated in our system with the value given on the site.

2. Run the following command to generate the checksum for the downloaded software. See the following screenshot:

   ```
   [root@localhost opt]# cksum apache-tomcat-7.0.12.zip
   ```

```
[root@localhost opt]# cksum apache-tomcat-7.0.12.zip
3514439228 7638243 apache-tomcat-7.0.12.zip
[root@localhost opt]#
```

Tomcat comes with different packages for installation such as binary, source, and RPM. Based on the requirement, the package should be taken from the official site. Let's have a brief discussion on which package should be implemented in real time and why.

Binary package

It comes with a pre-set library and customized configuration which are implemented and tested as per industry standards. A few advantages of using the binary package are:

- It is a standard package that suits most of the real-time environments
- In a non-DOS environment (such as Linux, UNIX, and so on), we can configure multiple Tomcat instances on a single OS
- It is path independent; we can configure Tomcat in any part of the OS based on our resources available (hardware)

RPM/exe

RPM is defined as a system installer, which is developed and compiled on each OS independently. It has a pre-defined library, which will work only on the respective OS. A few advantages of using RPM are:

- It does not require installation of any dependent libraries for the package
- RPM is built with the shared libraries for the respective OS
- It does not need to configure separate startup services

The only disadvantage is, we cannot configure multiple instances in a single operating system and it has predefined paths.

Source

You can customize the installation based on your requirements using the source package. Suppose you want to customize during installation of the software, it can be done in this package.

- Customization of Tomcat can be done very effectively (only required services are installed)
- In a non-DOS environment (such as Linux, UNIX, and so on), we can configure multiple Tomcat instances on a single OS
- It is path independent; we can configure Tomcat in any part of the OS based on our resources available (hardware)
- In a production environment, it's always recommended to use the source or binary instead of the RPM

Prerequisites for the Tomcat 7 installation

Before we begin with the Apache Tomcat 7 installation, we have to configure the prerequisites and they are very important for the Tomcat 7 installation to start. Following are the prerequisites mentioned for Apache Tomcat 7:

- Java SE 1.6 or later
- Configuration of the OS environment variables

Installation of Java

Java has been developed by many vendors. Based on the application requirement and type of architecture, different JVMs are used by various applications. Common JDK vendors are IBM, HP, Sun, OpenJDK, and so on. Sun holds a major stake in IT industries. JDK is widely used and accepted across various IT industries.

JDK packages are available for each OS and can be compiled on any system using a common set of libraries. These packages are easily available on the Internet or already integrated with different OS vendors.

JDK/JRE comes in 32 bit and 64 bit editions, so we can use it based on the application requirement. Some of the performance characteristics of the 64 bit versus 32 bit **Virtual Machine (VM)** are:

- The benefits of using 64 bit are being able to address larger amounts of memory which comes with a small performance loss in 64 bit VMs, versus running the same application on a 32 bit VM

- You can allocate more than 4 GB to JVM for memory intensive applications

In a 64 bit Java edition, you have to allocate more memory for JVM as compared to a 32 bit edition. In practice, a 64 bit Java requires 30 percent more memory than the 32 bit Java version.

Installation of Java in Linux

In this topic, we will discuss the steps performed during installation of Java on Linux:

1. Download the JDK from the Oracle site on the Linux system.

For more information about the version changes and releases, visit http://www.oracle.com/technetwork/java/javase/downloads/index.html.

We are doing the installation on the /opt partition of the hard drive and the Java version we are using is Java(TM) SE Runtime Environment (build 1.6.0_24-b07).

Once the download is complete, it will create the binary file in /opt (jdk-6u24-linux-i586.bin).

2. Change the permission of the package using the following command:

   chmod 0755 jdk-6u24-linux-i586.bin

 The chmod 0755 file is equivalent to u=rwx (4+2+1), go=rx (4+1 & 4+1). The 0 specifies no special modes.

3. Run the following command to install the JDK:

   [root@localhost opt]# ./jdk-6u24-linux-i586.bin

   You will see an output similar to the following screenshot:

```
[root@localhost opt]# ./jdk-6u24-linux-i586.bin
Unpacking...
Checksumming...
Extracting...
UnZipSFX 5.50 of 17 February 2002, by Info-ZIP (Zip-Bugs@lists.wku.edu).
   creating: jdk1.6.0_24/
   creating: jdk1.6.0_24/jre/
   creating: jdk1.6.0_24/jre/bin/
  inflating: jdk1.6.0_24/jre/bin/java
  inflating: jdk1.6.0_24/jre/bin/keytool
  inflating: jdk1.6.0_24/jre/bin/policytool
  inflating: jdk1.6.0_24/jre/bin/rmiregistry
  inflating: jdk1.6.0_24/jre/bin/rmid
  inflating: jdk1.6.0_24/jre/bin/tnameserv
  inflating: jdk1.6.0_24/jre/bin/orbd
  inflating: jdk1.6.0_24/jre/bin/servertool
  inflating: jdk1.6.0_24/jre/bin/unpack200
  inflating: jdk1.6.0_24/jre/bin/pack200
  inflating: jdk1.6.0_24/jre/bin/jcontrol
    linking: jdk1.6.0_24/jre/bin/ControlPanel  -> ./jcontrol
  inflating: jdk1.6.0_24/jre/bin/java_vm
  inflating: jdk1.6.0_24/jre/bin/javaws
   creating: jdk1.6.0_24/jre/lib/
   creating: jdk1.6.0_24/jre/lib/applet/
   creating: jdk1.6.0_24/jre/lib/ext/
  inflating: jdk1.6.0_24/jre/lib/ext/sunjce_provider.jar
  inflating: jdk1.6.0_24/jre/lib/ext/sunpkcs11.jar
  inflating: jdk1.6.0_24/jre/lib/ext/dnsns.jar
  inflating: jdk1.6.0_24/jre/lib/ext/localedata.pack
  inflating: jdk1.6.0_24/jre/lib/ext/meta-index
   creating: jdk1.6.0_24/jre/lib/i386/
   creating: jdk1.6.0_24/jre/lib/i386/native_threads/
  inflating: jdk1.6.0_24/jre/lib/i386/native_threads/libhpi.so
   creating: jdk1.6.0_24/jre/lib/i386/server/
  inflating: jdk1.6.0_24/jre/lib/i386/server/libjvm.so
```

4. During the installation, the binary will prompt for the acceptance of the agreement, then press *Enter*. See the following screenshot:

```
Java(TM) SE Development Kit 6 successfully installed.

Product Registration is FREE and includes many benefits:
* Notification of new versions, patches, and updates
* Special offers on Oracle products, services and training
* Access to early releases and documentation

Product and system data will be collected. If your configuration
supports a browser, the JDK Product Registration form will
be presented. If you do not register, none of this information
will be saved. You may also register your JDK later by
opening the register.html file (located in the JDK installation
directory) in a browser.

For more information on what data Registration collects and
how it is managed and used, see:
http://java.sun.com/javase/registration/JDKRegistrationPrivacy.html

Press Enter to continue.....
```

5. After pressing *Enter* it will exit from the command prompt, as shown in the following screenshot:

```
Press Enter to continue.....


Done.
[root@localhost opt]#
```

6. After the installation is complete, the binary will create the folder named `jdk1.6.0_24` in `/opt`. If the folder is present in `/opt`, that means the installation is successfully done. See the following screenshot:

```
root@localhost jdk1.6.0_24]# ls -ltrh
otal 19M
rw-r--r--  1 root root  19M Feb  2 17:30 src.zip
r--r--r--  1 root root   76 Feb  2 17:30 THIRDPARTYLICENSEREADME.txt
r--r--r--  1 root root  21K Feb  2 17:30 README_zh_CN.html
r--r--r--  1 root root  25K Feb  2 17:30 README_ja.html
r--r--r--  1 root root  28K Feb  2 17:30 README.html
r--r--r--  1 root root 3.3K Feb  2 17:30 COPYRIGHT
rwxr-xr-x  2 root root 4.0K Feb  2 19:36 bin
rwxr-xr-x 10 root root 4.0K Feb  2 19:36 jre
rwxr-xr-x  9 root root 4.0K Feb  2 19:36 lib
rwxr-xr-x  4 root root 4.0K Feb  2 19:36 man
rwxr-xr-x  3 root root 4.0K Feb  2 19:36 include
rwxr-xr-x  7 root root 4.0K Feb  2 19:36 db
rwxr-xr-x  3 root root 4.0K May 16 20:34 demo
rwxr-xr-x  7 root root 4.0K May 16 20:34 sample
r--r--r--  1 root root 4.8K May 16 20:35 register_zh_CN.html
r--r--r--  1 root root 6.6K May 16 20:35 register_ja.html
r--r--r--  1 root root 5.2K May 16 20:35 register.html
```

Let's quickly go through the JDK directory structure, shown in the previous screenshot:

- `bin`: It contains the entire executable for the JDK for java, javac, jmap, and so on.

- `jre`: It contains all the files necessary for Java to perform the function.

- `lib`: As the name suggests, it's a library directory for the JDK.

- `man`: This directory contains all the manual pages for Java (document directory).

- `demo`:-This folder contains working examples of different utilities. These utilities can be directly used.

- `sample`: This directory contains the code files for utilities provided in the demo directory.

- `include`: It contains the header files for different functions used in Java.h

- `db`: It contains the entire component of the Derby Database. Derby is a pure Java relational database engine.

 Tomcat 7 can be run on JRE, it means no need to install a JDK component; if there is a space issue in your environment that can be customized accordingly.

Installation of Java in Windows

In this topic, we will discuss the steps performed during installation of Java in the Windows operating system:

1. Download the JDK from the Oracle site on the Windows system from the following link: `http://www.oracle.com/technetwork/java/javase/downloads/index.html`.

 We are doing the installation on the C partition of the hard drive and the Java version we are using is Java(TM) SE Runtime Environment (build 1.6.0_24-b07).

2. Once the download is complete, `jdk-6u24-windows-i586.exe` is created in the download location.

3. By double-clicking the `jdk-6u24-windows-i586.exe` file, installation of Java will begin. It will open a new pop-up window for installation. See the following screenshot:

4. By clicking **Next** on the window, it will take us to a new window where we can customize the JDK installation based on the requirement, as well as define the installation path of the JDK. In the current environment, we are installing Java on the default location.

5. Check if the default path is `C:\Program Files\Java\jdk1.6.0_24`.

6. Check the field **Installation type: Default**.

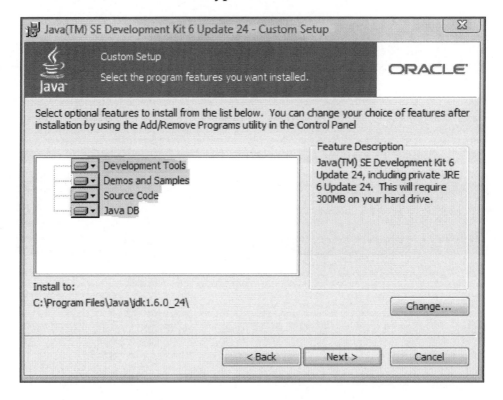

7. Once the installation is done, it will show the status as complete, similar to the following screenshot:

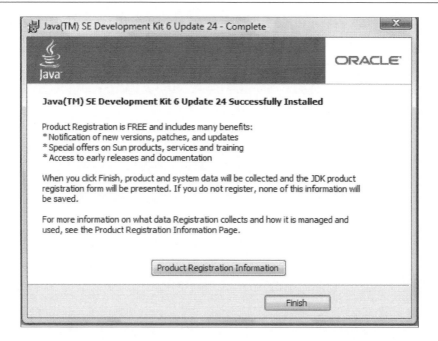

Configuration of OS environment variables

After the installation of Java on a different OS, it's now time to set the environment variables for Tomcat at the OS level. In order to run Tomcat, we have to define the JAVA_HOME as an environment variable and set the path for Java so that it can be accessed from any partition of OS.

What is JAVA_HOME?

JAVA_HOME is the JDK install directory, for example, `C:\jdk6`. It is meant to be set as an environment variable and referenced in Windows batch files or Unix scripts. In Tomcat, JAVA_HOME is defined in `catalina.sh` under TOMCAT_HOME/bin. The following screenshot shows the definition of JAVA_HOME in Tomcat 7. Once you execute `startup.sh`, it internally calls `catalina.sh` and invokes JAVA_HOME. In a production environment, it is always recommended to use the permanent environment variable.

```
# For Cygwin, ensure paths are in UNIX format before anything is touched
if $cygwin; then
  [ -n "$JAVA_HOME" ] && JAVA_HOME=`cygpath --unix "$JAVA_HOME"`
  [ -n "$JRE_HOME" ] && JRE_HOME=`cygpath --unix "$JRE_HOME"`
  [ -n "$CATALINA_HOME" ] && CATALINA_HOME=`cygpath --unix "$CATALINA_HOME"`
  [ -n "$CATALINA_BASE" ] && CATALINA_BASE=`cygpath --unix "$CATALINA_BASE"`
  [ -n "$CLASSPATH" ] && CLASSPATH=`cygpath --path --unix "$CLASSPATH"`
fi
```

Setting the JAVA_HOME and PATH variable in Windows

The environment variable and path can be set in Windows by performing the following steps:

1. Right-click on the **My Computer** icon on your desktop and then click **Properties**, as shown in the following screenshot:

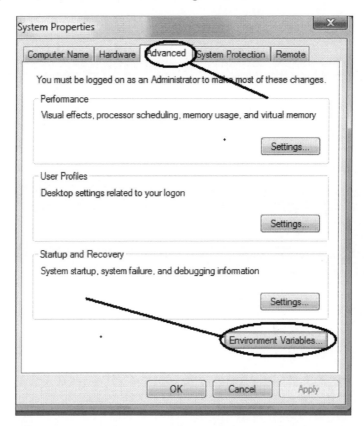

2. Click **Advanced | Environment Variables**.
3. Under **System Variables**, click **New**.
4. In the **Variable name** field, enter JAVA_HOME, as shown in the following screenshot:

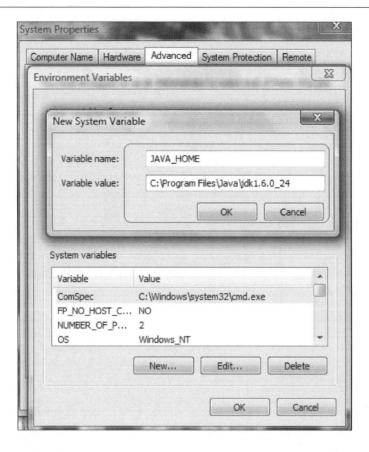

5. In the **Variable value** field, enter the installation path of the Java Development Kit.

6. Click **OK**.

7. Click on **Apply Changes**.

Setting the global path variable in Windows

After setting JAVA_HOME, now it is time to add the Java path in the global path variable. Following is a detailed procedure, which needs to be followed for creating the global path variable in Windows:

1. Right-click on the **My Computer** icon on your desktop and then click **Properties**.

2. Click **Advanced | Environment Variables**.

3. Under **System Variables**, click on **Path**.

4. Edit the path and add the Java path in the end.

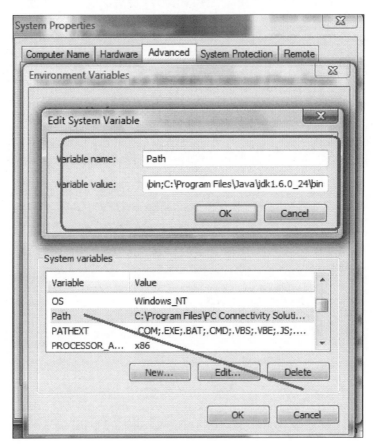

5. In the **Variable value** field, enter the installation path of the Java Development Kit, as shown in the previous screenshot.

6. Click **OK**.

7. Click on **Apply Changes**.

Setting the JAVA_HOME and the PATH environment variable in Linux

The environment variable and path are set differently in Linux as compared to Windows. Perform the following steps to set the environment variable in Linux:

1. Open the `.bash_profile` using the *vi* editor for the root user.

 You can put the environment variable in `bashrc` also. It will also execute at the time of the user login.

2. Add the following environment variable in the file. The following is the code snippet of `.bash_profile`. The highlighted code shows the declaration of JAVA_HOME and PATH. export will add the JAVA_HOME and PATH to the system parameter for every user login.

```
# .bash_profile
# Get the aliases and functions
if [ -f ~/.bashrc ];then . ~/.bashrc
fi
# User specific environment and start-up programs
JAVA_HOME=/opt/jdk1.6.0_24
PATH=$JAVA_HOME/bin:$PATH:$HOME/bin
export PATH JAVA_HOME
unset USERNAME
```

3. Save the `.bash_profile` using the `:wq` command.

4. Once you have saved the `.bash_profile`, then you have to logout and re-log in to the environment to activate the changes using the following command:

```
su - username
su - root (as our user is root)
```

 If we run the previous command for any user, then the profile of that user will be reloaded.

Also, you can run the `env` command to verify the environment variables are configured properly, as shown in the following screenshot:

```
[root@localhost ~]# env
HOSTNAME=localhost.localdomain
TERM=xterm
SHELL=/bin/bash
HISTSIZE=1000
SSH_CLIENT=192.168.169.1 54312 22
SSH_TTY=/dev/pts/4
USER=root
LS_COLORS=no=00:fi=00:di=00:34:ln=00:36:pi=40:33:so=00:35:bd=40:33:01:cd=40:33:01:or=01:05:37:41:mi=01:05:37:41:ex=00:32:*.cmd=00:32:*.exe=00:32:*.com=00:32:
*.btm=00:32:*.bat=00:32:*.sh=00:32:*.csh=00:32:*.tar=00:31:*.tgz=00:31:*.arj=00:31:*.taz=00:31:*.lzh=00:31:*.zip=00:31:*.z=00:31:*.Z=00:31:*.gz=00:31:*.bz2=0
0:31:*.bz=00:31:*.tz=00:31:*.rpm=00:31:*.cpio=00:31:*.jpg=00:35:*.gif=00:35:*.bmp=00:35:*.xbm=00:35:*.xpm=00:35:*.png=00:35:*.tif=00:35:
MAIL=/var/spool/mail/root
PATH=/opt/jdk1.6.0_24/bin:/usr/kerberos/sbin:/usr/kerberos/bin:/usr/local/sbin:/usr/local/bin:/sbin:/bin:/usr/sbin:/usr/bin:/root/bin
INPUTRC=/etc/inputrc
PWD=/root
JAVA_HOME=/opt/jdk1.6.0_24
LANG=en_US.UTF-8
SSH_ASKPASS=/usr/libexec/openssh/gnome-ssh-askpass
SHLVL=1
HOME=/root
LOGNAME=root
SSH_CONNECTION=192.168.169.1 54312 192.168.169.128 22
LESSOPEN=|/usr/bin/lesspipe.sh %s
G_BROKEN_FILENAMES=1
_=/bin/env
[root@localhost ~]# []
```

 It is always best practice to first take the backup of the existing profile. In case there are issues while doing the changes, then we can revert back the changes using the command `cp`

```
[root@localhost ~]# cp .bash_profile  .bash_profile_
backup.
```

Now we have set the environment variable for Windows and Linux environments, but how can we verify whether the environment is set properly or not?

Before we start installation of Apache Tomcat 7, let's quickly verify the environment variable on both the OSes.

In the Windows environment, variables can be verified using the following command:

echo %VARIABLE_NAME%

For JAVA_HOME:

C:\Users\user>echo %JAVA_HOME%

C:\Program Files\Java\jdk1.6.0_24

For PATH:

C:\Users\user>echo %PATH%

C:\Program Files\PC Connectivity
  Solution\;C:\Windows\system32;C:\Windows;C:\Windows\System32\Wbem;C:
  Program Files\Broadcom\Broadcom 802.11\Driver;

C:\Program Files\Java\jdk1.6.0_24\bin

In Linux, we can use the following command to verify the environment variables:

```
echo $VARIABLE_NAME
```

For JAVA_HOME:

```
[root@localhost ~]# echo $JAVA_HOME
/opt/jdk1.6.0_24
```

For PATH:

```
[root@localhost ~]# echo $PATH
/opt/jdk1.6.0_24/bin:/usr/kerberos/sbin:/usr/kerberos/bin:/usr/local/
  sbin:/usr/local/bin:/sbin:/bin:/usr/sbin:/usr/bin:/root/bin
```

After verifying the environment variable on both the OSes, we are sure that JAVA_HOME and PATH are properly set in the environment. We have completed the prerequisites of installation of Apache Tomcat 7. Now, we can proceed with the installation of Apache Tomcat 7.

Installation of Apache Tomcat 7

Let's start the installation of Tomcat 7 on different OSes. The steps involved to install the software on Windows are discussed first, and then we move on to the Linux environment.

Installation on a Windows environment

In this topic, we will discuss the steps involved during the software installation of Tomcat 7. Following are the steps:

1. Download the latest stable version from the Tomcat official site, http://tomcat.apache.org/download-70.cgi. We are downloading the **32-bit/64-bit Windows Service Installer (pgp, md5)**. Once the download is complete, save it in the software folder.

2. Double-click on apache-tomcat-7.0.14.exe. It will launch the setup wizard.

 If you don't find the exe file along with the downloaded folder, download it using the link, http://apache.osuosl.org/tomcat/tomcat-7/v7.0.23/bin/. Save the file in the apache-tomcat folder.

3. Then, click on **Next** button to continue, as shown in the following screenshot:

4. An agreement pop-up is displayed. Click on **I Agree**. It means we agree to use Tomcat 7 as per the GPL license, as shown in the following screenshot:

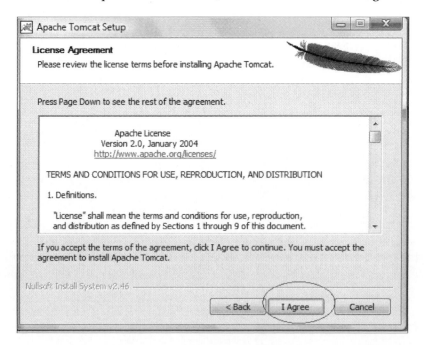

5. The following window shows us the different components we need to install:

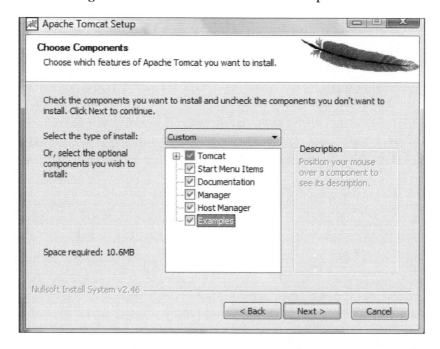

6. In the next step, we have to configure the username and password for the Tomcat Manager, as shown in the following screenshot. We have set the **Username** and **Password** to admin. Click on **Next**.

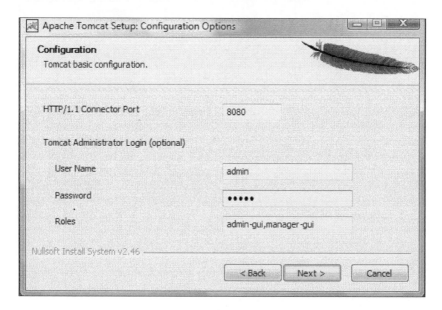

7. In the next window, it will pick up the Java version from the JAVA_HOME variable, if the variables are properly defined, as shown in the following screenshot:

8. The next window displays the installation path of Tomcat. By default, we use C:\Program Files\Apache Software Foundation\Tomcat 7.0. In case we want to change it, then we have to click on **Browse** and select the desired path. Click on **Install**, as shown in the following screenshot:

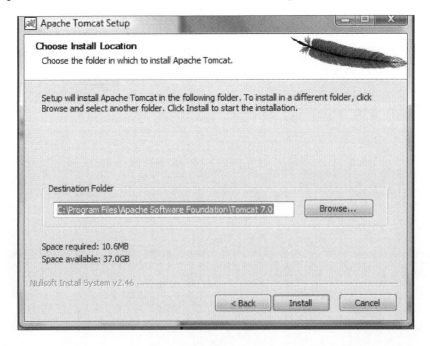

9. It's the final step of the Tomcat 7 installation. This will display the successful implementation of Tomcat, as shown in the following screenshot:

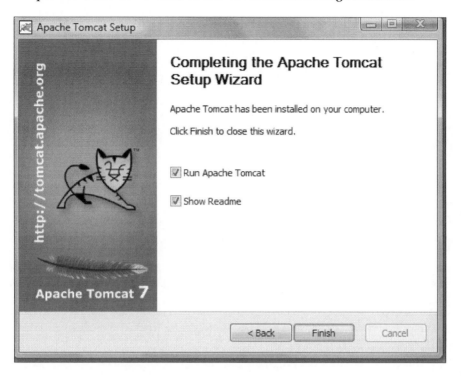

Installation on a Linux environment

Installation of Tomcat 7 is quite simple in a Linux environment as compared to Windows. It can be done in just three steps:

1. Download the latest stable version from Tomcat's official site http://tomcat.apache.org/download-70.cgi. Once the download is complete, save it in the /opt location. Unzip the Tomcat 7 source, that is, apache-tomcat-7.0.12.zip using the following command:

   ```
   [root@localhost opt]# unzip apache-tomcat-7.0.12.zip
   ```

2. After you unzip the apache-tomcat-7.0.12.zip, it will create the directory named apache-tomcat-7.0.12 in the opt directory. Go to the bin directories of apache-tomcat-7.0.12 using the following command:

   ```
   [root@localhost opt]# cd apache-tomcat-7.0.12/bin/
   ```

3. Run the following command. If you fail to run the following command, then Tomcat services will not come up. By default, the package comes with read/write permissions, but no execution permissions are given to the package. We have to manually change the permissions:

```
[root@localhost bin]# chmod 0755 *.sh
[root@localhost bin]# pwd
/opt/apache-tomcat-7.0.12/bin
```

 The chmod 0755 file is equivalent to u=rwx (4+2+1),go=rx (4+1 & 4+1). The 0 specifies no special modes.

After this step, the installation of Tomcat is complete in Linux.

Startup and shutdown of Tomcat services

We have now completed the installation of Apache Tomcat on both the OSes. Now, it's time to start the services and verify the setup we have created up to now. So why waste time, let's rock and roll.

Services in Windows

In Windows, we can start/stop the services using two methods:

- Through the **Microsoft Management Console (MMC)**: Go to **Start | Run | services.msc**. When the MMC opens, as shown in the following screenshot, you can start/stop services based on the requirement:

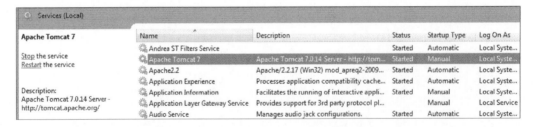

- **Apache monitor console**: Tomcat comes with a very handy tool for administration, which is popularly known as the Apache monitoring console. It's very useful in managing the Tomcat instance (service recycle, enabling logs, and JVM configuration).The following screenshot shows the recycle process using the Tomcat monitoring console. To start/stop services, go to **Start | Programs | Apache-Tomcat7 |apache-tomcat monitor Start/Stop**.

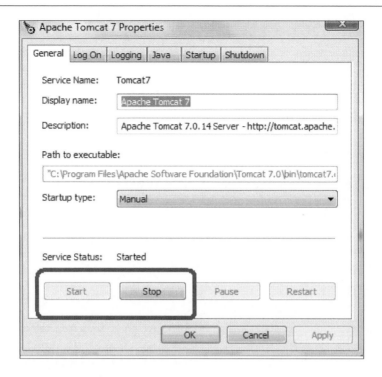

Services in Linux

The Linux startup process is completely different. Here, we have to run the startup/ shutdown scripts manually to bring the services online. Let us start the services on Linux to verify the installation.

Before that, let's quickly verify the configuration. Tomcat 7 comes with different scripts, through which we will verify the complete installation. There is a very good script placed in the Tomcat `bin` directory named as `version.sh`, through which we can verify the complete Tomcat version and system information. Let's run the script using the following command:

```
[root@localhost bin]# ./version.sh
Using CATALINA_BASE:    /opt/apache-tomcat-7.0.12
Using CATALINA_HOME:    /opt/apache-tomcat-7.0.12
Using CATALINA_TMPDIR: /opt/apache-tomcat-7.0.12/temp
Using JRE_HOME:         /opt/jdk1.6.0_24
Using CLASSPATH:        /opt/apache-tomcat-7.0.12/bin/bootstrap.jar:/opt/
apache-tomcat-7.0.12/bin/tomcat-juli.jar
Server version: Apache Tomcat/7.0.12
Server built:   Apr 1 2011 06:13:02
```

```
Server number:     7.0.12.0
OS Name:           Linux
OS Version:        2.6.18-8.el5
Architecture:      i386
JVM Version:       1.6.0_24-b07
JVM Vendor:        Sun Microsystems Inc.
```

There is one more script in the Tomcat `bin` directory that is very useful. `configtest.sh` is used to check any configuration changes in scripts. This script performs a quick configuration check on the system and finds the errors. Let's run the script using the following command:

```
[root@localhost bin]# ./configtest.sh
Using CATALINA_BASE:    /opt/apache-tomcat-7.0.12
Using CATALINA_HOME:    /opt/apache-tomcat-7.0.12
Using CATALINA_TMPDIR: /opt/apache-tomcat-7.0.12/temp
Using JRE_HOME:         /opt/jdk1.6.0_24
Using CLASSPATH:        /opt/apache-tomcat-7.0.12/bin/bootstrap.jar:/opt/
apache-tomcat-7.0.12/bin/tomcat-juli.jar
May 22, 2011 4:06:16 PM org.apache.coyote.AbstractProtocolHandler init
INFO: Initializing ProtocolHandler ["http-bio-8080"]
May 22, 2011 4:06:16 PM org.apache.coyote.AbstractProtocolHandler init
INFO: Initializing ProtocolHandler ["ajp-bio-8009"]
May 22, 2011 4:06:16 PM org.apache.catalina.startup.Catalina load
INFO: Initialization processed in 1401 ms
```

 `configtest.sh` is available in a Linux environment only.

After doing the configuration check, start the Tomcat services. The Tomcat services can be started using the `startup.sh` in the `bin` directory.

Startup script

To start the Tomcat services, you have to perform the following mentioned steps:

1. The first step is to change the directory from the current location to the Tomcat directory.

    ```
    [root@localhost bin]# cd /opt/apache-tomcat-7.0.12/bin/
    ```

2. In the `bin` directory, we will find the entire executable for Tomcat. To start the services, we have to use the following command. Once you execute the startup command, it will display the parameters which are essential for booting Tomcat. Some of them are CATALINA_BASE, CATALINA_HOME, JRE_HOME, and so on.

    ```
    [root@localhost bin]# ./startup.sh

    Using CATALINA_BASE:   /opt/apache-tomcat-7.0.12

    Using CATALINA_HOME:   /opt/apache-tomcat-7.0.12

    Using CATALINA_TMPDIR: /opt/apache-tomcat-7.0.12/temp

    Using JRE_HOME:        /opt/jdk1.6.0_24

    Using CLASSPATH:       /opt/apache-tomcat-
       7.0.12/bin/bootstrap.jar:/opt/apache-tomcat-7.0.12/bin/
       tomcat-juli.jar
    ```

Shutdown script

A Tomcat shutdown script is also available in the `bin` directory named as `./shutdown.sh`. Let's execute the script to know the output. The details are as follows:

```
[root@localhost bin]# cd /opt/apache-tomcat-7.0.12/bin/

[root@localhost bin]# ./shutdown.sh

Using CATALINA_BASE:   /opt/apache-tomcat-7.0.12

Using CATALINA_HOME:   /opt/apache-tomcat-7.0.12

Using CATALINA_TMPDIR: /opt/apache-tomcat-7.0.12/temp

Using JRE_HOME:        /opt/jdk1.6.0_24

Using CLASSPATH:       /opt/apache-tomcat-
   7.0.12/bin/bootstrap.jar:/opt/apache-tomcat-7.0.12/bin/tomcat-juli.jar
```

Verification of Tomcat status

Once we have executed the startup scripts, the next step is the verification of the Tomcat services, to check whether services are coming up fine or not. By default, Tomcat runs on HTTP port 8080 and can be accessed on the web browser using the URL, `http://localhost:8080`. We then find the Tomcat welcome page, which shows that Tomcat is installed correctly and running fine in the environment, as shown in the following screenshot:

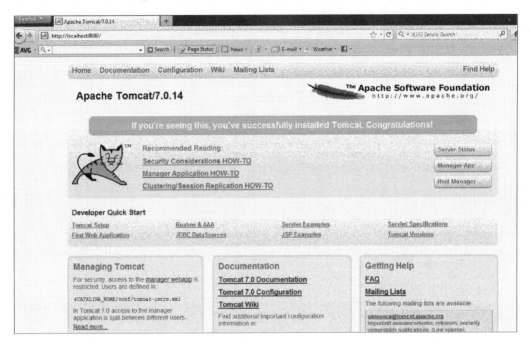

Once the welcome page for Tomcat 7 is displayed, we can verify the server status by clicking on **Server Status**.

It will prompt for the user ID/password. Remember, we have created a user admin that the user ID will be used here for access, as shown in the following screenshot:

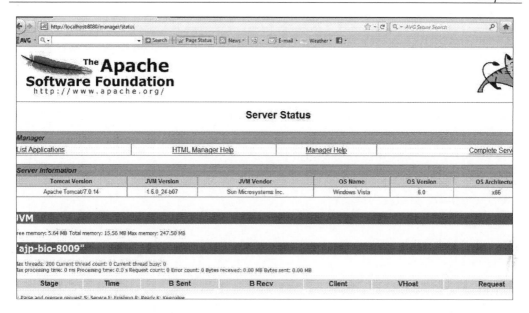

Common problems and troubleshooting in installation

There are multiple issues which may arise during the installation of Tomcat 7. Let's discuss these issues:

Error: Permission denied for the Java binary

Scenario 1: The Java installation is not working, while executing the Java binary.

```
[root@localhost opt]# ./jdk-6u24-linux-i586.bin
```

```
-bash: ./jdk-6u24-linux-i586.bin: Permission denied
```

Issue: The Java binary doesn't have execute permissions with a specific user.

Fix: Change the permission to 0755 for `./jdk-6u24-linux-i586.bin` using the following command:

```
chmod 0755 jdk-6u24-linux-i586.bin
```

> The `chmod 0755 file` is equivalent to `u=rwx (4+2+1)`, `go=rx` `(4+1 & 4+1)`. The 0 specifies no special modes.

Error: Tomcat is not able to find JAVA_HOME

Scenario 2: While starting the Tomcat startup script, the following error occurs:

```
[root@localhost bin]# ./startup.sh

Neither the JAVA_HOME nor the JRE_HOME environment variable is defined

At least one of these environment variables is needed to run this
  program
```

Fix: Check the `.bash_profile` and find out whether the following mentioned entry is present in the file:

```
JAVA_HOME=/opt/jdk1.6.0_24

PATH=$JAVA_HOME/bin:$PATH:$HOME/bin

export PATH JAVA_HOME
```

Error: Error in the logs showing port already in use

Scenario 3: Tomcat services is not displayed after running `startup.sh`.

Issue: This service is already running on the server.

Fix: Check for any Java process running in the system using the following command in Linux:

```
Ps -ef |grep tomcat
```

This command will show all Tomcat processes. If any process is running on an OS, kill it and run the startup scripts again.

In Windows, go to the **Task Manager** and check if any Java process is running for Tomcat. If any process is running, then kill the process and restart the Tomcat services.

Summary

In this chapter, we have covered the Apache Tomcat history and new features introduced in Tomcat 7. We have done a step-by-step installation of Tomcat on Windows and Linux operating systems. Also, we have discussed the common problems that may arise during the installation and their possible solutions.

In the next chapter, we will discuss the various methods used for deployment in Tomcat 7 and solution of issues that may occur during the deployment process.

2
Configuration and Deployment

In the previous chapter, you have installed Apache Tomcat 7 on DOS (Windows) and non-DOS (Linux/Unix,) operating systems. Now, it's time to discuss the different configuration and deployment strategy tools used by different IT industries.

In this chapter, we will discuss the following topics:

- Configuration of Tomcat
- Configuration of the virtual directory
- Deployment of an application on Tomcat 7

Configuration files and their usage

Apache Tomcat 7 comes with a default setup, which can be directly used for a QA environment. We can customize Tomcat based on the environment specification; components such as Services, Servers, Engine, Connectors, Realm, and Valve can be configured. The Tomcat configuration files are available in the conf folder. Let's discuss the configuration properties and their usage.

Tomcat 7, by default, comes with seven configuration files (usually in XML format), and these files are very useful in order to customize Tomcat, based on the environment needs. We shall install in the production or development environment.

The following screenshot shows the directory structure of the configuration directory for Tomcat 7:

```
root@localhost conf]# ls -l
otal 136
rwxr-xr-x 3 root root  4096 May 16 21:03
rw-r--r-- 1 root root 11888 Apr  1 18:15 catalina.policy
rw-r--r-- 1 root root  5089 Apr  1 18:15 catalina.properties
rw-r--r-- 1 root root  1428 Apr  1 18:15 context.xml
rw-r--r-- 1 root root  3213 Apr  1 18:15 logging.properties
rw-r--r-- 1 root root  6645 Apr  1 18:15 server.xml
rw-r--r-- 1 root root  1566 Apr  1 18:15 tomcat-users.xml
rw-r--r-- 1 root root 53273 Apr  1 18:15 web.xml
```

It's very important from an administrator's point of view, to know about the configuration files and their usage in the Tomcat environment. Let's discuss the configuration properties one-by-one, as follows:

- `catalina.policy`: This file describes the security policy permissions for Tomcat 7. It enforces the security policy permissions by JVM on the web application.

> When `catalina` is executed with the `-security` option, the security policy mentioned in the `catalina` file is used and the web application security policy also gets executed.

- `catalina.properties`: This file contains the shared definition of the server, shared loader, and JARs, which need to be scanned at the time of the server startup.

- `server.xml`: This is one of the important configuration files of Tomcat. It holds critical information, such as the IP address, port, virtual host, context path, and so on.

- `tomcat-users.xml`: This file is used for authentication, authorization, and role-based definitions. It is used to implement a database of users/passwords/roles for authentication and container-managed security. To add/remove users or assign/unassign roles to existing users, edit this file.

- `logging.properties`: As the name suggests, it defines the logging properties of the Tomcat instances (such as startup logs).

- `web.xml`: This defines the default values for all web applications loaded into this instance of Tomcat, at the time of startup of the Tomcat instance. If a web application has its own deployment descriptor, its content will always override the configuration settings specified in this default descriptor.

- context.xml: The contents of this file will load with every application. Configuration of parameters such as session persistence, Comet connection tracking, and so on, are done here.

> Any changes made in the server.xml file will be in effect after restarting the Tomcat instance.

> Application level resources are not defined in the web.xml of the configuration folder. It would be better to define these in the application web.xml.

Configuration of Tomcat 7

Until now, we have discussed the various configuration files of Tomcat 7. Now, the interesting part starts while implementing these in practical, or on live systems.

Before we learn the details of the Tomcat server configuration, let's quickly understand how the web application works from the following steps:

1. Whenever you hit the URL (for example, www.abc.com), the browser will contact the DNS server.
2. The DNS server will contact the ISP for the required information.
3. Once the web server accepts the request from the client browser, it will redirect it to the database server.
4. In turn, the database server will retrieve the query and respond it back to the web server.
5. The web server then forwards the same response to the client browser, and finally, the client browser will display the content to the user.

That's how the web browser gets the content generated by the web server. The following figure explains the web application functionality and different components, which play a vital role for the application to work:

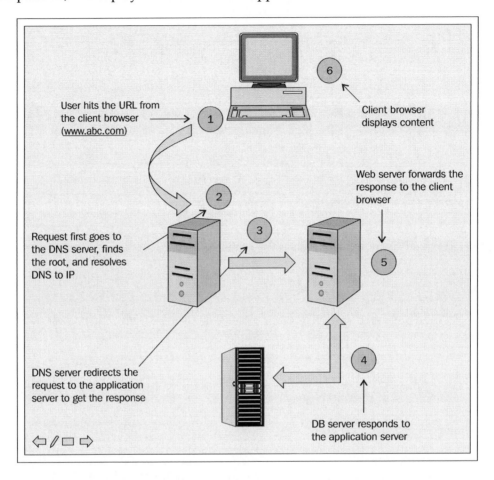

DataSource configuration

For any web application, the database plays a very vital role as it's the backbone for an enterprise application. For an application to perform well, the correct datasource configuration is necessary at the application layer.

Before moving further, let's quickly discuss how the web application gets the response from the database server.

1. Whenever you hit the URL (for example, www.abc.com), the request goes to the web server.

2. Once the web server accepts the request from the client browser, it will analyze the request based on the query. If it requires the database (DB) response, then it redirects the request to the database server.

3. Based on the query, the database server will retrieve the content and respond to the web server. The web server then forwards the response from the database server to the client browser.

This process flow is also explained in the following figure:

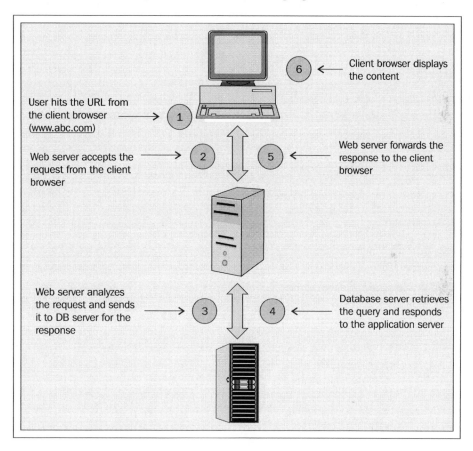

After all the previous discussions, we now understand how the database request flows in the web application. Now, it's time to do the real-time configuration of the datasource of Tomcat 7. Some of the terminologies used in the database connectivity are explained in the following content.

JDBC

Java Database Connectivity (JDBC) is a Java-based data access technology is an API through which the client accesses the server database. It is oriented towards a relational database and provides a way to query and update the database.

JNDI

Java Naming and Directory Interface (JNDI) services are an API for the Java platform, which provides naming and directory functionalities to applications written using the Java programming language.

DataSource

It is a Java object used to access relational databases through the JDBC API. It works well when integrated with the JNDI and after a datasource object is registered with a JNDI naming service. Objects can be accessed by the application itself and connect to the database.

The following are the parameters required for any database server to connect Tomcat 7 with the database and are also the prerequisites for datasource configuration:

- IP address
- Port number
- JNDI name
- Database user ID/password

> Database servers in production
>
> The applications which are hosted on the Internet, their web servers are always configured in the **Demilitarized Zone (DMZ)**. For more information on the DMZ zone, please refer to http://en.wikipedia.org/wiki/DMZ_(computing). Database servers are placed in an internal network. In this situation, the firewall port needs to be open between the web servers and the database server for communication.

Database Connection Pool (DBCP) configuration is located in the TOMCAT_HOME or CATALINA_HOME/lib/tomcat-dbcp.jar. This specific JAR is responsible for connection pooling. The following screenshot shows the location of tomcat-dbcp.jar. The following are the built-in properties of the Tomcat 7 server for accomplishing a connection with the database:

- Database Connection pool
- Common DBCP properties

```
root@localhost lib]# cd /opt/apache-tomcat-7.0.12/lib/
root@localhost lib]# ls -l tomcat-dbcp.jar
-rw-r--r-- 1 root root 234639 Apr  1 18:15 tomcat-dbcp.jar
root@localhost lib]# █
```

- Configuration of the database server details in `server.xml`
- The database specific JAR or JDBC driver needs to be placed in the `lib` directory
- The JNDI should be defined in the application `web.xml` file
- Application code should have proper JNDI configuration defined

There are many databases available in the market and every DB has its own advantage and disadvantage. We will discuss the most common databases used in the enterprise application and how to configure a datasource for these databases.

DataSource configuration consists of four major steps, irrespective of the database used.

DataSource for Oracle

The Oracle database holds a major share in the IT market because of its features. Following are the steps which you need to perform on the datasource configuration of Tomcat.

1. By default, the definition of datasource values are defined in the global section of `server.xml`. The following screenshot shows the datasource details in `server.xml`:

```
<!-- Global JNDI resources Documentation at /docs/jndi-resources-
    howto.html-->
<GlobalNamingResources>
<!-- Editable user database that can also be used by
UserDatabaseRealm to authenticate users-->
    <Resource name="jdbc/tomcat7" auth="Container"
        type="javax.sql.DataSource"
        driverClassName="oracle.jdbc.OracleDriver"
        url="jdbc:oracle:thin:@127.0.0.1:1521:test"
        description="test database for tomcat 7"
```

```
        username="admin" password="admin" maxActive="20" maxIdle="10"
        maxWait="-1"/>
</GlobalNamingResources>
```

```
<Resource name="jdbc/tomcat7" auth="Container"
         type="javax.sql.DataSource" driverClassName="oracle.jdbc.OracleDriver"
         url="jdbc:oracle:thin:@127.0.0.1:1521:mysid"
         description="User database that can be updated and saved"
         username="admin" password="admin" maxActive="20" maxIdle="10"
         maxWait="-1"/>
```

2. Oracle JDBC driver classes should be placed in the CATALINA_HOME/lib/ folder of the Tomcat instance. For Oracle, either class 12.jar or ojdbc14.jar is used.

> By default, Tomcat accepts only *.jar. If the driver is in ZIP format, then rename it to .jar and then deploy it in the jar directory. Based on the version used in the environment, you can download the Oracle JAR for free using the link, http://www.oracle.com/technetwork/database/enterprise-edition/jdbc-10201-088211.html.

> In case you have installed the Oracle database version 9i, then you should use the oracle.jdbc.driver.OracleDriver class for JDBC connections, and for versions above 9i, you should use oracle.jdbc.OracleDriver class. oracle.jdbc.driver.OracleDriver is deprecated and support for this driver will be discontinued from the next major release.

3. It's always mandatory to define the **Document Type Definition (DTD)** for the resource in the application web.xml. There is always a question that comes to the mind of the administrator, why can't we define the application specific DTD in the server web.xml? The answer to that question is very tricky. When the application is deployed, it will reference the application web.xml for the resource, but not for the server web.xml. The server web.xml should be used only for the server properties changes, such as the session parameter and so on, which references to the web/application server specific.

```
<resource-ref>
    <description>Oracle Datasource for tomcat </description>
    <res-ref-name>jdbc/tomcat7 </res-ref-name>
    <res-type>javax.sql.DataSource</res-type>
    <res-auth>Container</res-auth>
</resource-ref>
```

4. After the previous step, the developer has to reference the JNDI in their code file and connect it to the database.

DataSource for MySQL

MySQL is one of the biggest open source databases currently supported by Oracle. It follows the same process as Oracle, but a few parameters vary. The following steps are to be performed to configure the datasource for MySQL:

1. The following lines of code provide the definition of datasource in `server. xml` By default, these values are defined in the global section.

```
<Resource name="jdbc/tomcat7" auth="Container"
  type="javax.sql.DataSource"
  maxActive="100" maxIdle="30" maxWait="10000"
  username="tomcatuser" password="tomcat"
  driverClassName="com.mysql.jdbc.Driver"
  url="jdbc:mysql://localhost:3306/tomcat7"/>
```

2. The following lines of code provide the `web.xml` configuration for the application. This should be placed on the `WEB-INF/web.xml` for the application-specific content.

```
<web-app xmlns="http://java.sun.com/xml/ns/j2ee"
  xmlns:xsi="http://www.w3.org/2001/XMLSchema-instance"
  xsi:schemaLocation="http://java.sun.com/xml/ns/j2ee
  http://java.sun.com/xml/ns/j2ee/web-app_2_4.xsd"
  version="2.4">
<description>Tomcat 7 test DB</description>
<resource-ref>
   <description>DB Connection</description>
   <res-ref-name>jdbc/tomcat7</res-ref-name>
   <res-type>javax.sql.DataSource</res-type>
   <res-auth>Container</res-auth>
</resource-ref>
</web-app>
```

3. The MySQL JDBC driver is deployed in the `CATALINA_HOME/lib/` folder of Tomcat. `MySQL 3.23.47` or `Connector/J 3.0.11-stable` are the most common and widely used JAR files.

 You can download the MySQL JAR freely from the open source website, `http://dev.mysql.com/downloads/`.

4. One of the most important points which the Tomcat administrator should keep in mind is that, in MySQL, the DB should be configured with all privileges for the DB server user. Log in to the MySQL prompt and run the following command to grant the privileges:

```
mysql> GRANT ALL PRIVILEGES ON *.* TO tomcatuser@localhost
IDENTIFIED BY 'tomcat7' WITH GRANT OPTION;

mysql> create database tomcat7;

mysql> use tomcat7;

mysql> create table testdata ( id int not null auto_increment
primary key,foo varchar(25), bar int);
```

 If you create the MySQL user without password, then the JDBC driver will fail to connect and you will have an authentication error in `catalina.out`.

DataSource for PostgreSQL

PostgreSQL is an open source and relational database. It is one of the oldest databases (15 years old). It can be installed on multiple OSes, such as Windows, Unix, MAC, and so on.

It has a four step configuration rule similar to Oracle as follows:

1. The following code provides the definition of datasource in `server.xml`. By default, these values are defined in the global section.

```
<Resource name="jdbc/tomcat7" auth="Container"
  type="javax.sql.DataSource"
  driverClassName="org.postgresql.Driver"
  url="jdbc:postgresql://127.0.0.1:5432/tomcat7"
  username="tomcat7" password="tomcat" maxActive="20" maxIdle="10"
  maxWait="-1"/>
```

2. The PostgreSQL JDBC driver is deployed in the `CATALINA_HOME/lib/postgresql-9.0-801.jdbc3.jar` folder of Tomcat.

 Based on the version, the JDBC driver should be downloaded. For more reference on the driver version, refer to `http://jdbc.postgresql.org/download.html`.

3. For the `web.xml` configuration of the application, use the following lines of code. This should be placed in the `WEB-INF/web.xml` for the application-specific content.

```
<resource-ref>
  <description>postgreSQL Tomcat datasource </description>
  <res-ref-name>jdbc/tomcat7 </res-ref-name>
  <res-type>javax.sql.DataSource</res-type>
  <res-auth>Container</res-auth>
</resource-ref>
```

At the end of these steps, the developer will reference the JNDI in his/her code file and connect to the database.

Comparison of the datasource for common databases

Until now, we have seen how the datasource is configured on different databases. Let's quickly compare and find out what are the different syntaxes for each database:

- **Oracle**: The following mentioned code describes the datasource parameter for the Oracle database:

```
<Resource name="jdbc/tomcat7" auth="Container"
  type="javax.sql.DataSource"
  driverClassName="oracle.jdbc.OracleDriver"
  url="jdbc:oracle:thin:@127.0.0.1:1521:test"
  description="test database for tomcat 7"
  username="admin" password="admin" maxActive="20"
  maxIdle="10" maxWait="-1"/>
```

- **MySQL**: The following mentioned code describes the datasource parameter for the MySQL database:

```
<Resource name="jdbc/tomcat7" auth="Container"
  type="javax.sql.DataSource"
  driverClassName="org.postgresql.Driver"
  url="jdbc:postgresql://127.0.0.1:5432/tomcat7"
  username="tomcat7" password="tomcat" maxActive="20" maxIdle="10"
  maxWait="-1"/>
```

- **PostgreSQL**: The following mentioned code describes the datasource parameter for the PostgreSQL database:

```
<Resource name="jdbc/tomcat7" auth="Container"
  type="javax.sql.DataSource"
  driverClassName="org.postgresql.Driver"
  url="jdbc:postgresql://127.0.0.1:5432/tomcat7"
  username="tomcat7" password="tomcat" maxActive="20" maxIdle="10"
  maxWait="-1"/>
```

Database	oracle	Mysql	Postgresql
classes	oracle.jdbc.OracleDriver	com.mysql.jdbc.Driver	org.postgresql.Driver
Port	1521	3306	5432
JDBC driver	ojdbc14.jar	MySQL 3.23.47	postgresql-9.0-801.jdbc3.jar

In the previous figure, we have defined each `driverClassName`, port, and JDBC driver for each database and tabulated to conclude that if you know the details for connectivity with the database, you can configure any new database very easily.

 Every vendor has a predefined set of libraries through which you can connect to its database. If you need to connect to any other database, which is not mentioned here, then you can visit the vendor websites for support information.

Tomcat Manager configuration

The Tomcat Manager is a very powerful tool for Tomcat administration. In production server issues, it's not possible to be in the data center at all times. Sometimes, we have to connect to Tomcat remotely to resolve the issues and that is when the Tomcat Manager is very useful for handing a critical issue. It comes with the following features:

- Deployment of a new application remotely
- Idle session clearing
- Undeployment of an application without restarting the container
- Analysis of memory leaks
- JVM status
- Server status

Enabling the Tomcat Manager

By default, the Tomcat Manager is disabled in Tomcat 7. To enable the Tomcat Manager, you have to do the configuration in the default file, that is, `tomcat-users.xml` in the `conf` folder of Tomcat 7.

In this file, user roles and their authentication are configured. Let's quickly discuss the configuration parameters for enabling the Tomcat Manager.

Before enabling the Tomcat Manager, an authentication window will pop-up while browsing the Tomcat page, as shown in the following screenshot:

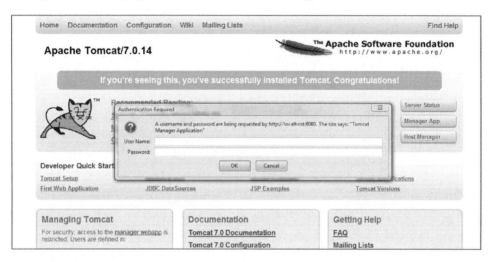

The following screenshot shows the `tomcat-users.xml` section before enabling the user properties:

```
<tomcat-users>
<!--
  NOTE:  By default, no user is included in the "manager-gui" role required
  to operate the "/manager/html" web application.  If you wish to use this ap
  you must define such a user - the username and password are arbitrary.
-->
<!--
  NOTE:  The sample user and role entries below are wrapped in a comment
  and thus are ignored when reading this file. Do not forget to remove
  <!.. ..> that surrounds them.
-->
<!--
  <role rolename="tomcat"/>
  <role rolename="role1"/>
  <user username="tomcat" password="tomcat" roles="tomcat"/>
  <user username="both" password="tomcat" roles="tomcat,role1"/>
  <user username="role1" password="tomcat" roles="role1"/>
-->
</tomcat-users>
```

After enabling the Tomcat Manager, the user will get a message in the command prompt, as shown in the following screenshot:

```
  <role rolename="tomcat"/>
  <role rolename="role1"/>
  <user username="admin" password="admin" roles="tomcat"/>
  <user username="both" password="admin" roles="tomcat,role1"/>
  <user username="role1" password="admin" roles="role1"/>
</tomcat-users>
```

By default, Tomcat 7 comes with two users, tomcat and role1. If you want to add more users based on your system requirement, you can add here and define the role. Once you enable the Tomcat user configurations, this configuration will be in effect after the Tomcat recycle.

You can browse the Tomcat Manager using the URL http://localhost:8080/ and click on **Manager App**, as shown in the the following screenshot:

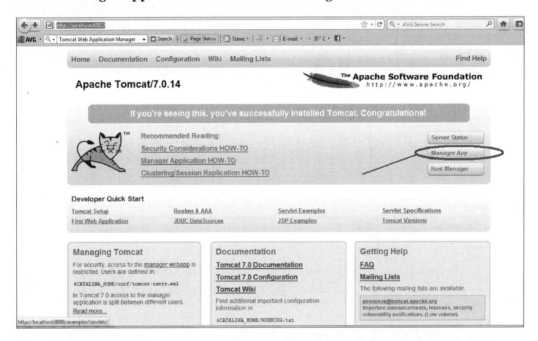

Once the authentication page is displayed, provide the user ID/password (user = admin, password = admin) as it's already defined in tomcat-users.xml. Click on **OK**. The pop-up will redirect it to the Tomcat Manager console, as shown in the following screenshot:

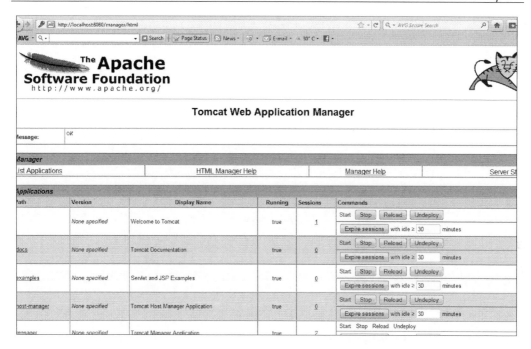

Through this console, we can deploy the new application or modify the current application's state to stop, undeploy, start, reload, clear sessions, and so on. Also, we can check the current status of the server by clicking on the **Server Status**, as shown in the following screenshot:

The following screenshot shows the **Server Status**:

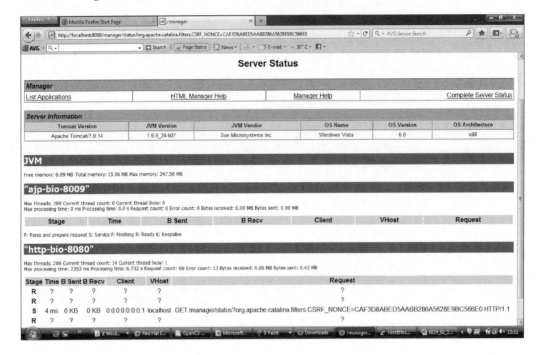

The server status will define the following details:

- JVM status
  - Max memory
  - Total memory
  - Free memory

- Connection of AJP port 8009
  - Connection state
  - Data sent
  - Data received
  - Client
  - Virtual host

- Connection on HTTP port 8080
  - ◦ Connection state
  - ◦ Data sent
  - ◦ Data received
  - ◦ Client
  - ◦ Virtual host

- Server information
  - ◦ Tomcat version
  - ◦ OS version
  - ◦ JVM version
  - ◦ System architecture

Context path

The context path is a key element of a web application. It's also used for a virtual host. Virtual hosting can be defined as a method through which you can host multiple domain names on the same web server or a single IP.

The context path is also used to define the URL mapping for the `.war` files.

Many people ask why we need the context path. Instead, can we deploy the application on one root directory? The answer is, by defining the context path, we minimize the load on the server. When the server gets the request with the URL, it will check the `server.xml` or context path for the defined URL. If it's found, then the URL will be served from here, otherwise the server has to search all the deployed WAR files. Hence, the context path reduces the CPU cycle.

The second important advantage is, it gives us freedom to customize the application based on our requirement, such as logging, appBase, DB connection, and so on.

Let's consider a scenario for a large enterprise where a single application needs to be deployed on 100 Tomcat servers. Now it's impossible to deploy the application on every server, and so, in that case Common NAS share is used for the application deployment.

Enabling the context path

The context path in Tomcat can be enabled in two ways:

- GUI using the Tomcat Web Application Manager
- Command-line configuration in `server.xml`

GUI using the Tomcat Web Application Manager

For enabling the context path in the Tomcat Manager, you have to first log in to the Tomcat Manager app using the URL `http://localhost:8080`. Then click on **Manager App**, as shown in the following screenshot:

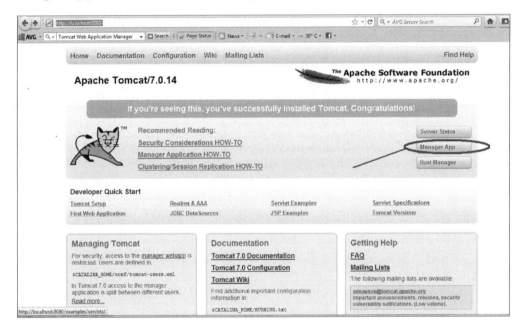

It then displays the **Tomcat Web Application Manager** console and its features, as shown in the following screenshot:

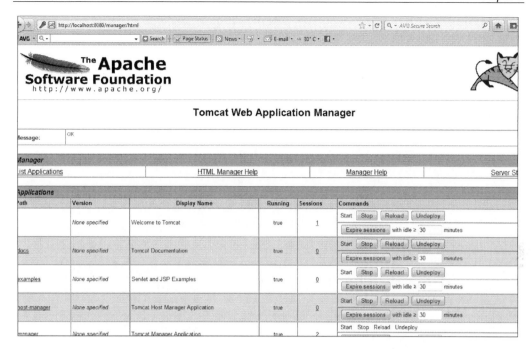

You can create the context path using the **Deploy** tab. Click on **Browse** and select the required WAR file. Then click on **Deploy**. It will take 10 to 15 seconds to deploy the application and you will see a page similar to the following screenshot:

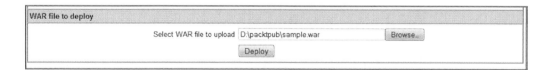

The following screenshot shows the application deployment status and administrative controls such as **Stop**, **Reload**, and **Undeploy**:

Once the application is deployed successfully, you can browse the application using the URL http://localhost:8080/sample, as shown in the following screenshot:

Command-line configuration in server.xml

Another way of adding the context path in Tomcat 7 is by editing server.xml. But, you need to have a good understanding of XML. Let's quickly discuss the changes that need to be done on the Tomcat server.

```
<Context path="/sample" docBase="/opt/" reloadable="true"
  swallowOutput="true">
  <WatchedResource>WEB-INF/web.xml</WatchedResource>
  <Logger className="org.apache.catalina.logger.FileLogger"
    prefix="www-sample-com-log." suffix=".txt"
    timestamp="true"/>
</Context>
```

```
<Context path="/sample" docBase="/opt/" reloadable="true"
      swallowOutput="true">
<WatchedResource>WEB-INF/web.xml</WatchedResource>
    <Logger className="org.apache.catalina.logger.FileLogger"
      prefix="www-example-com-log." suffix=".txt"
      timestamp="true"/>

  </Context>
```

Now, it's time to discuss the parameters defined in the context path. The previous screenshot shows the details for the context path.

- path="/sample": It defines the path URL for the server request, for example, http://localhost:8080/sample.

- docBase="/opt/": It defines the document root for the context path. In simple language, this parameter defines the place from where the deployment .war file gets picked up.

- `reloadable="true"`: If this parameter is `true`, then every change done on the WAR file will be in effect automatically without a Tomcat recycle.

- `swallowOutput="true"`: If this parameter is set to true, then the output for `System.out` and `System.err` will be redirected to the application log.

 It's always recommended to take the backup of the existing configuration file before performing changes in Tomcat.

Deployment in Tomcat 7

Deployment is basically defined as the installation of the WAR files in the web application. In other words, we can define the unpacking of the WAR file in the Tomcat `webapps` directory.

Structure of the WebArchive

You develop your web application within a specified directory structure so that it can be archived and deployed on Tomcat 7. All servlets, classes, static files, and other resources belonging to a web application are organized under a directory hierarchy. The root of this hierarchy defines the **document root** of your web application. All files under this root directory can be served to the client, except for files under the special directory `WEB-INF`, located under the root directory. The name of your web application is used to resolve requests for components of the application.

 Always place private files (files which are not required to serve to the client) in the `WEB-INF` directory, under the `root` directory. All files under `WEB-INF` are private, and are not served to the client.

- WebApplicationName/: In this directory (or a subdirectory), all the static files, such as HTML and JSP files are placed. This directory is the document root of your web application.

- /WEB-INF/web.xml: It contains the deployment descriptor for the web application. Resources specific to the application are placed here.

- /WEB-INF/classes: This contains all the server-side classes or your application-specific third-party classes.

- /WEB-INF/lib: This directory contains JAR files used for the JSP completion.

- `web.xml`: It contains the details of all your dynamic files (servlets and JSP) and also other configuration-related information such as session time out and defining the datasource (access to DB).

```
<servlet>
  <servlet-name>classB</servlet-name>
  <servlet-class>class.classB</servlet-class>
</servlet>
```

In the previous snippet, we are mapping the name to the servlet class (when Tomcat 7 starts, it will create an object of the class and map it to the name we have provided in the `servlet-name` field).

```
classB =new class.classB ()
<servlet-mapping>
<servlet-name> classB </servlet-name>
```

Archive Files

In most production environments, you receive a deployment unit as an archive file from the developer. An archive file is a single file that contains all of an application or module's classes, static files, directories, and deployment descriptor files. Archive files are typically created by using the JAR utility or Ant JAR tool.

Deployment units that are packaged using the JAR utility have a specific file extension depending on the type, as explained in the following points:

- EJBs are packaged as `.jar` files
- Web applications are packaged as `.war` files
- Resource adapters are packaged as `.rar` files
- Enterprise applications are packaged as `.ear` files, and can contain any combination of EJBs, web applications, and resource adapters
- Web services can be packaged either as `.ear` files or as `.war` files

Exploded archive directories

An exploded archive directory contains the same files and directories as a JAR archive. However, the files and directories reside directly in your filesystem and are not packaged into a single archive file with the JAR utility.

A deployment unit should be deployed as an exploded archive directory, rather than a single archive file, in the following circumstances:

- You want to perform partial updates to a deployed application without redeploying the entire application.

- You want to use the Tomcat Manager to dynamically edit and persist selected deployment descriptor values for the deployment.

 It's not possible to edit deployment descriptor values in the console for deployments from the archive files or .war files.

- You are deploying a web application that contains static files that you will periodically update. In this case, it is easier to deploy the application as an exploded directory, because you can update and refresh the static files without re-creating the archive.

Deployment operations

The deployment tools provide support for performing these common deployment operations:

- **Deploy**: It makes deployment source files available to target servers and loading classes into class loaders so that applications are available to clients.

- **Redeploy:** It updates a deployment unit or part of a deployment unit (for example, a WAR, a module within a WAR, or a static file in a Web Application) that is currently deployed and available to clients. When redeploying an entire application, all of the application's modules must redeploy successfully or the entire application is stopped.

 An application becomes unavailable to clients during redeployment. The Tomcat 7 server doesn't guarantee the operation of the application and deployment task if there is an access from the client at this time. For this reason, redeployment is not recommended for use in a production environment.

- **Stop:** This unloads an application's classes and makes an application unavailable to clients. Stopping still leaves the deployment files and deployment name available to the target servers for subsequent redeployment or starting.

- **Start**: It reloads an application's classes into class loaders and makes the application available to clients. Starting requires that the deployment files be available on the target servers as a result of an earlier deployment.

- **Undeploy**: This stops a deployment unit and then removes its deployment files and the deployment name from the target servers.

An application becomes unavailable to clients during undeployment. The Tomcat 7 server doesn't guarantee the operation of the application and deployment task if there is an access from the client at this time.

Types of deployment

The deployment staging mode determines how deployment files are made available to the target servers that must deploy an application or standalone module. The Tomcat 7 server provides three different options for staging files listed as follows:

- Stage mode
- Nostage mode
- External_stage mode

The following table describes the behavior and best practices for using the different deployment staging modes:

Deployment Staging Mode	Behavior	When to Use
Stage	The Tomcat administrator first copies the deployment unit source files to the staging directories of the target servers and then the target servers deploy them using their local copy of the deployment files.	Deploying small or moderate-sized applications to multiple Tomcat 7 server instances. Deploying small or moderate-sized applications to a cluster.
Nostage	The Tomcat administrator does not copy the deployment unit files. Instead, all servers deploy using the same physical copy of the deployment files, which must be directly accessible by the Tomcat administrator and target servers. Nostage deployments of exploded archive directories is not recommended	Deploying to a single server instance. Deploying to a cluster on a multi-homed machine. Deploying very large applications to multiple targets or to a cluster where deployment files are placed on the server.

Deployment Staging Mode	Behavior	When to Use
External_stage	The Tomcat administrator does not copy the deployment files. Instead, the administrator must ensure that deployment files are distributed to the correct staging directory location before deployment (for example, by manually copying files prior to deployment). With external_stage deployments, the Tomcat administrator requires a copy of the deployment files for validation purposes. Copies of the deployment files that reside in the target servers' staging directories are not validated before deployment.	Deployments where you want to manually control the distribution of deployment files to the target servers. Deploying to the server instance where third-party applications or scripts manage the copying of deployment files to the correct staging directories. Deployments that do not require a dynamic update of selected deployment descriptors via the Tomcat Manager (not supported in external_stage mode). Deployments that do not require partial redeployment of the application components.

Ways of application deployment in Tomcat 7

Deployment of applications can be done in many ways in Tomcat 7. There are five different ways which are widely known and accepted in the various industries displayed in the following figure:

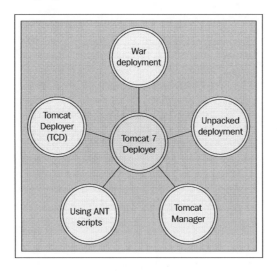

- **War deployment**: You can deploy the WAR file in the CATALINA_BASE directory of Tomcat and restart Tomcat to view the application. This approach is widely used in the production environment.

- **Unpacked deployment**: In this deployment method, the WAR file is extracted on the CATALINA_BASE directory for the instance. This method is commonly used in the development server.

- **Tomcat Manager**: It's a very good tool which is widely used in the production environment, mainly in remote infrastructure deployment. You can log in to the Tomcat browser from your system and deploy. Then click on the new web application deployment, as shown in the next screenshot:

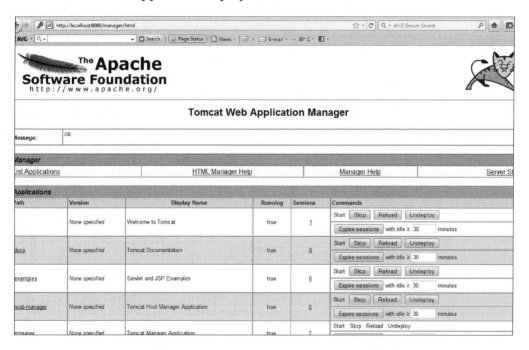

- You can create the context path using the **Deploy** tab. Click on **Browse** and select the required WAR file. Then click on **Deploy**. It will take 10 to 15 seconds to deploy the application and you will see a page similar to the following screenshot:

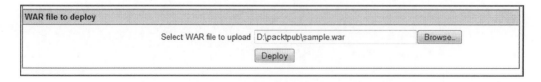

- The following screenshot shows the application deployment status and administrative control such as **Stop**, **Reload**, and **Undeploy**:

- Once the application is deployed successfully, as shown in the following screenshot, you can browse the application using the URL, `http://localhost:8080/sample`:

- **Using ANT scripts**: You can also deploy the application using the ANT scripts. These scripts contain the information of the source/destination and target file. For doing this deployment, the Tomcat instance should be running.

- **TCD (Tomcat Deployer)**: It is a tool which is used for application deployment. ANT should be installed for the TCD to be working and the Tomcat instance should be running. There is no need to install he TCD on the Tomcat instance.

Common issues in deployment, configuration, and their troubleshooting

There are multiple issues which may arise after the deployment and configuration on Tomcat. Let's discuss the different issues:

Scenario 1:

Issue: Users complain that after the deployment, they can still view the old code.

Troubleshooting steps:

- Check if the latest file is present on the doc base.
- Check the `catalina.out` in the `logs` directory of Tomcat 7 and whether the WAR filename is deployed or not.

- If both are checked and the issue still persists, then stop the Tomcat service and clear the content of the `temp` directory under the `work/Catalina/localhost` using the following command:

```
cd /opt/apache-tomcat-7.0.12/temp/
  rm -rf ../temp/*
```

```
cd /opt/apache-tomcat-7.0.12/work/Catalina/localhost/
  rm -rf ../localhost/*
```

- Restart the Tomcat service and ask the user to test the application.

Scenario 2:

Issue: Users complaining that they can view the current deployed code on one node and the other node still displays the previous version of the code.

Troubleshooting steps:

- Check if the latest file is present on the doc base.
- Check the `catalina.out` in the `logs` directory of Tomcat 7 and whether the WAR filename is deployed or not.

  If both are checked and the issue still persists, then stop the Tomcat service on node2. Replicate the code from node1 and clear the content of the `temp` directory under the `work/Catalina/localhost` using the following command:

```
cd /opt/apache-tomcat-7.0.12/temp/
  rm -rf ../temp/*
```

```
cd /opt/apache-tomcat-7.0.12/work/Catalina/localhost/
  rm -rf ../localhost/*
```

- Restart the Tomcat service and ask the user to test the application. Also, check the database status on node1 and node2, if they are in replication.
- Connect the database from both the nodes.

Scenario 3:

Issue: The Tomcat instance is not coming up after the changes made to `server.xml`.

Troubleshooting steps:

- Go to the Tomcat `bin` directory.
- Then, run the `configtest.sh`. It will give you the following output:

```
[root@localhost ~]# cd /opt/apache-tomcat-7.0.12/bin/
[root@localhost bin]# ./configtest.sh
Using CATALINA_BASE:   /opt/apache-tomcat-7.0.12
```

```
Using CATALINA_HOME:     /opt/apache-tomcat-7.0.12

Using CATALINA_TMPDIR:   /opt/apache-tomcat-7.0.12/temp

Using JRE_HOME:          /opt/jdk1.6.0_24

Using CLASSPATH:         /opt/apache-tomcat-7.0.12/bin/bootstrap.
jar:/opt/apache-tomcat-7.0.12/bin/tomcat-juli.jar

Error:-

org.apache.catalina.startup.Bootstrap.main(Bootstrap.java:435)

Caused by: java.net.BindException: Address already in use

        at java.net.PlainSocketImpl.socketBind(Native Method)

        at java.net.PlainSocketImpl.bind(PlainSocketImpl.java:383)

        at java.net.ServerSocket.bind(ServerSocket.java:328)

        at java.net.ServerSocket.<init>(ServerSocket.java:194)

        at java.net.ServerSocket.<init>(ServerSocket.java:150)
```

- It means that Tomcat is already running. Then, stop the web server and clear the `temp` directory.
- Restart the services again.

Summary

In this chapter, we have discussed the configuration of Tomcat including data source configuration for the different databases (Oracle, MySQL, and PostgreSQL) and the context path creation using a sample application, various ways to perform deployment including deployment using the Tomcat Manager for the sample application. We also discussed troubleshooting of common issues.

In the next chapter, we will discuss performance tuning for Tomcat 7 in terms of the JVM and OS level.

3
Performance Tuning

Visualize that you are on a vacation, enjoying the trip, and at 2 o'clock in the morning, your phone rings. You quickly pick up your phone to find out that your boss is calling to say that ABC Company's web system is down and you have to come online and fix the issue. If you don't want to face these sort of situations, please read this chapter with more attention.

In this chapter, we will cover the major topics of performance tuning including the following:

- Memory related issues
- JVM parameter optimization
- OS level optimization to improve the performance

Performance tuning for Tomcat 7

Performance tuning plays a vital role to run a web application without downtime. Also, it helps in improving the performance of Tomcat while running the applications. Tuning of the Tomcat server may vary from application to application. Since every application has its own requirements, it is a very tricky task to tune Tomcat 7 for every application. In this topic, we will discuss tuning of various components of Tomcat, and how they are useful in the server performance. Before we start with the configuration changes, let us quickly discuss why we need to tune Tomcat.

Why we need performance tuning?

People always ask, why do we need to do performance tuning for Tomcat 7 when, by default, Tomcat 7 packages are customized for the production run.

The answer to this question is very subjective; every web application has its own requirement. Some of the applications require high memory while others require less memory but a high GC pause. It varies from application to application and the administrator has to tune Tomcat based on the application's requirement.

Performance tuning is still incomplete with JVM tuning. There are multiple other things which also play a key role in the performance of an application, such as database configuration, OS level setting, and the hardware used for the application. The following figure shows the different types of performance tuning done on Tomcat 7:

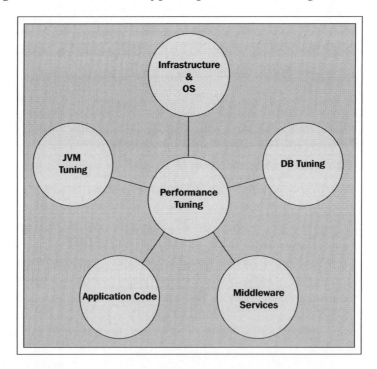

There are different aspects, which have an impact on the performance of Tomcat 7, mentioned as follows:

- **Application Code**: If the application code is not developed properly, it may cause performance issues. For example, if the database connection from the application code is not closed properly, then it will create a stale connection in the database, hence, causing the application to run slowly.

- **Database Tuning**: The database can cause major issues in the performance of the application hosted in Tomcat. For example, if the database response is slow, then it sends a delayed response to the application query, hence, causing the application to run slowly in Tomcat 7.

- **JVM Tuning**: Every application has its own memory requirement. If an application (say abc) has a very huge memory requirement and you have allocated less memory, then you might face OOM (out of memory) issues, hence, causing performance issues.

- **Middleware Services**: Middleware services may lead to application connectivity issues with the external interface. For example, nowadays, mobile applications use web services to connect to the server and fetch the application data. In this way, we are only exposing web services to the Internet and not the entire application server.

- **Infrastructure and OS**: Infrastructure issues may also lead to performance degradation. For example, if there is an Internet connectivity issue with the network or there is a packet drop in the network, it causes degraded performance.

We will discuss different ways of troubleshooting the previously mentioned issues in *Chapter 7, Troubleshooting in Tomcat*.

 In 70 percent of cases, the reason for bad performance of the application is incorrect code. There are various reasons such as improper closing of loops, connections are not closed, and so on.

How to start performance tuning

Performance tuning starts from the day the application deployment stage begins. One may ask, as the application is only in the development phase, why do we need to do performance tuning now?

At the time of the application development, we are in the state to define the architecture of the application, how the application is going to perform in reality, and how many resources are required for an application. There are no predefined steps for performance tuning. But there are certain thumb rules which all administrators should follow for performance tuning.

The following figure shows the process flow for performance tuning:

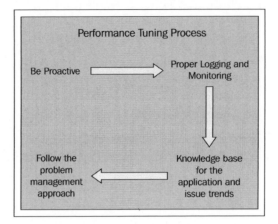

- **Be Proactive**: Think about the various ways an application failure may arise in future (bottlenecks for the application). Then prepare a solution for the application to avoid the failure. Keep track of application issues and use the latest profiling tool available in the market.

 If you are proactively checking the application and avoid bottlenecks for the application, then around 70 percent of the issues are solved in the production environment. This approach will give your customers great satisfaction when using the application.

- **Proper Logging and Monitoring**: Proper logging should be enabled for Tomcat, this will be really helpful in tracing the potential issues which are about to occur in the production system. We will discuss different methods of enabling logger in *Chapter 6, Logging in Tomcat 7*. It is always recommended to monitor the system on a regular basis.

 There are many monitoring tools available in the market, which give you a real picture of the application. Major enterprises use these kind of tools for profiling the application. For example, JON(Jboss on Network), CA Wily, Nagios, Panorama, and so on.

- **Knowledge base for the application and issue trends**: It is always recommended to have a knowledge base for the application as the application is running 24x7. Also, we should have a good documentation for the application's support, so that everyone who is working on this application has the same information on the issues.

- **Follow the problem management approach**: Make it good practice to perform the **Root Cause Analysis (RCA)** for every issue. This way recurrence of this issue can be avoided in the future.

We have discussed the approaches for tuning Tomcat 7. Now, it's time to do real-time performance tuning for Tomcat 7.

Tomcat components tuning

In Tomcat 7, you can do many configurations to improve the server performance, threads tuning, port customization, and JVM tuning. Let's quickly discuss the major components of Tomcat 7 which are important for performance improvement.

Types of connectors for Tomcat 7

Connectors can be defined as a point of intersection where requests are accepted and responses are returned. There are three types of connectors used in Tomcat 7, as shown in the following figure. These connectors are used according to different application requirements. Let's discuss the usability of each connector:

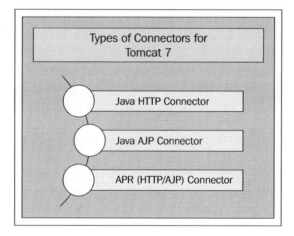

Java HTTP Connector

The Java HTTP Connector is based on the HTTP Protocol, which supports only the HTTP/1.1 protocol. It makes the Tomcat server act as a standalone web server and also enables the functionality to host the JSP/servlet.

 For more information on the HTTP Connector, please visit http://tomcat.apache.org/tomcat-7.0-doc/config/http.html.

Java AJP Connector

The Java AJP Connector is based on the **AJP (Apache JServ Protocol)** and communicates with the web server through the AJP. This connector is mainly used when you don't want to expose your Java servlet container to the Internet (using a different frontend server) and is also very helpful where SSL is not terminating in Tomcat 7. Some of the examples where the AJP is implemented are, mod_jk, mod _proxy, and so on.

 For more information on AJP Connectors, please visit the URL http://tomcat.apache.org/tomcat-7.0-doc/config/ajp.html.

APR (AJP/HTTP) Connector

Apache Portable Runtime (APR) is very helpful where scalability, performance, and better collaboration are required with different web servers. It provides additional functionalities such as Open SSL, Shared memory, Unix sockets, and so on. It also enables Java to emerge as a web server technology rather than being absorbed on backend technology. We will discuss the real-time implementation of the Tomcat Connector in *Chapter 4, Integration of Tomcat with the Apache Web Server*.

 For more details on the APR Connector, please visit the link http://tomcat.apache.org/tomcat-7.0-doc/apr.html.

Thread optimization for Tomcat 7

Thread tuning plays a major role in Tomcat's performance. In most cases, we have seen that a particular application works very well on other industries, but when we implement the same application, its performance is degraded (application performance issues). The reason being that there may be the chance that we have done an improper tuning of the thread, which may lead to server-degraded performance. Let's discuss the different components of thread tuning thread pools.

The thread pool can be defined as the capacity of the web server to accept the number of connections or requests handled in Tomcat 7. We can configure two types of thread pool; Shared pool and Dedicated pool. These configurations need to be done in `server.xml` placed in `TOMCAT_HOME/conf/server.xml`. Let us discuss these methods and their configurations.

Shared thread pool (shared executor)

It can be defined as a thread pool which is shared among many connectors. For example, if you have a four connector configuration, then you can share the same thread pool for all connectors. Following is the process to configure a shared thread pool:

1. Edit the `server.xml` and add the definition of the shared thread pool inside the services section. The following highlighted code shows the thread pool:

```
<Executor name="tomcatThreadPool"
   namePrefix="catalina-exec-"
   maxThreads="150"
   minSpareThreads="4"/>
```

2. Once you have defined the shared thread pool, call the reference of the thread setting in the Connector definition for the services section of `server.xml`, as shown in the following code:

```
<Connector executor="tomcatThreadPool"
   port="8080" protocol="HTTP/1.1"
   connectionTimeout="20000"
   redirectPort="8443" />
```

We have taken the default example given in `server.xml` to explain the shared pool. In practice, you can define the shared pool based on the business requirement.

Dedicated thread pool

It can be defined as a thread pool which is dedicated to only one connector definition. For example, if the application is expecting a high load, then using a dedicated thread pool is better for the connector, to manage the Tomcat instance smoothly. Following is the process to configure a dedicated thread pool. The highlighted code defines the values of a dedicated connection pool:

1. Edit the `server.xml` and define the configuration of the dedicated thread pool inside the Connector section. The following highlighted code shows the thread pool:

    ```
    <Connector port="8443" protocol="HTTP/1.1"
      SSLEnabled="true"
      maxThreads="150"
      scheme="https"
      secure="true"
      clientAuth="false" sslProtocol="TLS" />
    ```

Shared thread pool versus dedicated thread pool

Let us do a quick comparison between shared thread pool and dedicated thread pool to find out where they can be used. The following table shows the comparison between both the thread pooling methods for Tomcat 7:

Features	Shared thread pool	Dedicated thread pool
Number of users	Less	High
Environment	Development	Production
Performance	Low	Good

maxThreads

maxThreads can be defined as the highest number of requests a server can accept. By default, Tomcat 7 comes with `maxThreads=150`. In a production environment, we have to tune the `maxThreads` based on the server performance.

Let's perform a real time `maxThreads` tuning. Let us assume we have `maxThreads=300` for an application. Now, it's time to determine the impact of the thread tuning on the server. If the `maxThreads` is not configured properly, it may degrade the server performance. How to find the impact on the server?

The solution is to check the CPU utilization for the server. If the CPU utilization is high, then decrease the value of the threads. This means the thread had degraded the server performance, but if the CPU utilization is normal, then increase the value of the threads to accommodate more concurrent users.

 While setting the maxThreads, you have to consider other resources as well, such as the database connection, network bandwidth, and so on.

maxKeepAlive

It is defined as the number of concurrent TCP connections waiting in Tomcat 7. By default, maxKeepAlive is set to 1, which also means it is disabled.

If maxKeepAlive = 1 then,

- SSL is not terminated in Tomcat
- Load balancer technique is used
- Concurrent users are more

If maxKeepAlive > 1 then,

- SSL is terminated in Tomcat
- Concurrent users are less

JVM tuning

Before we start with JVM tuning, we should note that there are various vendors available in the market for JVM. Based on the application requirement, we should select the JDK from the vendor.

 Sun JDK is widely used in the IT industries.

Why do we need to tune the JDK for Tomcat?

Tomcat 7 comes with a heap size of 256 MB. Applications today need a large memory to run. In order to run the application, we have to tune the JVM parameter for Tomcat 7. Let's quickly discuss the default JVM configurations for Tomcat. The following steps describe the method to find out the Tomcat **Process ID (PID)** and memory values as shown in the next screenshot:

Run the following command on the terminal in Linux:

```
ps -ef |grep java
```

This will return all the Java processes running in the system, with all information such as the PID, where Tomcat is running, and so on:

```
root@localhost bin}# ps -ef |grep java
root      4306      1  0 14:09 pts/1    00:00:04 /opt/jdk1.6.0_24/bin/java -Djava.util.logging.config.file=/opt/apache-tomcat-7.0.12/conf/logging.
}java.util.logging.manager=org.apache.juli.ClassLoaderLogManager -Djava.endorsed.dirs=/opt/apache-tomcat-7.0.12/endorsed -classpath /opt/apache-t
bin/bootstrap.jar:/opt/apache-tomcat-7.0.12/bin/tomcat-juli.jar -Dcatalina.base=/opt/apache-tomcat-7.0.12 -Dcatalina.home=/opt/apache-tomcat-7.0
.tmpdir=/opt/apache-tomcat-7.0.12/temp org.apache.catalina.startup.Bootstrap start
root@localhost bin}# 
```

```
root      4306      1  0 14:09 pts/1        00:00:04 /opt/jdk1.6.0_24/bin/java
 -Djava.util.logging.config.file=/opt/apache-
 tomcat-7.0.12/conf/logging.properties -
 Djava.util.logging.manager=org.apache.juli.ClassLoaderLogManager -
 Djava.endorsed.dirs=/opt/apache-tomcat-7.0.12/endorsed -classpath
 /opt/apache-tomcat-7.0.12/bin/bootstrap.jar:/opt/apache-tomcat-
 7.0.12/bin/tomcat-juli.jar -Dcatalina.base=/opt/apache-tomcat-7.0.12 -
 Dcatalina.home=/opt/apache-tomcat-7.0.12 -Djava.io.tmpdir=/opt/apache-
 tomcat-7.0.12/temp org.apache.catalina.startup.Bootstrap start
```

In the previous output, 4306 is the PID for the Tomcat process. Now, we know the process ID for Tomcat, let's find out the memory allocated to the Tomcat instance using the command jmap.

For checking the process ID for Tomcat on Windows, you have to run the following command:

```
tasklist |find "tomcat"
```

The following screenshot shows the output of the previous command, where 2112 is the process ID for the Tomcat process:

```
C:\Users\user>tasklist |find "tomcat"
tomcat7.exe                    2112 Services              0      38,656 K
```

JMAP (Memory Map)

JMAP prints the complete picture for the shared Java Virtual Memory. It is a very good utility for the administrators to check the status of the shared memory. This command provides different options for executing the command. The following table describes the useful options of JMAP:

Options	Description
-dump	Dumps the Java heap in hprof binary format
-finalizer info	Prints information on objects awaiting finalization
-heap	Prints a heap summary
-histo	Prints a histogram of the heap
-permstat	Prints class loader-wise statistics of permanent generation of the Java heap

 For more information on the JMAP command, please visit http://docs.oracle.com/javase/6/docs/technotes/tools/share/jmap.html.

Syntax for jmap

The syntax for using the jmap command is ./jmap -heap <process id> where <process id> is the Java process for which we want to check the memory.

In the previous syntax, the -heap option prints a heap summary, the GC algorithm used, the heap configuration, and the generation-wise heap usage.

 If you want to run the jmap command for a 64 bit VM, then use the command jmap -J-d64 -heap pid.

In our current scenario, the PID is 4306:

```
[root@localhost bin]# ./jmap -heap 4306
```

The output of the previous command is as follows:

```
Attaching to process ID 4306, please wait...
Debugger attached successfully.
Client compiler detected.
JVM version is 19.1-b02
using thread-local object allocation.
Mark Sweep Compact GC
```

```
Heap Configuration:

   MinHeapFreeRatio = 40

   MaxHeapFreeRatio = 70

   MaxHeapSize       = 268435456 (256.0MB)

   NewSize           = 1048576 (1.0MB)

   MaxNewSize        = 4294901760 (4095.9375MB)

   OldSize           = 4194304 (4.0MB)

   NewRatio          = 2

   SurvivorRatio     = 8

   PermSize          = 12582912 (12.0MB)

   MaxPermSize       = 67108864 (64.0MB)

Heap Usage:
New Generation (Eden + 1 Survivor Space):

   capacity = 5111808 (4.875MB)

   used     = 3883008 (3.703125MB)

   free     = 1228800 (1.171875MB)

   75.96153846153847% used

Eden Space:

   capacity = 4587520 (4.375MB)

   used     = 3708360 (3.5365676879882812MB)

   free     = 879160 (0.8384323120117188MB)

   80.83583286830357% used

From Space:

   capacity = 524288 (0.5MB)

   used     = 174648 (0.16655731201171875MB)

   free     = 349640 (0.33344268798828125MB)

   33.31146240234375% used

To Space:

   capacity = 524288 (0.5MB)

   used     = 0 (0.0MB)

   free     = 524288 (0.5MB)

   0.0% used

tenured generation:

   capacity = 11206656 (10.6875MB)

   used     = 3280712 (3.1287307739257812MB)

   free     = 7925944 (7.558769226074219MB)
```

```
    29.274673908077485% used
Perm Generation:
    capacity = 12582912 (12.0MB)
    used     = 6639016 (6.331459045410156MB)
    free     = 5943896 (5.668540954589844MB)
    52.762158711751304% used
```

The previous command returns the following details:

- The heap configuration for the application (the highlighted code describes the heap configuration)
- The heap utilization for each JVM component
- The algorithm used for the garbage collection

If you see the previous heap allocation, then you can clearly differentiate the memory allocated to Tomcat 7. It is 256 MB, with 12 MB of Perm Generation.

How to increase the heap size in Tomcat 7

To increase the heap size for Tomcat 7, we need to add the JAVA_OPTS parameter in catalina.sh, which can be found in TOMCAT_HOME/bin.

Let us take an example of increasing the max heap size to 512 MB instead 256 MB. Also setting the Perm Gen = 256 MB.

```
JAVA_OPTS="-Xms128m -Xmx512m -XX:MaxPermSize=256m"
```

 Every change in configuration for the JVM parameter will be in effect after restarting the Tomcat server. You can verify the change done in the JVM parameter by running the jmap command.

[root@localhost bin]# jmap -heap 21091

The output of the previous command is as follows:

```
Attaching to process ID 21091, please wait...
Debugger attached successfully.
Client compiler detected.
JVM version is 19.1-b02
using thread-local object allocation.
Mark Sweep Compact GC
Heap Configuration:
    MinHeapFreeRatio = 40
```

```
MaxHeapFreeRatio = 70
MaxHeapSize       = 536870912 (512.0MB)
NewSize           = 1048576 (1.0MB)
MaxNewSize        = 4294901760 (4095.9375MB)
OldSize           = 4194304 (4.0MB)
NewRatio          = 2
SurvivorRatio     = 8
PermSize          = 12582912 (12.0MB)
MaxPermSize       = 268435456 (256.0MB)
```

The highlighted line of code in the previous code snippet is reflecting the value changed after the recycle in the JVM parameter.

We can also define JRE_HOME, JAVA_OPTS, JAVA_ENDORSED_DIRS, JPDA_TRANSPORT, JPDA_ADDRESS, JPDA_SUSPEND, JPDA_OPTS, LOGGING_CONFIG, LOGGING_MANAGER parameters in catalina.sh.

After doing the real-time implementation of increasing the memory, we will understand the need to tune JVM and how the heap value increases and decreases in Tomcat 7. Another term which people often talk about is **Garbage Collection** (GC). JVM tuning is not complete without garbage collection.

Garbage collection

Garbage means waste, but let's find out how this *waste* term fits in JVM.

What is garbage in JVM?

Garbage is nothing but an object that resides in the JVM memory and is not currently used by any program.

Garbage collector is an algorithm which runs periodically, collects the status of active and inactive objects in the memory, and deletes the inactive objects to release memory.

Following are the facts for garbage collection:

- Garbage collection doesn't work properly with large memory applications
- Garbage collection doesn't consider the fact that some of the objects have a very short life, but some of them remain active for years until the recycle of Tomcat 7

How garbage collection works

When the GC algorithm is called, it collects all the inactive objects present in the memory and, hence, cleans the memory. It can be explained as the opposite of manual memory management:

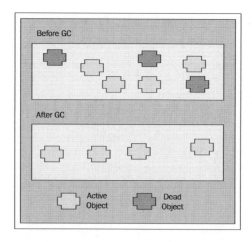

It removes all inactive objects from the memory and all active threads will remain in the memory. The previous figure shows the state of the memory before and after the GC. There are mainly three types of GC collectors used in the real-time environment:

- Serial collector
- Parallel collector
- Concurrent low pause collector

The following table describes the features of the serial collector:

Features	Serial collector
Process	Single thread is used for GC
GC pause	High
Threading	Single threaded
Application	Small application (data less than 100 MB)
Advantage	There is single thread communication

The following table describes the features of the parallel collector:

Features	Parallel collector
Process	Parallel thread does minor GC
GC pause	Less than Serial
Threading	Multithreaded
Application	Mid-large
Advantage	Used in applications when peak performance is needed

The following table describes the features of the concurrent collector:

Features	Concurrent collector
Process	GC is done concurrently
GC pause	Short pause
Threading	Multithreaded
Application	Mid-large
Advantage	Used in applications when a response is needed

 The three algorithms will work in JDK 1.5 or later.

 Parallel and concurrent collector algorithms should not be used together.

JVM options

The Java HotSpot VM options are classified in two categories; standard and non-standard options.

Standard options

Standard options are acknowledged by the Java HotSpot VM mentioned in the Java application launcher page for each OS. The following screenshot shows the standard option for the Java application launcher reference page:

```
[root@localhost ~]# java -showversion
java version "1.6.0_24"
Java(TM) SE Runtime Environment (build 1.6.0_24-b07)
Java HotSpot(TM) Client VM (build 19.1-b02, mixed mode, sharing)

Usage: java [-options] class [args...]
           (to execute a class)
   or  java [-options] -jar jarfile [args...]
           (to execute a jar file)

where options include:
    -d32          use a 32-bit data model if available

    -d64          use a 64-bit data model if available
    -client       to select the "client" VM
    -server       to select the "server" VM
    -hotspot      is a synonym for the "client" VM  [deprecated]
                  The default VM is client.

    -cp <class search path of directories and zip/jar files>
    -classpath <class search path of directories and zip/jar files>
                  A : separated list of directories, JAR archives,
                  and ZIP archives to search for class files.
    -D<name>=<value>
                  set a system property
    -verbose[:class|gc|jni]
                  enable verbose output
    -version      print product version and exit
    -version:<value>
                  require the specified version to run
    -showversion  print product version and continue
    -jre-restrict-search | -jre-no-restrict-search
                  include/exclude user private JREs in the version search
    -? -help      print this help message
    -X            print help on non-standard options
    -ea[:<packagename>...|:<classname>]
    -enableassertions[:<packagename>...|:<classname>]
                  enable assertions
    -da[:<packagename>...|:<classname>]
    -disableassertions[:<packagename>...|:<classname>]
                  disable assertions
    -esa | -enablesystemassertions
                  enable system assertions
    -dsa | -disablesystemassertions
                  disable system assertions
```

Non-standard options

Non-standard options are defined with -x or -xx options in the JVM. These options are grouped into three categories:

- **Behavioral options**: It changes the basic behavior of the VM.
- **Performance tuning options**: It triggers the performance optimization for the VM. also, these options are very useful for server tuning.

- **Debugging options**: It displays the output and printing information of the VM. In addition to that, it enables tracing in logs (these options are very useful in troubleshooting critical issues).

 Options that begin with -X are non-standard (not guaranteed to be supported on all VM implementations). Options that are specified with -XX are not stable and are not recommended for casual use.

The following table describes very commonly used options for JVM:

Options	Parameter	Description
Behavioral Options	-XX:+ScavengeBeforeFullGC	Do young generation GC prior to a full GC
Behavioral Options	--XX:-UseParallelGC	Use parallel garbage collection for scavenges
Performance Options	-XX:MaxNewSize=size	Maximum size of new generation (in bytes)
Performance Options	-XX:MaxPermSize=64m	Size of the Permanent Generation (after exceeding –Xmx value)
Performance Options	-Xms	Minimum heap memory for the startup of Tomcat
Performance Options	–Xmx	Maximum memory allocated to the instance
Performance Options	-Xss	Stack size for the heap
Debugging Options	-XX:-CITime	Prints time spent in the JIT Compiler
Debugging Options	-XX:ErrorFile=./hs_err_pid<pid>.log	If an error occurs, save the error data to this file
Debugging Options	-XX:HeapDumpPath=./java_pid<pid>.hprof	Path to the directory or filename for the heap dump
Debugging Options	-XX:-HeapDumpOnOutOfMemoryError	Dump the heap to the file when java.lang.OutOfMemoryError is thrown

Options	Parameter	Description
Debugging Options	`-XX:OnError="<cmd args>;<cmd args>"`	Run user-defined commands on fatal error
Debugging Options	`-XX:OnOutOfMemoryError="<cmd args>;`	Run user-defined commands when an OutOfMemoryError is first thrown
Debugging Options	`-XX:-PrintClassHistogram`	Print a histogram of class instances on *Ctrl-Break*

 For more information on the JVM non-standard options, please visit the link `http://www.oracle.com/technetwork/java/javase/tech/vmoptions-jsp-140102.html`.

Parameters displayed in the logs for GC

GC prints the output of the garbage collection to the `stdout` stream. At every garbage collection, the following five fields are printed:

```
[%T %B->%A(%C), %D]
```

- `%T`: This is "GC" when the garbage collection is a scavenge, and "Full GC:" is performed, then scavenge collects live objects from the new generation only, whereas a full garbage collection collects objects from all spaces in the Java heap.
- `%B`: It is the size of the Java heap used before the garbage collection, in KB.
- `%A`: It is the size of the Java heap after the garbage collection, in KB.
- `%C`: It is the current capacity of the entire Java heap, in KB.
- `%D`: It is the duration of the collection in seconds.

SurvivorRatio

It is defined as a ratio of eden to the survivor space size. The default value is 8, meaning that eden is 8 times bigger than from and to, each. The syntax for the SurvivorRatio is `-XX:SurvivorRatio=<size>`.

The following are some examples:

```
Xmn / (SurvivorRatio + 2) = size of from and to, each
( Xmn / (SurvivorRatio + 2) ) * SurvivorRatio = eden size
```

OS tuning

Every OS has its own prerequisites to run Tomcat 7 and the system has to be tuned based on the application's requirement, but there are some similarities between each OS. Let's discuss the common module used for optimization of Tomcat 7 for every OS. The OS plays a vital role for increasing the performance. Depending on the hardware, the application's performance will increase or decrease. Some of the points which are very much useful for the application are:

- **Performance characteristics of the 64 bit versus 32 bit VM**: The benefits of using 64 bit VMs are being able to address larger amounts of memory, which comes with a small performance loss in 64 bit VMs versus running the same application on a 32 bit VM. You can allocate more than 4 GB JVM for a memory-intensive application.

 In case you are using a 64 bit JVM edition, then you have to add 30 percent more memory as compared to a 32 bit JVM edition.

- **Files size**: Based on the application requirement, the file size is set in the OS. If the application is using a very high number of transactions, then the file limit needs to be increased.

- **Ulimits**: Based on the sessions, a user can increase the limits.

 These values are defined in /etc/sysctl.conf. If you need to update any of the above parameters then update it in etc/sysctl.conf, otherwise all the details will be flushed after the reboot of the OS.

- **Huge page size**: Many applications send a huge page size causing the application to run slow. In this case, you can increase the page size based on the application needs. You can check the page size by running the following command:

```
[root@localhost bin]# cat /proc/meminfo
MemTotal:      1571836 kB
MemFree:        886116 kB
Buffers:         74712 kB
Cached:         430088 kB
SwapCached:          0 kB
Active:         308608 kB
Inactive:       331944 kB
HighTotal:      671680 kB
```

```
HighFree:           97708 kB
LowTotal:          900156 kB
LowFree:           788408 kB
SwapTotal:        2040212 kB
SwapFree:         2040212 kB
Dirty:                 36 kB
Writeback:              0 kB
AnonPages:         135764 kB
Mapped:             54828 kB
Slab:               33840 kB
PageTables:          3228 kB
NFS_Unstable:           0 kB
Bounce:                 0 kB
CommitLimit:      2826128 kB
Committed_AS:      496456 kB
VmallocTotal:      114680 kB
VmallocUsed:         4928 kB
VmallocChunk:      109668 kB
HugePages_Total:        0
HugePages_Free:         0
HugePages_Rsvd:         0
Hugepagesize:        4096 kB
```

It will show you the complete details of the memory. Based on the current utilization, you can increase the value.

Summary

In this chapter, we have covered the different ways of performance improvement and techniques in Apache Tomcat 7. We went through step-by-step configuration for connectors, JVM performance tuning, and OS parameter optimization.

In the next chapter, we will discuss the various ways of integrating different web servers with Tomcat 7 and solutions for common problems faced in a real-time environment.

4

Integration of Tomcat with the Apache Web Server

The Apache HTTP server is one of the most widely used frontend web servers across the IT industry. This project was open sourced in 1995 and is owned by The Apache Software Foundation.

This chapter is very useful for the web administrator who works on enterprise-level web integration. It gives a very good idea about how integration is implemented in IT organizations. So, if you are thinking of enhancing your career in enterprise-level integrations of applications, then read this chapter carefully.

In this chapter, we will discuss the following topics:

- The Apache HTTP installation
- The various modules of Apache
- Integration of Apache with Tomcat 7
- How IT industry environments are set up

User request flow (web/application level)

Before we discuss the installation of Apache, let's discuss a high-level overview of how the request flows from the web and application server for an application in IT industries. The following figure shows the process flow for a user request, in a web application. The step-by-step involvement of each component is as follows:

1. The user hits the URL in the browser and the request goes to the HTTP server instead of Tomcat.

2. The HTTP server accepts the request and redirects it to Tomcat for business logic processing.

3. Tomcat internally contacts the database server to fetch the data, and sends the response back to the user through the same channel of request:

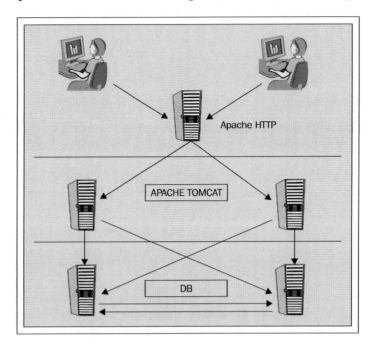

Why the Apache HTTP server

The Apache HTTP server is one of the most successful and common web servers used in IT industries. The reason being that it is supported by open source communities. In IT industries, the Apache HTTP server is heavily used as a frontend web server for the following reasons:

- **Efficiently serves static content**: Static content such as images, JS, CSS, and HTML files are more efficiently served by the HTTP server in a heavy user environment. Tomcat is also capable, but it increases the response time.

- **Increase the speed by 10 percent**: As compared to Tomcat, Apache serves static content 10 percent more efficiently. Integration of Apache is very helpful in the scenario of a high user load.

- **Clustering**: Apache is one of the most cost-effective and stable solutions to connect multiple instances of Tomcat. The biggest advantage of this feature is that the application will be online in case one of the instances goes down. Also, during deployment, we can deploy the code on one instance while the other instance is still online, serving requests to users. In simple terms, there is no downtime for the application.

- **Security**: Apache can enable user and host-based security. It can be done on Tomcat too. We have to decide where security needs to be enabled, either on Apache or Tomcat, based on the application's requirement

- **Multiple website hosting**: One of the best features of the Apache HTTP server is the capability of hosting multiple websites. This feature is also introduced for the first time in Tomcat 7. We can create 32 virtual hosts using `httpd.conf`. In case you want to configure more than 32 virtual hosts, then we have to create a separate `virtual.conf` file and include it in `httpd.conf` (`httpd.conf` and `virtual.conf` are the configuration files of the Apache HTTP server).

- **Modules**: Apache is very flexible with reference to modules. We can compile and decompile any module based on the application's requirement. This feature is very useful in terms of application scalability and integration with third-party tools.

- **Decorator**: This can be defined as the application URL (Redirects and Rewrites) rule designed to serve the user request based on the application's content. The Apache web server supports both, Redirects and Rewrites rules very effectively.

 We can create Redirect and Rewrites in application code also. These rules are in the form of servlet classes.

Installation of the Apache HTTP

The Apache installation can be done using various methods, based on the requirement of the infrastructure. For example, if you want to run multiple Apache instances on a single machine, then the Source installation will be used. There are mainly three types of installations done in various web environments:

- Source
- Binary
- RPM/exe

 Source is preferred by web administrators, as it can be customized based on system requirements.

Apache HTTP installation on Windows

In this topic, we will discuss the installation of the Apache HTTP as a service. The installation of the Apache HTTP server on the Windows platform is quite simple. Following are the steps to be performed:

1. The Apache HTTP server can be downloaded from various different sites, but it is always recommended to download it from its official site http:// httpd.apache.org/download.cgi. On this site, you can find the stable and beta release details. Download the latest **Win32 Binary without crypto (no mod_ ssl) (MSI Installer)** given in the website. Click on **httpd-2.2.X-win32-x86- no_ssl.msi** to begin the download. Here 2.2 is the major version and X is the minor version, which changes almost every month. The following screenshot shows the different versions available for the download:

Apache HTTP Server (httpd) 2.2.19 is the best available version   2011-05-22

The Apache HTTP Server Project is pleased to announce the release of Apache HTTP Server (httpd) version 2.2.19. This release represents fifteen years of innovation by the project, and is recommended over all previous releases!

For details see the Official Announcement and the CHANGES_2.2 or condensed CHANGES_2.2.19 lists

Add-in modules for Apache 2.0 are not compatible with Apache 2.2. If you are running third party add-in modules, you must obtain modules compiled or updated for Apache 2.2 from that third party, before you attempt to upgrade from these previous versions. Modules compiled for Apache 2.2 should continue to work for all 2.2.x releases.

- Unix Source: httpd-2.2.19.tar.gz [PGP] [MD5] [SHA1]
- Unix Source: httpd-2.2.19.tar.bz2 [PGP] [MD5] [SHA1]
- Win32 Source: httpd-2.2.19-win32-src.zip [PGP] [MD5] [SHA1]
- Win32 Binary without crypto (no mod_ssl) (MSI Installer): httpd-2.2.19-win32-x86-no_ssl.msi [PGP] [MD5] [SHA1]
- Win32 Binary including OpenSSL 0.9.8r (MSI Installer): httpd-2.2.19-win32-x86-openssl-0.9.8r.msi [PGP] [MD5] [SHA1]
- NetWare Binary: apache_2.2.19-netware.zip [PGP] [MD5] [SHA1]
- Other files

 We are using **httpd-2.2.X-win32-x86-no_ssl.msi** for the installation of Apache here and the installation steps will not change with the update of the minor version.

2. Once you have downloaded the required exe file. (**http-2.2.X-win32-x86- no_ssl.exe**), double-click on the exe and you will see a welcome screen as a pop-up. Click **Next**, as shown in the following screenshot:

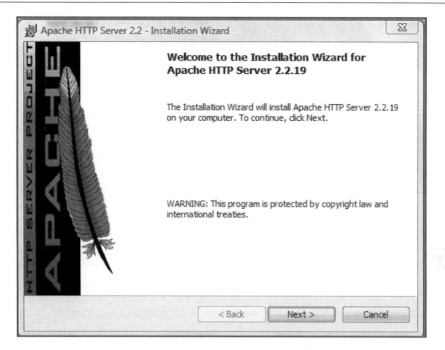

3. The next screen shows the **License Agreement**. Click on **I accept**, as shown in the following screenshot, it will show the server information screen:

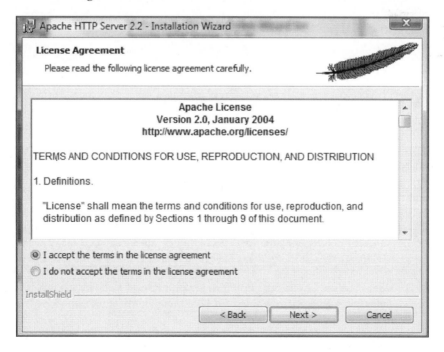

4. As shown in the following screenshot, you have to enter the following details
   - ○ **Server Domain**
   - ○ **Server name**: In a real-time environment, server name is the host name of the machine.
   - ○ **Administrator e-mail ID**: It is the SMTP address on the local server.

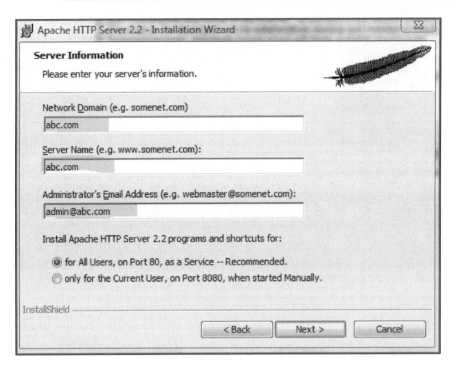

5. Once you fill in the details shown in the previous screenshot, click on **Next**. It takes you to the installation screen. Choose **Typical**, as shown in the following screenshot:

In a Typical installation, entire libraries and modules, which are required for installation of Tomcat 7 in Windows, are installed automatically. Also, a Typical installation contains predefined modules, which are necessary for the web server to perform their functionality. This method is recommended for beginners and intermediate users. In a Custom installation, we have the freedom to choose the modules, which are necessary for the application to perform their function properly, the rest of the module can be ignored, hence, taking less space and memory. This method is recommended for those who have a good knowledge of Apache.

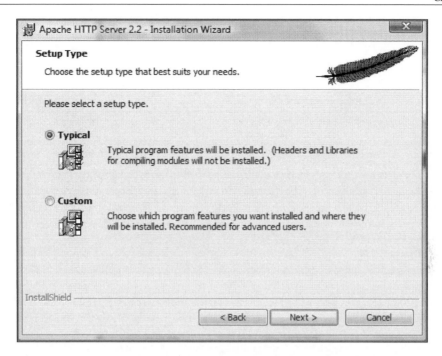

6. In the next screen, the installation directory of the HTTP server is displayed:

 It is recommended to use D drive for critical websites. The reason being that if the server crashes, Apache can still be recovered without any issue.

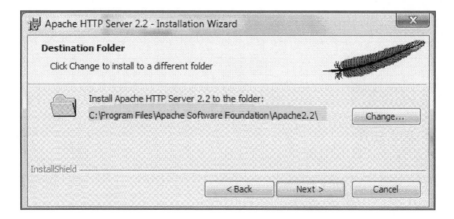

7. After clicking on **Next**, the installation process starts, as shown in the following screenshot:

8. Then a screen comes up indicating that it's completed, as shown in the following screenshot:

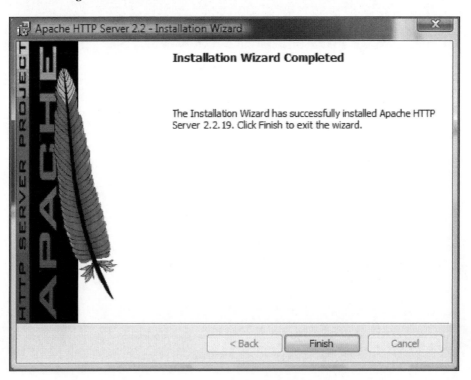

How to monitor the Apache service

Once Apache is installed, you can start and stop the services in two ways:

- Apache monitoring service
- services.msc

By default, Apache comes with a tool called Apache Monitor, through which Apache systems can be monitored. The following screenshot shows the Apache services status as green. It means the server is running. If you want to restart the services, you can use the **Restart** button to do the same.

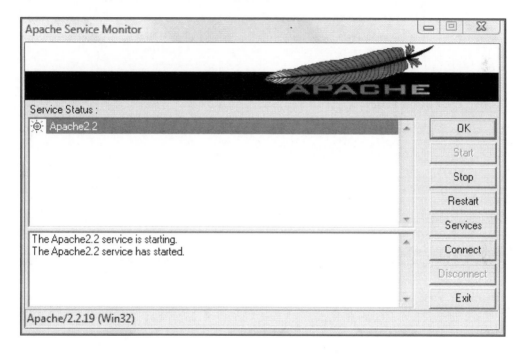

Another way of recycling Apache is through the **services.msc**, which can be accessed by clicking **Start | Run | services.msc**

The services console will open. Click on **Apache2.2** services, a services properties console window is displayed. It shows the **Start** and **Stop** prompt, and the current status of the server instance, as shown in the following screenshot:

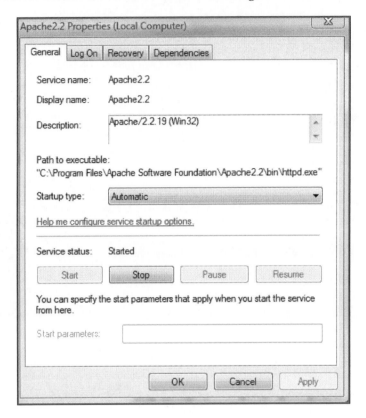

Installation of Apache HTTP on Linux (non-DOS environment)

The Apache HTTP installation in a non-DOS environment is different, as compared to a Windows environment. In the previous section, *Installation of the Apache HTTP*, we have discussed about binary files. In this installation, we will discuss the Source installation. Following are the steps involved in Source installation:

1. Download the Apache httpd server from the Apache official site. `http://httpd.apache.org/download.cgi`. The following screenshot shows the file to be downloaded (**httpd-2.2.X.tar.gz** where 2.2 is the major version and X is the minor version):

Apache HTTP Server (httpd) 2.2.19 is the best available version   2011-05-22

The Apache HTTP Server Project is pleased to announce the release of Apache HTTP Server (httpd) version 2.2.19. This release represents fifteen years of innovation by the project, and is recommended over all previous releases!

For details see the Official Announcement and the CHANGES_2.2 or condensed CHANGES_2.2.19 lists

Add-in modules for Apache 2.0 are not compatible with Apache 2.2. If you are running third party add-in modules, you must obtain modules compiled or updated for Apache 2.2 from that third party, before you attempt to upgrade from these previous versions. Modules compiled for Apache 2.2 should continue to work for all 2.2.x releases.

- Unix Source: httpd-2.2.19.tar.gz [PGP] [MD5] [SHA1]
- Unix Source: httpd-2.2.19.tar.bz2 [PGP] [MD5] [SHA1]
- Win32 Source: httpd-2.2.19-win32-src.zip [PGP] [MD5] [SHA1]
- Win32 Binary without crypto (no mod_ssl) (MSI Installer): httpd-2.2.19-win32-x86-no_ssl.msi [PGP] [MD5] [SHA1]
- Win32 Binary including OpenSSL 0.9.8r (MSI Installer): httpd-2.2.19-win32-x86-openssl-0.9.8r.msi [PGP] [MD5] [SHA1]
- NetWare Binary: apache_2.2.19-netware.zip [PGP] [MD5] [SHA1]
- Other files

2. Once the download is complete, the source file is stored in the home directory of the user (in our case it's /root). The source file comes in the form of tar.gz. Run the following command to unzip the source. First create a folder httpd and then extract the content in the httpd directory.

```
tar -zxvf  httpd-2.2.X.tar.gz
```

 We have extracted the httpd-2.2.19.tar.gz in the /opt directory.

```
root@localhost:/opt
httpd-2.2.19/srclib/apr-util/dbm/NWGNUdbmgdbm
httpd-2.2.19/srclib/apr-util/dbm/NWGNUmakefile
httpd-2.2.19/srclib/apr-util/dbm/apr_dbm_sdbm.c
httpd-2.2.19/srclib/apr-util/dbm/apr_dbm_db.mak
httpd-2.2.19/srclib/apr-util/dbm/NWGNUdbmdb
httpd-2.2.19/srclib/apr-util/dbm/apr_dbm_db.dep
httpd-2.2.19/srclib/apr-util/dbm/sdbm/
httpd-2.2.19/srclib/apr-util/dbm/sdbm/sdbm_lock.c
httpd-2.2.19/srclib/apr-util/dbm/sdbm/sdbm_private.h
httpd-2.2.19/srclib/apr-util/dbm/sdbm/sdbm.c
httpd-2.2.19/srclib/apr-util/dbm/sdbm/sdbm_pair.c
httpd-2.2.19/srclib/apr-util/dbm/sdbm/sdbm_hash.c
httpd-2.2.19/srclib/apr-util/dbm/sdbm/sdbm_tune.h
httpd-2.2.19/srclib/apr-util/dbm/sdbm/sdbm_pair.h
httpd-2.2.19/srclib/apr-util/dbm/apr_dbm.c
httpd-2.2.19/srclib/apr-util/aprutil.mak
httpd-2.2.19/srclib/apr-util/misc/
httpd-2.2.19/srclib/apr-util/misc/apu_dso.c
httpd-2.2.19/srclib/apr-util/misc/apr_thread_pool.c
httpd-2.2.19/srclib/apr-util/misc/apr_date.c
httpd-2.2.19/srclib/apr-util/misc/apr_queue.c
httpd-2.2.19/srclib/apr-util/misc/apu_version.c
httpd-2.2.19/srclib/apr-util/misc/apr_reslist.c
httpd-2.2.19/srclib/apr-util/misc/apr_rmm.c
httpd-2.2.19/srclib/apr-util/aprutil.dep
httpd-2.2.19/srclib/apr-util/libaprutil.rc
httpd-2.2.19/srclib/apr-util/apu-config.in
```

3. You can check the directory using the following command. The result displayed is similar to the following screenshot:

   `ls -ltrh`

```
[root@localhost opt]# ls -ltrh
total 124M
-rw-r--r--  1 root root   81M May 16 20:28 jdk-6u24-linux-i586.bin
-rw-r--r--  1 root root  7.3M May 16 20:29 apache-tomcat-7.0.12.zip
drwxr-xr-x 10 root root  4.0K May 16 20:35 jdk1.6.0_24
drwxr-xr-x 11 root root  4.0K May 20 10:01 httpd-2.2.19
drwxr-xr-x  9 root root  4.0K Jun 23 02:23 apache-tomcat-7.0.12
-rw-r--r--  1 root root   36M Jul 25 10:58 httpd-2.2.19.tar
[root@localhost opt]#
```

4. Then access the extracted directory using the following command. The result is similar to the following screenshot:

   `cd httpd-2.2.19`

   `ls -ltrh`

```
[root@localhost httpd-2.2.19]# ls -ltrh
total 1.4M
-rw-r--r--  1 root root   403 Nov 21  2004 emacs-style
-rw-r--r--  1 root root   11K Nov 21  2004 config.layout
-rw-r--r--  1 root root   15K Nov 21  2004 ABOUT_APACHE
-rw-r--r--  1 root root   10K Mar 13  2005 ROADMAP
-rw-r--r--  1 root root  8.0K Oct 17  2005 VERSIONING
-rw-r--r--  1 root root  5.1K Nov 29  2005 LAYOUT
-rw-r--r--  1 root root  2.9K Dec  7  2006 InstallBin.dsp
-rw-r--r--  1 root root  5.9K Jan  9  2007 README
-rw-r--r--  1 root root   17K Jan 12  2007 libhttpd.dsp
-rw-r--r--  1 root root  2.6K Aug 23  2007 BuildAll.dsp
-rw-r--r--  1 root root   29K Jan 18  2008 LICENSE
-rw-r--r--  1 root root  4.1K Jun 11  2008 httpd.dsp
-rw-r--r--  1 root root  4.7K Sep 18  2008 INSTALL
-rw-r--r--  1 root root   19K Nov 24  2008 acinclude.m4
-rw-r--r--  1 root root  8.6K Nov 25  2008 Makefile.in
-rw-r--r--  1 root root   828 Jan  5  2009 NOTICE
-rw-r--r--  1 root root  2.7K Jul 29  2009 BuildBin.dsp
-rw-r--r--  1 root root  5.3K Oct 13  2009 README.platforms
-rw-r--r--  1 root root   34K Oct  5  2010 Makefile.win
-rw-r--r--  1 root root   56K Oct  5  2010 Apache.dsw
-rw-r--r--  1 root root  2.5K Dec 20  2010 README-win32.txt
-rwxr-xr-x  1 root root  5.7K Feb  9 04:13 buildconf
-rw-r--r--  1 root root   13K Apr  1 06:47 NWGNUmakefile
-rw-r--r--  1 root root   24K Apr 16 12:09 configure.in
-rw-r--r--  1 root root   28K May  6 10:28 libhttpd.mak
-rw-r--r--  1 root root  8.8K May  6 10:28 httpd.mak
-rw-r--r--  1 root root   30K May  6 21:37 libhttpd.dep
-rw-r--r--  1 root root  1.3K May  6 21:37 httpd.dep
-rw-r--r--  1 root root  114K May 20 09:54 CHANGES
drwxr-xr-x  9 root root  4.0K May 20 09:59 os
drwxr-xr-x  3 root root  4.0K May 20 10:00 server
drwxr-xr-x 20 root root  4.0K May 20 10:00 modules
drwxr-xr-x  2 root root  4.0K May 20 10:00 test
drwxr-xr-x  4 root root  4.0K May 20 10:00 support
drwxr-xr-x  5 root root  4.0K May 20 10:00 srclib
drwxr-xr-x  9 root root  4.0K May 20 10:00 docs
drwxr-xr-x  5 root root  4.0K May 20 10:01 build
drwxr-xr-x  2 root root  4.0K May 20 10:01 include
-rwxr-xr-x  1 root root  646K May 20 10:01 configure
-rw-r--r--  1 root root   12K May 20 10:01 httpd.spec
```

5. After the verification of the directory, it's time to install the Apache HTTP server on Linux. By default, the execution permission is not set to `true` on the source folder. For that, we have to run the `chown` command to make it `true`.

```
[root@localhost httpd-2.2.19]# chown 0755 configure
```

By default **Apache Portable Runtime (APR)** is not installed in the 2.2 version, we have to install it. Let's discuss APR and its utilities in detail.

> 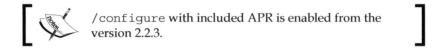 `/configure` with included APR is enabled from the version 2.2.3.

Apache Portable Runtime

Apache Portable Runtime is an open source project, which is supported by the Apache Foundation software. The main goal of this project is to provide the developer with an API, through which they can code and predict the identical behavior, regardless of different platforms. It eliminates the requirement of additional code dependency for different operating systems. For more information on this project, please visit `http://apr.apache.org/`.

Tomcat 7 uses APR to provide the capability of scalability, performance, and best collaboration with native technologies.

The Apache Portable Runtime project is again divided into three subprojects, to enhance and simplify the capability of this project. The following figure shows the different subprojects for APR:

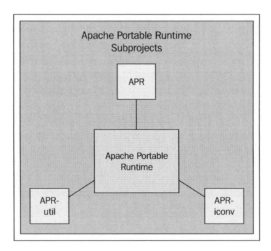

APR is a portable runtime library, through which Apache integrates with other native technologies. It is also helpful in resolving the problem of threads and processes. For more information on APR, please visit http://apr.apache.org/docs/apr/trunk/index.html.

Apache Portable Runtime Utility (APR-util) is a companion library for APR. To install this utility, the GCC++ package should be installed to the OS (http://apr.apache.org/docs/apr-util/trunk/).

APR-iconv is a portable implementation of the iconv() library (http://apr.apache.org/docs/apr-iconv/trunk/).

Installation of APR/APR-util

APR/APR-util comes with the source of the Apache package, and they can be found in the following directories as shown in the following screenshot:

- APR: Installdir/srclib/apr
- APR-util: Instaldir/srclib/apr-util

As we have extracted the source in /opt/httpd-2.2.19, the source directory is also found in the same directory.

```
[root@localhost httpd-2.2.19]# cd srclib/
[root@localhost srclib]# ls -lrh
total 32K
drwxr-xr-x  4 root root 4.0K May 20 10:01 pcre
-rw-r--r--  1 root root  121 Feb 11  2005 Makefile.in
drwxr-xr-x 19 root root 4.0K May 20 10:01 apr-util
drwxr-xr-x 25 root root 4.0K Jul 25 11:55 apr
[root@localhost srclib]#
```

Let's start with the installation of APR, followed by the installation of APR-util.

The APR installation can be done in three steps using three commands. The steps are as follows:

1. Enter the source directory of apr and apr-util, then configure the code using the following commands:

    ```
    [root@localhost srclib]# cd /opt/httpd-2.2.19/srclib/apr
    [root@localhost apr]# ./configure --prefix=/opt/httpd/apr-httpd/
    [root@localhost apr-util]# /configure --prefix=/usr/local/apr-util-httpd/ --with-apr=/usr/local/apr-httpd/
    Make
    Make install
    ```

The APR/APR-util installation should be done first, if we are compiling the source code of Apache manually. If we miss installing APR/APR-util, then at the `make` command execution for Apache, source will produce an error.

2. You can configure Apache using the following command. The following screenshot shows the output of the command when executed:

```
[root@localhost httpd-2.2.19]#./configure --with-included-apr
  --prefix=/opt/apache-2.2.19
```

```
[root             httpd-2.2.19]# ./configure --with-included-apr
checking for chosen layout... Apache
checking for working mkdir -p... yes
checking build system type... i686-pc-linux-gnu
checking host system type... i686-pc-linux-gnu
checking target system type... i686-pc-linux-gnu

Configuring Apache Portable Runtime library ...

configuring package in srclib/apr now
checking build system type... i686-pc-linux-gnu
checking host system type... i686-pc-linux-gnu
checking target system type... i686-pc-linux-gnu
Configuring APR library
Platform: i686-pc-linux-gnu
checking for working mkdir -p... yes
APR Version: 1.4.5
checking for chosen layout... apr
checking for gcc... gcc
checking for C compiler default output file name... a.out
checking whether the C compiler works... yes
checking whether we are cross compiling... no
checking for suffix of executables...
checking for suffix of object files... o
checking whether we are using the GNU C compiler... yes
checking whether gcc accepts -g... yes
checking for gcc option to accept ISO C89... none needed
checking for a sed that does not truncate output... /bin/sed
Applying APR hints file rules for i686-pc-linux-gnu
  setting CPPFLAGS to "-DLINUX=2"
```

```
make[3]: Nothing to be done for 'local-all'.
make[3]: Leaving directory '/opt/httpd-2.2.19/srclib/apr'
/opt/httpd-2.2.19/srclib/apr/build/mkdir.sh /opt/apache-2.2.19/lib /opt/apache-2.2.19/bin /opt/apache-2.2.19/build \
                /opt/apache-2.2.19/lib/pkgconfig /opt/apache-2.2.19/include
/usr/bin/install -c -m 644 /opt/httpd-2.2.19/srclib/apr/include/apr.h /opt/apache-2.2.19/include
for f in /opt/httpd-2.2.19/srclib/apr/include/apr_*.h; do \
        /usr/bin/install -c -m 644 ${f} /opt/apache-2.2.19/include; \
    done
/bin/sh /opt/httpd-2.2.19/srclib/apr/libtool --mode=install /usr/bin/install -c -m 755 libapr-1.la /opt/apache-2.2.19/lib
/usr/bin/install -c -m 755 .libs/libapr-1.so.0.4.5 /opt/apache-2.2.19/lib/libapr-1.so.0.4.5
(cd /opt/apache-2.2.19/lib && { ln -s -f libapr-1.so.0.4.5 libapr-1.so.0 || { rm -f libapr-1.so.0 && ln -s libapr-1.so.0.4.5 libapr-1.so.0; }; })
(cd /opt/apache-2.2.19/lib && { ln -s -f libapr-1.so.0.4.5 libapr-1.so || { rm -f libapr-1.so && ln -s libapr-1.so.0.4.5 libapr-1.so; }; })
/usr/bin/install -c -m 755 .libs/libapr-1.lai /opt/apache-2.2.19/lib/libapr-1.la
/usr/bin/install -c -m 755 .libs/libapr-1.a /opt/apache-2.2.19/lib/libapr-1.a
chmod 644 /opt/apache-2.2.19/lib/libapr-1.a
ranlib /opt/apache-2.2.19/lib/libapr-1.a
PATH="$PATH:/sbin" ldconfig -n /opt/apache-2.2.19/lib
----------------------------------------------------------------------
Libraries have been installed in:
   /opt/apache-2.2.19/lib
```

3. The previous screenshot describes the progress of the `configure` command. Once the command is executed, it will get the return code `0` otherwise you will see an error on the screen. Then, run the `make` command on the server to compile the code. The following figure shows the output of the `make` command:

    [root@localhost httpd-2.2.X]#make

```
Making all in srclib
make[1]: Entering directory '/opt/httpd-2.2.19/srclib'
Making all in apr
make[2]: Entering directory '/opt/httpd-2.2.19/srclib/apr'
make[3]: Entering directory '/opt/httpd-2.2.19/srclib/apr'
/bin/sh /opt/httpd-2.2.19/srclib/apr/libtool --silent --mode=compile gcc -g -O2 -pthread   -DHAVE_CONFIG_H -DLINUX=2 -D_REENTRANT -D_G
4_SOURCE   -I./include -I/opt/httpd-2.2.19/srclib/apr/include/arch/unix -I./include/arch/unix -I/opt/httpd-2.2.19/srclib/apr/include/a
.2.19/srclib/apr/include  -o passwd/apr_getpass.lo -c passwd/apr_getpass.c && touch passwd/apr_getpass.lo
/bin/sh /opt/httpd-2.2.19/srclib/apr/libtool --silent --mode=compile gcc -g -O2 -pthread   -DHAVE_CONFIG_H -DLINUX=2 -D_REENTRANT -D_G
4_SOURCE   -I./include -I/opt/httpd-2.2.19/srclib/apr/include/arch/unix -I./include/arch/unix -I/opt/httpd-2.2.19/srclib/apr/include/a
.2.19/srclib/apr/include  -o strings/apr_cpystrn.lo -c strings/apr_cpystrn.c && touch strings/apr_cpystrn.lo
/bin/sh /opt/httpd-2.2.19/srclib/apr/libtool --silent --mode=compile gcc -g -O2 -pthread   -DHAVE_CONFIG_H -DLINUX=2 -D_REENTRANT -D_G
4_SOURCE   -I./include -I/opt/httpd-2.2.19/srclib/apr/include/arch/unix -I./include/arch/unix -I/opt/httpd-2.2.19/srclib/apr/include/a
.2.19/srclib/apr/include  -o strings/apr_fnmatch.lo -c strings/apr_fnmatch.c && touch strings/apr_fnmatch.lo
/bin/sh /opt/httpd-2.2.19/srclib/apr/libtool --silent --mode=compile gcc -g -O2 -pthread   -DHAVE_CONFIG_H -DLINUX=2 -D_REENTRANT -D_G
4_SOURCE   -I./include -I/opt/httpd-2.2.19/srclib/apr/include/arch/unix -I./include/arch/unix -I/opt/httpd-2.2.19/srclib/apr/include/a
.2.19/srclib/apr/include  -o strings/apr_snprintf.lo -c strings/apr_snprintf.c && touch strings/apr_snprintf.lo
/bin/sh /opt/httpd-2.2.19/srclib/apr/libtool --silent --mode=compile gcc -g -O2 -pthread   -DHAVE_CONFIG_H -DLINUX=2 -D_REENTRANT -D_G
4_SOURCE   -I./include -I/opt/httpd-2.2.19/srclib/apr/include/arch/unix -I./include/arch/unix -I/opt/httpd-2.2.19/srclib/apr/include/a
.2.19/srclib/apr/include  -o strings/apr_strings.lo -c strings/apr_strings.c && touch strings/apr_strings.lo
/bin/sh /opt/httpd-2.2.19/srclib/apr/libtool --silent --mode=compile gcc -g -O2 -pthread   -DHAVE_CONFIG_H -DLINUX=2 -D_REENTRANT -D_G
4_SOURCE   -I./include -I/opt/httpd-2.2.19/srclib/apr/include/arch/unix -I./include/arch/unix -I/opt/httpd-2.2.19/srclib/apr/include/a
.2.19/srclib/apr/include  -o strings/apr_strnatcmp.lo -c strings/apr_strnatcmp.c && touch strings/apr_strnatcmp.lo
```

 It is very important to check the output of the `make` command, as it gives an error most of the times.

```
/opt/httpd-2.2.19/srclib/apr/libtool --silent --mode=link gcc -g -O2 -pthread        -o mod_speling.la -rpath /opt/apache-2.2.19/modules -module -avoi
sion  mod_speling.lo
/opt/httpd-2.2.19/srclib/apr/libtool --silent --mode=compile gcc -g -O2 -pthread     -DLINUX=2 -D_REENTRANT -D_GNU_SOURCE -D_LARGEFILE64_SOURCE    -I/opt
d-2.2.19/srclib/pcre -I. -I/opt/httpd-2.2.19/os/unix -I/opt/httpd-2.2.19/server/mpm/prefork -I/opt/httpd-2.2.19/modules/http -I/opt/httpd-2.2.19/modules
ers -I/opt/httpd-2.2.19/modules/proxy -I/opt/httpd-2.2.19/include -I/opt/httpd-2.2.19/modules/generators -I/opt/httpd-2.2.19/modules/mappers -I/opt/http
.19/modules/database -I/opt/httpd-2.2.19/srclib/apr/include -I/opt/httpd-2.2.19/srclib/apr-util/include -I/opt/httpd-2.2.19/srclib/apr-util/xml/expat/li
opt/httpd-2.2.19/modules/proxy/../generators -I/opt/httpd-2.2.19/modules/ssl -I/opt/httpd-2.2.19/modules/dav/main -prefer-pic -c mod_alias.c && touch mo
as.slo
/opt/httpd-2.2.19/srclib/apr/libtool --silent --mode=link gcc -g -O2 -pthread        -o mod_alias.la -rpath /opt/apache-2.2.19/modules -module -avoid-
n  mod_alias.lo
/opt/httpd-2.2.19/srclib/apr/libtool --silent --mode=compile gcc -g -O2 -pthread     -DLINUX=2 -D_REENTRANT -D_GNU_SOURCE -D_LARGEFILE64_SOURCE    -I/opt
d-2.2.19/srclib/pcre -I. -I/opt/httpd-2.2.19/os/unix -I/opt/httpd-2.2.19/server/mpm/prefork -I/opt/httpd-2.2.19/modules/http -I/opt/httpd-2.2.19/modules
ers -I/opt/httpd-2.2.19/modules/proxy -I/opt/httpd-2.2.19/include -I/opt/httpd-2.2.19/modules/generators -I/opt/httpd-2.2.19/modules/mappers -I/opt/http
.19/modules/database -I/opt/httpd-2.2.19/srclib/apr/include -I/opt/httpd-2.2.19/srclib/apr-util/include -I/opt/httpd-2.2.19/srclib/apr-util/xml/expat/li
opt/httpd-2.2.19/modules/proxy/../generators -I/opt/httpd-2.2.19/modules/ssl -I/opt/httpd-2.2.19/modules/dav/main -prefer-pic -c mod_rewrite.c && touch
rewrite.slo
/opt/httpd-2.2.19/srclib/apr/libtool --silent --mode=link gcc -g -O2 -pthread        -o mod_rewrite.la -rpath /opt/apache-2.2.19/modules -module -avo
sion  mod_rewrite.lo
make[4]: Leaving directory '/opt/httpd-2.2.19/modules/mappers'
make[3]: Leaving directory '/opt/httpd-2.2.19/modules/mappers'
make[2]: Leaving directory '/opt/httpd-2.2.19/modules'
make[2]: Entering directory '/opt/httpd-2.2.19/support'
make[2]: Leaving directory '/opt/httpd-2.2.19/support'

make[1]: Leaving directory '/opt/httpd-2.2.19'
```

4. The previous and the following screenshots show the completion without any error. To proceed with the installation of `make`, we have to run the following command:

    [root@localhost httpd-2.2.X]#make install

```
make[3]: Nothing to be done for 'local-all'.
make[3]: Leaving directory '/opt/httpd-2.2.19/srclib/apr'
/opt/httpd-2.2.19/srclib/apr/build/mkdir.sh /opt/apache-2.2.19/lib /opt/apache-2.2.19/bin /opt/apache-2.2.19/build \
                /opt/apache-2.2.19/lib/pkgconfig /opt/apache-2.2.19/include
/usr/bin/install -c -m 644 /opt/httpd-2.2.19/srclib/apr/include/apr.h /opt/apache-2.2.19/include
for f in /opt/httpd-2.2.19/srclib/apr/include/apr_*.h; do \
        /usr/bin/install -c -m 644 ${f} /opt/apache-2.2.19/include; \
    done
/bin/sh /opt/httpd-2.2.19/srclib/apr/libtool --mode=install /usr/bin/install -c -m 755 libapr-1.la /opt/apache-2.2.19/lib
/usr/bin/install -c -m 755 .libs/libapr-1.so.0.4.5 /opt/apache-2.2.19/lib/libapr-1.so.0.4.5
(cd /opt/apache-2.2.19/lib && { ln -s -f libapr-1.so.0.4.5 libapr-1.so.0 || { rm -f libapr-1.so.0 && ln -s libapr-1.so.0.4.5 libapr-1.so.0; }
(cd /opt/apache-2.2.19/lib && { ln -s -f libapr-1.so.0.4.5 libapr-1.so || { rm -f libapr-1.so && ln -s libapr-1.so.0.4.5 libapr-1.so; }; })
/usr/bin/install -c -m 755 .libs/libapr-1.lai /opt/apache-2.2.19/lib/libapr-1.la
/usr/bin/install -c -m 755 .libs/libapr-1.a /opt/apache-2.2.19/lib/libapr-1.a
chmod 644 /opt/apache-2.2.19/lib/libapr-1.a
ranlib /opt/apache-2.2.19/lib/libapr-1.a
PATH="$PATH:/sbin" ldconfig -n /opt/apache-2.2.19/lib
----------------------------------------------------------------------
Libraries have been installed in:
   /opt/apache-2.2.19/lib

If you ever happen to want to link against installed libraries
in a given directory, LIBDIR, you must either use libtool, and
specify the full pathname of the library, or use the '-LLIBDIR'
flag during linking and do at least one of the following:
   - add LIBDIR to the 'LD_LIBRARY_PATH' environment variable
     during execution
```

5. The previous command installs the Apache HTTP on the server, as shown in the following screenshot. It shows the completion on the server. If you view the previous screenshot, you will find that it creates the directory structure, files, manpage and `htdocs`, as shown in the next screenshot:

```
Installing configuration files
mkdir /opt/apache-2.2.19/conf
mkdir /opt/apache-2.2.19/conf/extra
mkdir /opt/apache-2.2.19/conf/original
mkdir /opt/apache-2.2.19/conf/original/extra
Installing HTML documents
mkdir /opt/apache-2.2.19/htdocs
Installing error documents
mkdir /opt/apache-2.2.19/error
Installing icons
mkdir /opt/apache-2.2.19/icons
mkdir /opt/apache-2.2.19/logs
Installing CGIs
mkdir /opt/apache-2.2.19/cgi-bin
Installing header files
Installing build system files
Installing man pages and online manual
mkdir /opt/apache-2.2.19/man
mkdir /opt/apache-2.2.19/man/man1
mkdir /opt/apache-2.2.19/man/man8
mkdir /opt/apache-2.2.19/manual
make[1]: Leaving directory '/opt/httpd-2.2.19'
```

6. After the `make` install is complete, the directory structure of the Apache HTTP server is created in the current path of the installation. Let's quickly see how the directory looks. The following screenshot shows the directory structure of the Apache HTTP server. In 90 percent of cases, Apache administrators work on the `conf`, `modules`, and `htdocs` directories for performing day-to-day operations.

```
[root@              apache-2.2.19]# ls -ltrh
total 60K
drwxr-xr-x  2 root root  4.0K May 20 12:59 htdocs
drwxr-xr-x 14 root root   12K May 20 13:01 manual
drwxr-xr-x  3 root root  4.0K Jul 25 16:05 lib
drwxr-xr-x  2 root root  4.0K Jul 25 16:05 modules
drwxr-xr-x  2 root root  4.0K Jul 25 16:05 bin
drwxr-xr-x  4 root root  4.0K Jul 25 16:05 conf
drwxr-xr-x  3 root root  4.0K Jul 25 16:05 error
drwxr-xr-x  2 root root  4.0K Jul 25 16:05 logs
drwxr-xr-x  3 root root  4.0K Jul 25 16:05 icons
drwxr-xr-x  2 root root  4.0K Jul 25 16:05 cgi-bin
drwxr-xr-x  2 root root  4.0K Jul 25 16:05 include
drwxr-xr-x  4 root root  4.0K Jul 25 16:06 man
drwxr-xr-x  2 root root  4.0K Jul 25 16:06 build
```

7. Before we end the installation, it is necessary to start the services of HTTP to verify the instance is properly installed. The best way to check the configuration is by running the `configtest` script. This script comes by default with Apache httpd, only in a non-DOS environment. The script can be found in APACHE_HOME/bin.

    [root@localhost bin]# ./apachectl configtest

    Syntax OK

    Then restart Apache using the following command:

    [root@root@localhost bin]# ./apachectl start

    Once you start Apache, it's very important to verify the instance status. You can verify the system using the `ps` command:

    ps -ef |grep httpd

```
root       6334     1  0 16:11 ?        00:00:00 /opt/apache-2.2.19/bin/httpd -k start
daemon     6335  6334  0 16:11 ?        00:00:00 /opt/apache-2.2.19/bin/httpd -k start
daemon     6336  6334  0 16:11 ?        00:00:00 /opt/apache-2.2.19/bin/httpd -k start
daemon     6337  6334  0 16:11 ?        00:00:00 /opt/apache-2.2.19/bin/httpd -k start
daemon     6338  6334  0 16:11 ?        00:00:00 /opt/apache-2.2.19/bin/httpd -k start
daemon     6339  6334  0 16:11 ?        00:00:00 /opt/apache-2.2.19/bin/httpd -k start
root       6343 27394  0 16:11 pts/1    00:00:00 grep httpd
```

The previous screenshot shows the status of the HTTP process, this means the HTTP server is running properly.

> We can directly install the Apache package in Debain Linux (Ubuntu), using the apt-get command. The following command shows the syntax for the installation:
>
> ```
> sudo apt-get install apache2
> ```
>
> Also, you can install the Apache using the yum utility. This utility is used mainly in CentOS using the command:
>
> ```
> yum -y install httpd
> ```

Apache Jserv protocol

This protocol was mainly developed to transfer data over the network in binary format instead of plain text. It uses TCP and a packet-based protocol, hence, increasing the performance of the web servers. Another informational point is that decryption of requests is done on the web server end so that the application server doesn't have a high load.

> If you are using AJP, the network traffic is reduced, as the tariff passes over the TCP protocol.

mod_jk and mod_proxy are based on the AJP protocol. They are also helpful in transmitting a high content response over the browser.

> If we use the latest version of mod_jk for integration of Apache and Tomcat, then we can store the response header of 64k in the web browsers. This process is very useful in the case of SSO enabled applications or storing Java session values in the browser.

Installation and configuration of mod_jk

mod_jk is an AJP connector which is used to integrate web servers such as Apache or IIS to Tomcat 7. In case we don't install mod_jk, then we cannot use frontend web servers for Tomcat. This module is very helpful in order to hide Tomcat behind the frontend web server and also eliminates the port number while browsing the URL. It involves multiple steps starting from installation and configuration. Let's first discuss the installation of mod_jk.

Installation of mod_jk

The mod_jk source can be downloaded from its official site, `http://tomcat.apache.org/download-connectors.cgi`. It is always recommended to download the latest stable version from the site for the implementation.

1. Once the source is downloaded we have to extract it in the server directory using the following command:

   ```
   [root@localhost opt]# tar -zxvf tomcat-connectors-1.2.x-src.tar
   ```

   where x is the minor version number.

2. Once the code is extracted, a directory is created in the current path named as `tomcat-connectors-1.2.32`. It's the home directory of the mod_jk source. The following screenshot shows the extracted code in the `tomcat-connectors-1.2.32` directory, which is created after the execution of the previous command:

   ```
   total 52K
   -rw-r--r--  1 root bin  14K May   4  2008 LICENSE
   -rw-r--r--  1 root bin  269 Jan   3  2011 NOTICE
   -rw-r--r--  1 root bin 1.5K Jun  30 15:16 BUILD.txt
   drwxr-xr-x  4 root bin 4.0K Jul   2 01:47 tools
   drwxr-xr-x  6 root bin 4.0K Jul   2 01:47 jkstatus
   drwxr-xr-x  2 root bin 4.0K Jul   2 01:47 support
   drwxr-xr-x  9 root bin 4.0K Jul   2 01:47 xdocs
   drwxr-xr-x 10 root bin 4.0K Jul   2 01:47 docs
   drwxr-xr-x  2 root bin 4.0K Jul   2 01:47 conf
   drwxr-xr-x 11 root bin 4.0K Jul   2 01:47 native
   ```

3. Go to the native directory of the mod_jk source using the following command and then run the `configure` command:

   ```
   [root@localhost opt]# cd /opt/tomcat-connectors-1.2.32-src/native
       ./configure --with-apxs=/opt/apache-2.2.19/bin/apxs
   ```

Tip for configuration

mod_jk is specific to the Apache version and the **Apache Extension Tool (APXS)** should be used for the current version of Apache, which we will use in the environment.

Once mod_jk is compiled on one server, there is no need to generate for another Apache instance. It can be directly copied to the other instance.

This trick is tested on Linux only.

4. The following screenshot shows the installation process using the APXS module. Installation of `mod_jk` begins by running the `configure` command:

```
[root@          native]# ./configure --with-apxs=/opt/apache-2.2.19/bin/apxs
checking build system type... i686-pc-linux-gnu
checking host system type... i686-pc-linux-gnu
checking target system type... i686-pc-linux-gnu
checking for a BSD-compatible install... /usr/bin/install -c
checking whether build environment is sane... yes
checking for gawk... gawk
checking whether make sets $(MAKE)... yes
checking for test... /usr/bin/test
checking for rm... /bin/rm
checking for grep... /bin/grep
checking for echo... /bin/echo
checking for sed... /bin/sed
checking for cp... /bin/cp
checking for mkdir... /bin/mkdir
need to check for Perl first, apxs depends on it...              100%
checking for perl... /usr/bin/perl
APRINCLUDEDIR is  -I/opt/apache-2.2.19/include -I/opt/apache-2.2.19/include
building connector for "apache-2.0"
checking for gcc... gcc
checking for C compiler default output file name... a.out
checking whether the C compiler works... yes
checking whether we are cross compiling... no
checking for suffix of executables...
checking for suffix of object files... o
checking whether we are using the GNU C compiler... yes
checking whether gcc accepts -g... yes
checking for gcc option to accept ANSI C... none needed
checking for style of include used by make... GNU
checking dependency style of gcc... none
checking for a sed that does not truncate output... /bin/sed
```

5. Once the configuration is done, you need to run the `make` command, which compiles the source code, as shown in the following screenshot:

```
[root@localhost apache-2.0]# make
```

```
root@           native]# make
aking all in common
ake[1]: Entering directory `/opt/tomcat-connectors-1.2.32-src/native/common'
opt/apache-2.2.19/build/libtool --silent --mode=compile gcc -I/opt/apache-2.2.19/include  -DHAVE_CONFIG_H -g -O2 -pthread
clude -I/opt/apache-2.2.19/include  -DHAVE_CONFIG_H -DLINUX=2 -D_REENTRANT -D_GNU_SOURCE -D_LARGEFILE64_SOURCE -I /opt/jo
1/include/ -c jk_ajp12_worker.c -o jk_ajp12_worker.lo
opt/apache-2.2.19/build/libtool --silent --mode=compile gcc -I/opt/apache-2.2.19/include  -DHAVE_CONFIG_H -g -O2 -pthread
clude -I/opt/apache-2.2.19/include  -DHAVE_CONFIG_H -DLINUX=2 -D_REENTRANT -D_GNU_SOURCE -D_LARGEFILE64_SOURCE -I /opt/jo
1/include/ -c jk_connect.c -o jk_connect.lo
opt/apache-2.2.19/build/libtool --silent --mode=compile gcc -I/opt/apache-2.2.19/include  -DHAVE_CONFIG_H -g -O2 -pthread
clude -I/opt/apache-2.2.19/include  -DHAVE_CONFIG_H -DLINUX=2 -D_REENTRANT -D_GNU_SOURCE -D_LARGEFILE64_SOURCE -I /opt/jo
1/include/ -c jk_msg_buff.c -o jk_msg_buff.lo
opt/apache-2.2.19/build/libtool --silent --mode=compile gcc -I/opt/apache-2.2.19/include  -DHAVE_CONFIG_H -g -O2 -pthread
clude -I/opt/apache-2.2.19/include  -DHAVE_CONFIG_H -DLINUX=2 -D_REENTRANT -D_GNU_SOURCE -D_LARGEFILE64_SOURCE -I /opt/jo
1/include/ -c jk_util.c -o jk_util.lo                          100%
opt/apache-2.2.19/build/libtool --silent --mode=compile gcc -I/opt/apache-2.2.19/include  -DHAVE_CONFIG_H -g -O2 -pthread
clude -I/opt/apache-2.2.19/include  -DHAVE_CONFIG_H -DLINUX=2 -D_REENTRANT -D_GNU_SOURCE -D_LARGEFILE64_SOURCE -I /opt/jo
1/include/ -c jk_ajp13.c -o jk_ajp13.lo
opt/apache-2.2.19/build/libtool --silent --mode=compile gcc -I/opt/apache-2.2.19/include  -DHAVE_CONFIG_H -g -O2 -pthread
clude -I/opt/apache-2.2.19/include  -DHAVE_CONFIG_H -DLINUX=2 -D_REENTRANT -D_GNU_SOURCE -D_LARGEFILE64_SOURCE -I /opt/jo
1/include/ -c jk_pool.c -o jk_pool.lo
opt/apache-2.2.19/build/libtool --silent --mode=compile gcc -I/opt/apache-2.2.19/include  -DHAVE_CONFIG_H -g -O2 -pthread
clude -I/opt/apache-2.2.19/include  -DHAVE_CONFIG_H -DLINUX=2 -D_REENTRANT -D_GNU_SOURCE -D_LARGEFILE64_SOURCE -I /opt/jo
1/include/ -c jk_worker.c -o jk_worker.lo
opt/apache-2.2.19/build/libtool --silent --mode=compile gcc -I/opt/apache-2.2.19/include  -DHAVE_CONFIG_H -g -O2 -pthread
clude -I/opt/apache-2.2.19/include  -DHAVE_CONFIG_H -DLINUX=2 -D_REENTRANT -D_GNU_SOURCE -D_LARGEFILE64_SOURCE -I /opt/jo
1/include/ -c jk_ajp13_worker.c -o jk_ajp13_worker.lo
opt/apache-2.2.19/build/libtool --silent --mode=compile gcc -I/opt/apache-2.2.19/include  -DHAVE_CONFIG_H -g -O2 -pthread
clude -I/opt/apache-2.2.19/include  -DHAVE_CONFIG_H -DLINUX=2 -D_REENTRANT -D_GNU_SOURCE -D_LARGEFILE64_SOURCE -I /opt/jo
1/include/ -c jk_lb_worker.c -o jk_lb_worker.lo
```

6. After the code is compiled using the make command then installation of the code is done using the command `make install`:

```
root@localhost apache-2.0]# make install
```

```
make[1]: Leaving directory `/opt/tomcat-connectors-1.2.32-src/native'
target="all"; \                                                      100%
        list='common apache-2.0'; \
        for i in $list; do \
            echo "Making $target in $i"; \
            if test "$i" != "."; then \
                (cd $i && make $target) || exit 1; \
            fi; \
        done;
Making all in common
make[1]: Entering directory `/opt/tomcat-connectors-1.2.32-src/native/common'
make[1]: Nothing to be done for `all'.
make[1]: Leaving directory `/opt/tomcat-connectors-1.2.32-src/native/common'
Making all in apache-2.0
make[1]: Entering directory `/opt/tomcat-connectors-1.2.32-src/native/apache-2.0'
make[1]: Nothing to be done for `all'.
make[1]: Leaving directory `/opt/tomcat-connectors-1.2.32-src/native/apache-2.0'
```

7. Once the execution is complete, it will create the module in the `apache-2.0` directory of the source, as shown in the following screenshot:

```
total 2.3M
-rw-r--r-- 1 root bin   11K Jun 21  2007 bldjk.qclsrc
-rw-r--r-- 1 root bin   11K Jun 21  2007 bldjk54.qclsrc
-rw-r--r-- 1 root bin  1.4K Sep 13  2010 config.m4
-rw-r--r-- 1 root bin   12K Sep 14  2010 mod_jk.dsp
-rw-r--r-- 1 root bin  3.0K Oct 21  2010 Makefile.in
-rw-r--r-- 1 root bin  1.5K Oct 21  2010 Makefile.apxs.in
-rw-r--r-- 1 root bin  6.5K Mar 18 02:05 NWGNUmakefile
-rw-r--r-- 1 root bin  129K May 23 12:03 mod_jk.c
-rw-r--r-- 1 root bin  7.0K Jun 30 12:13 Makefile.vc
-rw-r--r-- 1 root root 1.6K Jul 25 16:30 Makefile.apxs
-rw-r--r-- 1 root root 3.2K Jul 25 16:30 Makefile
-rw-r--r-- 1 root root 124K Jul 25 16:33 mod_jk.o
-rw-r--r-- 1 root root  309 Jul 25 16:33 mod_jk.lo
-rwxr-xr-x 1 root root 858K Jul 25 16:33 mod_jk.so
-rw-r--r-- 1 root root  788 Jul 25 16:33 mod_jk.la
-rw-r--r-- 1 root root 1.1M Jul 25 16:33 mod_jk.a
```

Configuration of mod_jk in Apache

Configuration of `mod_jk` is a little complicated in Apache. There are various ways of performing the configuration, but the most commonly used option is the concept of creation of `workers.properties` and `mod_jk.conf`. The steps to be performed are mentioned below:

1. Copy the `mod_jk.so` from the `apache 2.0` directory of the connector source to the modules directory of the Apache httpd server by using the following command:

```
[root@localhost apache-2.0]# cp mod_jk.so /opt/apache-2.2.19/
modules/

chmod 755 mod_jk.so
```

The previous command sets the execution permission.

```
chown root:root mod_jk.so
```

The previous command sets the the ownership to root.

2. To edit the configuration of the httpd server, you have to create the new file called as `mod_jk.conf` in the `conf` directory of `$APACHE_HOME/conf` as follows:

```
[root@localhost apache-2.0]# cd /opt/apache-2.2.19/conf

vi mod-jk.conf

LoadModule jk_module modules/mod_jk.so
JkWorkersFile conf/workers.properties
JkLogFile logs/mod_jk.log
JkLogLevel info
JkMount /sample/* node1
```

The `mod_jk.conf` file contains the following details:

   ○ **Module path**: It defines the location of the module from where Apache loads the module during the startup process, for example, `LoadModule jk_module modules/mod_jk.so`.

   ○ **Worker file path**: It defines the location of the worker file, this file contains the information of the Tomcat instance details such as the IP, port and load balancing methods such as `JkWorkersFile conf/workers.properties`.

   ○ **Log file**: It records the activity for Apache Tomcat integration, it also records the connectivity health check run between Apache/Tomcat (`JkLogFile logs/mod_jk.log`).

   ○ **URL mapping**: It defines the context path for Apache and also sets the rules such as redirecting the request if you get any request with the defined URL, for example, `JkMount /sample/* node1`. This means whenever the user hit the URL `http://localhost/sample`, the request will redirect to the Tomcat node1.

- ◦ **Log level**: This parameter captures the different events performed by mod_jk in the logs (JkLogLevel info).

```
LoadModule jk_module modules/mod_jk.so
JkWorkersFile conf/workers.properties
JkLogFile logs/mod_jk.log
JkLogLevel info
JkMount /sameple/* node1
JkMount /* node1
```

3. Create a new file named as workers.properties in the conf using the following command:

[root@localhost conf]# vi workers.properties

```
worker.list=node1
worker.node1.port=8009
worker.node1.host=10.130.240.51
worker.node1.type=ajp13
worker.node1.lbfactor=1
```

workers.properties contain the following details:

- ◦ Node name (common name for the host)
- ◦ AJP port details for Tomcat (the port on which Tomcat accepts the request for AJP)
- ◦ Host IP for Tomcat (the IP address where the Tomcat instance is running)
- ◦ Protocol used (the protocol used for communication by default is AJP)
- ◦ Load balancing method (Round robin, persistence, and so on)

```
worker.list=node1
worker.node1.port=8009
worker.node1.host=10.130.240.51
worker.node1.type=ajp13
worker.node1.lbfactor=1
worker.node1.cachesize=10
```

4. The last step is to include the mod_jk.conf in the main configuration file of the httpd, that is, httpd.conf.

[root@localhost conf]# vi httpd.conf

 Include conf/mod_jk.conf should be added at the end of httpd.conf.

Now we are done with configuration of `mod_jk` in the Apache HTTP configuration file (`httpd.conf`). But `mod_jk` will not work until we recycle the Apache httpd services. So why wait? Let's recycle by running the following command:

```
[root@localhost bin]# ./apachectl stop
[root@root@localhost bin]# ./apachectl start
```

 In case the Apache services are not displayed after the configuration, then we will run the `configtest.sh` placed in the `bin` directory that shows the issues with configuration.

Once we are done with the Apache web server configurations, followed by the web server service restart, it's now time to test the application. In *Chapter 1, Installation of Tomcat 7*, we had tested the application by using the host and port number on which Tomcat services were running `http://localhost:8080/applicationname`, as shown in the following screenshot:

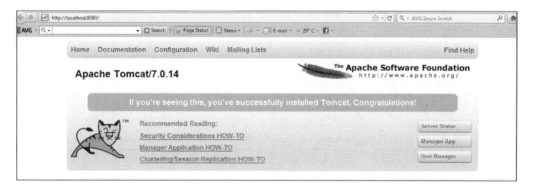

After enabling the `mod_jk` configuration, you can check the URL without using the port number (`http://localhost/applicationname`). The following screenshot shows the application with the application's URL:

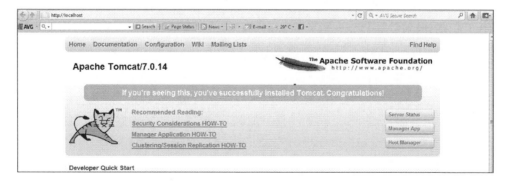

mod_proxy configuration

mod_proxy configuration is very simple as compared to mod_jk configuration. Here, we need to add the module and redirect the URL to a virtual host.

Open the httpd.conf and place the following entry:

1. Place the following lines of code after the other LoadModule directives:

    ```
    LoadModule proxy_module modules/mod_proxy.so
    LoadModule proxy_http_module modules/mod_proxy_http.so
    ```

2. Place the following lines of code with your other VirtualHost, or at the bottom of the file:

    ```
    NameVirtualHost *
    <VirtualHost *>
      ServerName abc.com
      ProxyRequests Off
      <Proxy *>
        Order deny,allow
        Allow from all
      </Proxy>
      ProxyPass / http://localhost:8080/
      ProxyPassReverse / http://localhost:8080/
      <Location />
        Order allow,deny
        Allow from all
      </Location>
    </VirtualHost>
    ```

Save the configuration file. Based on the Rule of Thumb, every configuration change is reflected only after a recycle.

```
[root@localhost bin]# ./apachectl stop
[root@root@localhost bin]# ./apachectl start
```

Comparison between mod_jk and mod_proxy

We have discussed `mod_jk` and `mod_proxy` but we still don't know when to use which module to increase the speed of the web server. Let's compare both modules and find out which can be used in a real-time environment:

Feature	mod_jk	mod_proxy
Load balancing	High level	Basic
Management interface	Yes	No
Compilation	Separate process	Not required. By default comes with Apache
Configuration	Huge	Basic
Protocol	AJP	HTTP/HTTPS/AJP
Node failure	Advance	NA

The previous table shows the comparison of `mod_jk` and `mod_proxy`. Based on the features, the web administrator can decide which module should be used.

 In 90 percent of cases, `mod_jk` is used with `Apache Tomcat`.

IIS integration with Tomcat 7

IIS versions vary with different versions of Windows OS, such as Windows 2003 comes with IIS 6 and Windows 2008 comes with IIS 7. Here, we discuss the integration of IIS 7 with Tomcat 7, but before we proceed, there are some sets of configuration which we need to configure to make sure the integration works well.

Prerequisites

The prerequisites for integration are:

- .NET 3.5 should be installed on the server
- The new site with a common virtual directory for IIS and Tomcat. We need to create a website, which accepts the request from the user and redirects it to Tomcat 7 internally. In order to integrate IIS with Tomcat, we have to create a common virtual directory for IIS and Tomcat, and then share the module.
- `isapi_redirect.dll`: It is a dynamic linking library for the Windows platform.

- `isapi_redirect iplugin`: It is used to redirect the request from IIS to Tomcat.

- `workers.properties`: It should have all the definitions for the configuration, such as the hostname, AJP port, and load balancing method.

- `uriworkermap.properties`: It contains the URI mapping information for the application, such as `/sample`.

Steps for installation

Download the latest `mod_jk` from `http://tomcat.apache.org/download-connectors.cgi`. Extract it to C and rename it to `Tomcat`. On double-clicking the folder, you will find a directory structure, as shown in the following screenshot:

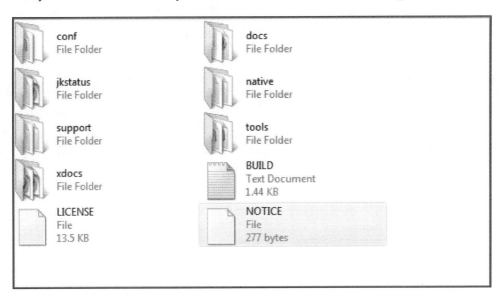

Go to the directory `C:\tomcat\native\iis` and double-click on the `isapi _redirect`. An entry in the registry will be created, as shown in the following screenshot:

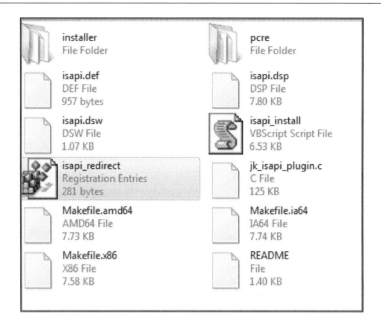

Let us quickly see the contents in the registry by editing the file:

```
REGEDIT4
[HKEY_LOCAL_MACHINE\SOFTWARE\Apache Software Foundation\Jakarta Isapi
    Redirector\1.0]
"log_file"="C:\\tomcat\\logs\\isapi.log"
"log_level"="debug"
"worker_file"="C:\\tomcat\\conf\\workers.properties"
"worker_mount_file"="C:\\tomcat\\conf\\uriworkermap.properties"
```

It shows the different parameters for the Tomcat connection such as `workers.properties`, URI mapping, log location, and so on.

Once the registry is saved, you have to restart the IIS server using the following commands from the command prompt:

`iisreset stop`

`iisreset start`

Let's discuss about the `workers.properties` and URI mapping files. There is a sample `workers.properties` available at `C:\tomcat\native\iis\installer\conf`.

The following screenshot shows the different configuration files, which are used for mod_jk configuration in IIS:

The workers.properties file consists of the following code:

```
workers.properties
# The workers that jk should create and work with
#worker.list=wlb,jkstatus
# Defining a worker named ajp13w and of type ajp13
# Note that the name and the type do not have to match.
worker.ajp13w.type=ajp13
worker.ajp13w.host=localhost
worker.ajp13w.port=8009
# Defining a load balancer
worker.wlb.type=lb
worker.wlb.balance_workers=ajp13w
# Define status worker
worker.jkstatus.type=status
```

The uriworkermap.properties file consists of the following code:

```
uriworkermap.properties
# uriworkermap.properties - IIS
# This file provides sample mappings for example wlb
# worker defined in workermap.properties.minimal
# The general syntax for this file is:
# [URL]=[Worker name]
/admin/*=wlb
/manager/*=wlb
/jsp-examples/*=wlb
/servlets-examples/*=wlb
/examples/*=wlb
# Optionally filter out all .jpeg files inside that context
# For no mapping the url has to start with exclamation (!)
!/servlets-examples/*.jpeg=wlb
# Mount jkstatus to /jkmanager
# For production servers you will need to
# secure the access to the /jkmanager url
/jkmanager=jkstatus
```

Common issues and troubleshooting for integration

There are many issues which may arise during the integration of Apache Tomcat or IIS Tomcat integration. Some of them are mentioned in the following section and we will find out the reason for these issues and their solutions These issues are very common with the integration of Tomcat.

Scenario 1: The httpd server is not able to compile, and this results in the exit from the compilation mode.

Error:

```
configure: error: in `/opt/httpd-2.2.19/srclib/apr':
configure: error: no acceptable C compiler found in $PATH
See `config.log' for more details.
configure failed for srclib/apr
```

Reason: C compilers are missing, such as the GCC and GCC+.

Solution: Download the GCC compiler from the Internet and compile it, as per the instructions given there:

```
[root@localhost httpd-2.2.19]# ./configure
checking for chosen layout... Apache
checking for working mkdir -p... yes
checking build system type... i686-pc-linux-gnu
checking host system type... i686-pc-linux-gnu
checking target system type... i686-pc-linux-gnu

Configuring Apache Portable Runtime library ...

checking for APR... reconfig
configuring package in srclib/apr now
checking build system type... i686-pc-linux-gnu
checking host system type... i686-pc-linux-gnu
checking target system type... i686-pc-linux-gnu
Configuring APR library
Platform: i686-pc-linux-gnu
checking for working mkdir -p... yes
APR Version: 1.4.5
checking for chosen layout... apr
checking for gcc... no
checking for cc... no
checking for cl.exe... no
configure: error: in `/opt/httpd-2.2.19/srclib/apr':
configure: error: no acceptable C compiler found in $PATH
See `config.log' for more details.
configure failed for srclib/apr
```

Scenario 2: Apache is not able to compile the make command, displaying an error and exiting the process.

Error: make is not able to compile the code.

Reason: make is not able to execute its functions.

Solution: Run the following command:

```
make clean
#Then
make
make install
```

```
gcc -E -DHAVE_CONFIG_H -DLINUX=2 -D_REENTRANT -D_GNU_SOURCE -D_LARGEFILE64_SOURCE    -I/opt/httpd-2.2.19/srcl
r-util/include/private  -I/opt/httpd-2.2.19/srclib/apr/include  -I/opt/httpd-2.2.19/srclib/apr-util/xml/expa
*[)]\{.*\};$/\1/' >> aprutil.exp
gcc -E -DHAVE_CONFIG_H -DLINUX=2 -D_REENTRANT -D_GNU_SOURCE -D_LARGEFILE64_SOURCE    -I/opt/httpd-2.2.19/srcl
r-util/include/private  -I/opt/httpd-2.2.19/srclib/apr/include  -I/opt/httpd-2.2.19/srclib/apr-util/xml/expa
d -e '/^$/d' >> aprutil.exp
sed 's,^\(location=\}.*$,\1installed,' < apu-1-config > apu-config.out
make[3]: Leaving directory `/opt/httpd-2.2.19/srclib/apr-util'
make[2]: Leaving directory `/opt/httpd-2.2.19/srclib/apr-util'
Making all in pcre
make[2]: Entering directory `/opt/httpd-2.2.19/srclib/pcre'
Makefile:7: /build/ltlib.mk: No such file or directory
make[2]: *** No rule to make target `/build/ltlib.mk'.  Stop.
make[2]: Leaving directory `/opt/httpd-2.2.19/srclib/pcre'
make[1]: *** [all-recursive] Error 1
make[1]: Leaving directory `/opt/httpd-2.2.19/srclib'
```

Scenario 3: The Apache HTTP server is unable to connect to Tomcat 7.

Error: Unable to connect through AJP.

Reason: Port might get blocked or the AJP configuration is not correct.

Solution: Check the logs for more errors using the following command:

```
[root@localhost logs]# cat error_log
```

[Mon Jul 25 16:11:00 2011] [notice] Apache/2.2.19 (Unix) DAV/2 configured -- resuming normal operations

[Mon Jul 25 16:52:16 2011] [notice] caught SIGTERM, shutting down

[Mon Jul 25 16:52:23 2011] [warn] No JkShmFile defined in httpd.conf. Using default /opt/apache-2.2.19/logs/jk-runtime-status

[Mon Jul 25 16:52:23 2011] [warn] No JkShmFile defined in httpd.conf. Using default /opt/apache-2.2.19/logs/jk-runtime-status

[Mon Jul 25 16:52:23 2011] [notice] Apache/2.2.19 (Unix) DAV/2 mod_jk/1.2.32 configured -- resuming normal operations

```
[root@localhost logs]# cat mod_jk.log
```

```
[Mon Jul 25 16:52:23.555 2011] [13355:3086857920] [warn] jk_map_validate_
property::jk_map.c (411): The attribute 'worker.node1.cachesize' is
deprecated - please check the documentation for the correct replacement.

[Mon Jul 25 16:52:23.555 2011] [13355:3086857920] [info] init_jk::mod_
jk.c (3252): mod_jk/1.2.32 () initialized

[Mon Jul 25 16:52:23.564 2011] [13356:3086857920] [warn] jk_map_validate_
property::jk_map.c (411): The attribute 'worker.node1.cachesize' is
deprecated - please check the documentation for the correct replacement.

[Mon Jul 25 16:52:23.564 2011] [13356:3086857920] [info] init_jk::mod_
jk.c (3252): mod_jk/1.2.32 () initialized
```

Then, run the `configtest` command on the server to verify the configuration using the following command:

```
[root@root@localhost bin]# ./apachectl configtest
```

```
Syntax OK
```

Summary

In this chapter, we have discussed the integration of Apache/IIS with Tomcat 7 and their various component integrations. Also, you can use ready made solutions for Apache and Tomcat using the link `http://www.apachefriends.org/en/xampp-windows.html`. After reading this chapter, the reader can expect to have a good command on the integration and the different issues they may encounter during the installation of the integration.

In the next chapter, we will discuss the security enhancement of Tomcat and their features such as application with their own security setting, server security SSL, and so on.

5
Securing Tomcat 7

The Internet has created a revolution in the 21st century; it provides us the capability of collecting information in seconds, whereas it would have taken months to collect the information previously. This has also raised security concerns for information privacy and has created the requirement of securing information over the Internet.

Everyday, new technologies are emerging to improve Internet usage for applications. With these technologies in the market, it becomes a tricky job for hackers and other communities to access secure information.

In this chapter, we will discuss the following topics:

- Tomcat security permissions
- Catalina properties
- SSL implementation on Tomcat 7

Tomcat Manager

The security being a major concern for IT companies, a separate department for IT security administration is created in every company. Their major responsibility is to make sure that there are no vulnerabilities in terms of the networks, web, and OS infrastructure.

We should download Tomcat from the Tomcat website or any secure, known host. There is a chance that malicious software is shipped with Tomcat if we download it from an unknown source. Once the download is complete, verify the integrity of Tomcat using MD5/PGP. In case of Linux, the MD5 can be verified with **Open Specification for Pretty Good Privacy (OpenPGP)**. This is a must in the process of production systems.

Tomcat security permissions

Apache Tomcat comes with good security-enabled options, but every environment has its own requirement for security, based on the usage of the application. For example, banking sites require a high level of security, on the other hand, user-based applications require little security.

In Tomcat 7, the default permission is configured in TOMCAT_HOME/Conf directory. The security is a collective effort of four files which make the system. Let's discuss about each file and their functionality.

catalina.properties

This file contains information related to the access of the package, package definition, common loader, shared loader, and a list of JAR files, which are not necessary to be scanned at the startup of Tomcat. It helps in improving the performance, as adding too many JAR files to the skip list improves memory consumption. If you want to add any common JAR, you have to define it under catalina.properties.

In a production environment, some of the library JARs are shared across many instances of Tomcat, and in that case we can use the shared loader parameter. By default, the Tomcat 7 policy comes with the following packages to enhance security. We can customize the policy based on the application's requirement and usage type. Following are the key syntaxes used in catalina.properties:

```
package.access=sun.,org.apache.catalina.,org.apache.coyote.,org.apache.
  tomcat.,org.apache.jasper.

package.definition=sun.,java.,org.apache.catalina.,org.apache.coyote.,
  org.apache.tomcat.,org.apache.jasper

common.loader=${catalina.base}/lib,${catalina.base}/lib/*.jar,
  ${catalina.home}/lib,${catalina.home}/lib/*.jar

tomcat.util.scan.DefaultJarScanner.jarsToSkip=
  \bootstrap.jar,commons-daemon.jar,tomcat-juli.jar,
  \annotations-api.jar,el-api.jar,jsp-api.jar,servlet-api.jar,
  \catalina.jar,catalina-ant.jar,catalina-ha.jar,
  catalina-tribes.jar,\jasper.jar,jasper-el.jar,ecj-*.jar,
  \tomcat-api.jar,tomcat-util.jar,tomcat-coyote.jar,
  tomcat-dbcp.jar,\tomcat-i18n-en.jar,tomcat-i18n-es.jar,
  tomcat-i18n-fr.jar,tomcat-i18n-ja.jar,\
  commons-beanutils*.jar,commons-collections*.jar,commons-dbcp*.jar,
  \commons-digester*.jar,commons-fileupload*.jar,commons-logging*.jar,
  \commons-pool*.jar,\ant.jar,jmx.jar,jmx-
  tools.jar,\xercesImpl.jar,xmlParserAPIs.jar,xml-apis.jar,
  \dnsns.jar,ldapsec.jar,localedata.jar,sunjce_provider.jar,
```

```
sunpkcs11.jar,tools.jar,\apple_provider.jar,AppleScriptEngine.jar,
CoreAudio.jar,dns_sd.jar,\j3daudio.jar,j3dcore.jar,j3dutils.jar,
jai_core.jar,jai_codec.jar,\mlibwrapper_jai.jar,MRJToolkit.jar,
vecmath.jar
```

catalina.policy

This file contains the Tomcat permission details and their deployed application, which is used at runtime. If you want to access any system parameter, such as the OS details, Tomcat internal code, or web application code from different directories, you can define the permission here. There are basically three kinds of permissions you can implement on Tomcat 7. The following figure shows the different types of polices for Catalina:

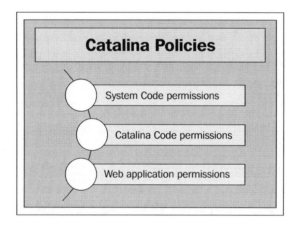

System Code permissions

This policy gives you access the Java library, which need to be verified at runtime by the Tomcat instance. Following code shows that full access permissions are granted for the Java library:

```
grant codeBase "file:${java.home}/lib/-"
  {permission java.security.AllPermission;
```

 There are a few more policy options you can implement in Catalina, such as System Code, Catalina Code, and Web application permissions.

The following points describe the different customized policies we can add in Tomcat 7:

- Read/write access(R/W) to the document root of the web application.
- Read, write, and delete access to the user for the web application directory. The following screenshot shows the different options:

```
// ============ SYSTEM CODE PERMISSIONS ==================================


// These permissions apply to javac
grant codeBase "file:${java.home}/lib/-" {
        permission java.security.AllPermission;
};

// These permissions apply to all shared system extensions
grant codeBase "file:${java.home}/jre/lib/ext/-" {
        permission java.security.AllPermission;
};

// These permissions apply to javac when ${java.home] points at $JAVA_HOME/jre
grant codeBase "file:${java.home}/../lib/-" {
        permission java.security.AllPermission;
};

// These permissions apply to all shared system extensions when
// ${java.home} points at $JAVA_HOME/jre
grant codeBase "file:${java.home}/lib/ext/-" {
        permission java.security.AllPermission;
};
```

Catalina Code permissions (Tomcat core permission)

This section contains the Tomcat internal file permissions to access the code. It helps in controlling the internal functionality of Tomcat. The following policy shows that `Catalina/lib` has given all the permissions:

```
grant codeBase "file:${catalina.home}/lib/-"
  {permission java.security.AllPermission;
```

This means that Tomcat has all the permissions to access the `lib` folder.

 The previous permission is used for the servlet API and their class loader, which are shared among the different codes.

The following screenshot shows the Catalina Code permissions:

```
// =========== CATALINA CODE PERMISSIONS ==================================


// These permissions apply to the daemon code
grant codeBase "file:${catalina.home}/bin/commons-daemon.jar" {
        permission java.security.AllPermission;
};

// These permissions apply to the logging API
// Note: If tomcat-juli.jar is in ${catalina.base} and not in ${catalina.home},
// update this section accordingly.
//   grant codeBase "file:${catalina.base}/bin/tomcat-juli.jar" {..}
grant codeBase "file:${catalina.home}/bin/tomcat-juli.jar" {
        permission java.io.FilePermission
          "${java.home}${file.separator}lib${file.separator}logging.properties", "read";

        permission java.io.FilePermission
          "${catalina.base}${file.separator}conf${file.separator}logging.properties", "read";
        permission java.io.FilePermission
          "${catalina.base}${file.separator}logs", "read, write";
        permission java.io.FilePermission
          "${catalina.base}${file.separator}logs${file.separator}*", "read, write";

        permission java.lang.RuntimePermission "shutdownHooks";
        permission java.lang.RuntimePermission "getClassLoader";
        permission java.lang.RuntimePermission "setContextClassLoader";

        permission java.util.logging.LoggingPermission "control";

        permission java.util.PropertyPermission "java.util.logging.config.class", "read";
        permission java.util.PropertyPermission "java.util.logging.config.file", "read";
        permission java.util.PropertyPermission "catalina.base", "read";
```

Web application permissions

This section contains the policy with reference to the application's resource utilization, such as JVM, JNDI, and so on. If you enable the following code, then the Tomcat classes can be accessed from the root directory of the code:

```
// grant codeBase "file:${catalina.base}/webapps/examples/
  WEB-INF/classes/-" {// };
```

The following screenshot displays the Web application permissions:

```
// ========== WEB APPLICATION PERMISSIONS ==========================================


// These permissions are granted by default to all web applications
// In addition, a web application will be given a read FilePermission
// and JndiPermission for all files and directories in its document root.
grant {
    // Required for JNDI lookup of named JDBC DataSource's and
    // javamail named MimePart DataSource used to send mail
    permission java.util.PropertyPermission "java.home", "read";
    permission java.util.PropertyPermission "java.naming.*", "read";
    permission java.util.PropertyPermission "javax.sql.*", "read";

    // OS Specific properties to allow read access
    permission java.util.PropertyPermission "os.name", "read";
    permission java.util.PropertyPermission "os.version", "read";
    permission java.util.PropertyPermission "os.arch", "read";
    permission java.util.PropertyPermission "file.separator", "read";
    permission java.util.PropertyPermission "path.separator", "read";
    permission java.util.PropertyPermission "line.separator", "read";

    // JVM properties to allow read access
    permission java.util.PropertyPermission "java.version", "read";
    permission java.util.PropertyPermission "java.vendor", "read";
    permission java.util.PropertyPermission "java.vendor.url", "read";
    permission java.util.PropertyPermission "java.class.version", "read";
    permission java.util.PropertyPermission "java.specification.version", "read";
    permission java.util.PropertyPermission "java.specification.vendor", "read";
    permission java.util.PropertyPermission "java.specification.name", "read";

    permission java.util.PropertyPermission "java.vm.specification.version", "read";
    permission java.util.PropertyPermission "java.vm.specification.vendor", "read";
    permission java.util.PropertyPermission "java.vm.specification.name", "read";
    permission java.util.PropertyPermission "java.vm.version", "read";
    permission java.util.PropertyPermission "java.vm.vendor", "read";
    permission java.util.PropertyPermission "java.vm.name", "read";
```

This policy will run from the root directory of the web application. If you want to access it from outside, then you need to customize the application.

tomcat-users.xml

This file contains the roles and security password for Tomcat.

The following screenshot shows the different roles, users, and passwords for Tomcat 7:

```
  <role rolename="tomcat"/>
  <role rolename="role1"/>
  <user username="tomcat" password="tomcat" roles="tomcat"/>
  <user username="both" password="tomcat" roles="tomcat,role1"/>
  <user username="role1" password="tomcat" roles="role1"/>
</tomcat-users>
```

server.xml

This is the main configuration file for Tomcat and it mainly contains the Connector port configuration.

The following screenshot shows the connector configuration, where Tomcat 7 runs on 8080 and has 20000 as the timeout setting:

```
      Define a non-SSL HTTP/1.1 Connector on port 8080
  -->
  <Connector port="8080" protocol="HTTP/1.1"
             connectionTimeout="20000"
             redirectPort="8443" />
  <!-- A "Connector" using the shared thread pool-->
  <!--
  <Connector executor="tomcatThreadPool"
             port="8080" protocol="HTTP/1.1"
             connectionTimeout="20000"
             redirectPort="8443" />
  -->
```

Enabling Tomcat Manager

By default, the Tomcat Manager is disabled in Tomcat 7. It is a very powerful tool, but if it goes to the wrong hands, then it can create a problem for the system administrator or the application administrator. So it's very important that you enable Tomcat Manager with proper security.

How to enable the Tomcat Manager

For enabling the Manager, we have to edit `tomcat-users.xml`, which is present in `TOMCAT_HOME/conf`. You will see that Tomcat users are commented out, as shown in the following screenshot:

```
<---
  <role rolename="tomcat"/>
  <role rolename="role1"/>
  <user username="tomcat" password="tomcat" roles="tomcat"/>
  <user username="both" password="tomcat" roles="tomcat,role1"/>
  <user username="role1" password="tomcat" roles="role1"/>
-->
```

Uncomment the user and save the file, followed by reloading Apache Tomcat 7, as shown in the following screenshot:

```
<role rolename="tomcat"/>
<role rolename="role1"/>
<user username="tomcat" password="tomcat" roles="tomcat"/>
<user username="both" password="tomcat" roles="tomcat,role1"/>
<user username="role1" password="tomcat" roles="role1"/>
```

> If you enable Tomcat Manager in a production environment, make sure it can be accessed only from the internal environment and not the **DMZ**.

Securing Tomcat 7 for production

In this topic, we will discuss the best practices used for securing Tomcat 7. Securing Tomcat does not mean only Tomcat, it includes both Tomcat configurations and other infrastructure configurations. Let's first start with the Tomcat configurations.

Tomcat settings

There are different methods of securing Tomcat 7 and these come into picture based on the application's requirement and the security policy used by an IT organization.

> Every organization has their own security policies and the IT administrator follows them while implementing the security in Tomcat.

In Tomcat 7, there are different configurations, which need to be changed or enabled in order to secure Tomcat for the external environment. Let's discuss each configuration and their usage for a real-time environment.

Connector Port

By default, Tomcat 7 runs on port 8080 using the HTTP protocol. As everyone knows the default port, it is easier for hackers to hit the port and trap the server. So it's always recommended to change the connector port and also the AJP port, which runs on 8009, to secure Tomcat.

> Connectors are configured in `server.xml` in the `conf` directory.

```
<Connector executor="tomcatThreadPool" port="8080" protocol="HTTP/1.1"
    connectionTimeout="20000" redirectPort="8443" />
<Connector port="8009" protocol="AJP/1.3" redirectPort="8443" />
```

We can check the port used by different services by viewing the `services` file in Windows and Linux. The following table gives us details of the location of the `services` file in Windows and Linux. This information is very useful in order to avoid port conflict between the two services.

The following screenshot shows the different ports used by various applications:

Operating system	Location of the `services` file
Linux	`/etc/services`
Windows	`C:\Windows\System32\drivers\etc`

```
# service-name   port/protocol   [aliases ...]    [# comment]

tcpmux           1/tcp                             # TCP port service multiplexer
tcpmux           1/udp                             # TCP port service multiplexer
rje              5/tcp                             # Remote Job Entry
rje              5/udp                             # Remote Job Entry
echo             7/tcp
echo             7/udp
discard          9/tcp           sink null
discard          9/udp           sink null
systat           11/tcp          users
systat           11/udp          users
daytime          13/tcp
daytime          13/udp
qotd             17/tcp          quote
qotd             17/udp          quote
msp              18/tcp                            # message send protocol
msp              18/udp                            # message send protocol
chargen          19/tcp          ttytst source
chargen          19/udp          ttytst source
ftp-data         20/tcp
ftp-data         20/udp
# 21 is registered to ftp, but also used by fsp
ftp              21/tcp
ftp              21/udp          fsp fspd
ssh              22/tcp                            # SSH Remote Login Protocol
ssh              22/udp                            # SSH Remote Login Protocol
```

The network administrator is responsible for allocating new ports and updating assigned ports in the previous code, which will be in effect after the recycle.

Slimming of Tomcat application

Tomcat 7 comes with many applications and examples built-in with the packages. It is always recommended to remove the application packages which are not used. Following are the advantages of removing a package:

- Reduction in the JVM memory utilization
- Chances of any vulnerability will be less, as unwanted applications (libraries/JAR) are not available
- Easier maintenance of applications

```
[root@localhost webapps]# ls -ltrh
total 40K
drwxr-xr-x  3 root root 4.0K May 22 15:08 ROOT
drwxr-xr-x 13 root root 4.0K May 22 15:08 docs
drwxr-xr-x  5 root root 4.0K May 22 15:08 manager
drwxr-xr-x  5 root root 4.0K May 22 15:08 host-manager
drwxr-xr-x  5 root root 4.0K May 22 15:08 examples
```

You can remove as many applications as you want to, the Tomcat Manager can also be removed if it is not in use.

Disable hot deployment

Hot deployment or autodeployment is a process through which code will be deployed to the application automatically, without recycling the services. To disable the hot deployment, you have to edit `server.xml` for the following parameter:

```
<Host name="localhost" appBase="webapps"
  unpackWARs="true" autoDeploy="true">
```

Change the `autoDeploy` to `false`.

```
<Host name="localhost" appBase="webapps"
  unpackWARs="true" autoDeploy="false">
```

After making the change, the application will get deployed to the web server only after the recycle.

Non-Tomcat settings

In the previous section, *Tomcat settings*, we have discussed about the Tomcat-level configuration to implement security policies for Tomcat 7. In a real-time environment, with new and the latest technologies, these settings are not enough to deal with security threats. To make the system more secure, we have to secure our infrastructure. Let's discuss a few best practices for securing the web infrastructure.

Service as a separate user

We should not run Tomcat as a root user. Instead, create a new user and give the privileges to that user to run the Tomcat server. The configuration file should also have the privileges of the root and user groups, and other directories such as `logs`, should have read/write permissions for this user/group.

Firewall

Tomcat should be configured in the internal zone if it's not a frontend application and only the connector port—AJP port—should be open from the external DMZ server. If in any case, Tomcat is configured in a frontend application, then the DB server should be placed in the internal zone with complete firewall restrictions. In order to create a strong firewall, we can enable or disable the port at the OS level using the system firewall. You can also verify whether the firewall rules are placed properly or not.

In Windows, we can verify the firewall settings by using the `netsh` command in the following manner:

```
netsh firewall show state
```

The previous command shows the current status of the firewall rules.

```
netsh firewall show config
```

The previous command shows the operation mode status of the firewall. The following screenshot shows the output of the previous two commands:

```
C:\Users\user>netsh firewall show state

Firewall status:
-------------------------------------------------------------------
Profile                               = Standard
Operational mode                      = Disable
Exception mode                        = Enable
Multicast/broadcast response mode     = Enable
Notification mode                     = Enable
Group policy version                  = Windows Firewall
Remote admin mode                     = Disable

Ports currently open on all network interfaces:
Port    Protocol   Version    Program
-------------------------------------------------------------------
No ports are currently open on all network interfaces.


C:\Users\user>netsh firewall show config

Domain profile configuration:
-------------------------------------------------------------------
Operational mode                      = Disable
Exception mode                        = Enable
Multicast/broadcast response mode     = Enable
Notification mode                     = Enable
```

In order to add or remove any firewall policies, we can run the following command:

```
netsh firewall set opmode enable
```

The previous command allows us to edit the configuration rule.

The following command adds the TCP port 8085 over the subnet. Hence, this port is accessible outside the system.

```
netsh firewall add portopening TCP 8085 HTTP enable subnet
```

In Linux, we can verify the firewall settings using the `iptables` command in the following manner:

```
[root@localhost etc]# iptables -L
```

The following screenshot shows the firewall rule for a Linux environment. Currently, no firewall rule is defined:

```
[root@localhost etc]# iptables -L
Chain INPUT (policy ACCEPT)
target      prot opt source              destination

Chain FORWARD (policy ACCEPT)
target      prot opt source              destination

Chain OUTPUT (policy ACCEPT)
target      prot opt source              destination
```

In case we have to edit the firewall rule, then the following command needs to be executed:

```
iptables -A INPUT -s 0/0 -i eth0 -d 192.168.1.2  -p TCP -j ACCEPT
```

The previous command defines the firewall rule, that accepts all requests originating from anywhere to the destination 192.168.1.2, through the TCP protocol.

 For more information on the DMZ, please visit `http://en.wikipedia.org/wiki/Demilitarized_zone`.

Password

We should not use any plain text password for the application or configuration level and always use an encrypted password using MD5 or a hashing algorithm. In order to enable the encryption password in Tomcat, we have to follow a sequence of steps.

Let's discuss each step briefly and enforce the password encryption policy for the Tomcat Manager.

1. We have to define the password encryption algorithm in the Realm section of server.xml, as in the following line of code:

```
<Realm className=
   "org.apache.catalina.realm.MemoryRealm"digest="MD5" />
```

```
        <Realm className="org.apache.catalina.realm.UserDatabaseRealm"
               resourceName="UserDatabase"/>
     </Realm>
<Realm className="org.apache.catalina.realm.MemoryRealm"
               digest="MD5" />

     <Host name="localhost"  appBase="webapps"
           unpackWARs="true" autoDeploy="true">
```

 We can define the algorithm based on the OS requirement, such as SHA, RSA, MD5, and so on.

2. Now go to tomcat_home/bin and run the following command, it will generate the encrypted algorithm, as shown in the following screenshot:

[root@localhost bin]# ./digest.sh -a MD5 secret

```
[root@localhost bin]# ./digest.sh -a MD5 secret
secret:5ebe2294ecd0e0f08eab7690d2a6ee69
```

The previous command can be described as ./digest.sh = script, which generates the password for Tomcat realm and -a = algorithm used, currently we are using MD5 algorithm.

3. Copy the MD5 string and replace the password text from tomcat_user.xml with the following line of code:

```
<user name="admin" password="5ebe2294ecd0e0f08eab7690d2a6ee69 "
   roles="manager-gui" />
```

4. Reload the Tomcat services and log in to the Tomcat Manager using the password.

 The password will not change here, we have only changed the method of storing passwords.

SSL configuration on Tomcat 7

Secure Socket Layer (SSL) is another way of securing data communication. It is a cryptographic protocol, in which data travels through a secure channel. The server sends a secure key to the client browser, the client browser decrypts it and a handshake takes place between the server and the client or we can say it's a two-way handshake over the secure layer.

When is SSL required for Tomcat?

SSL will be more efficient if you are using Tomcat as a frontend server. In case you are using Apache or IIS, then it's recommended to install SSL on Apache or the IIS server.

Types of SSL certificates

Before we go ahead and install SSL, let's discuss the two types of SSL certificates, which are explained as follows:

- **Self-signed certificate**: This certificate is used for testing purposes by applications which are hosted in the internal environment, where no verification is required and in this only data travel will be secure.

- **Signed certificate**: This certificate is basically used in real-time external environments, where authentication is required and also data should travel over the secure channel. For this kind of certificate, we have various third parties who generate the signed certificate and send it to us.

Process of installing SSL

The process of installing SSL varies for every server, but there are certain parameters which are common to every server for generation of the **Certificate Signing Request (CSR)**. The method of generating the CSR may vary, but information required for generating the CSR remains the same. The following table provides the CSR template:

CSR Attributes	Domain information as to which CSR needs to be generated
Common Name	Define the domain name
Organization	Organization name
Department	Department name of the organization
City	City where this organization is located
State	State where this organization is located
Country	Country where this organization is located
Key size	2048 (encryption bit)

Common name: It is the hostname for which CSR needs to be generated.

Key size: It is the size of the encryption keys.

Let's do a real-time implementation for installation of the SSL certificate on Tomcat 7. We will install SSL certificate for host `tomcat7packtpub.com` in Tomcat 7 by performing the following steps:

1. Create a CSR template for the `tomcat7packtpub.com`.

CSR Attributes	Domain information as to which CSR needs to be generated
Common Name	tomcat7packtpub.com
Organization	tomcat7packtpub.com
Department	Tomcat
City	Hyd
State	AP
Country	IN
Key size	2048

2. We need to create the CSR for the host `tomcat7packtpub.com`. For creating the CSR, we need to run the `keytool` present in `JAVA_HOME/bin`. The following command will capture parameters for the CSR:

By default, `keytool` will be executed from `JAVA_HOME/bin`. But if we have set the Java path, then you can run it from anywhere.

```
[root@localhost conf] # keytool -genkey -alias tomcat7
    -keyalg RSA -keysize 2048 -keystore tomcat.jks
```

```
[root@localhost conf]# keytool -genkey -alias tomcat7 -keyalg RSA -keysize 2048 -keystore tomcat.jks
Enter keystore password:
Re-enter new password:
What is your first and last name?
  [Unknown]:  tomcat7packtpub.com
What is the name of your organizational unit?
  [Unknown]:  tomcat7packtpub.com
What is the name of your organization?
  [Unknown]:  tomcat7
What is the name of your City or Locality?
  [Unknown]:  hyd
What is the name of your State or Province?
  [Unknown]:  AP
What is the two-letter country code for this unit?
  [Unknown]:  IN
Is CN=tomcat7packtpub.com, OU=tomcat7packtpub.com, O=tomcat7, L=hyd, ST=AP, C=IN correct?
  [no]:  yes

Enter key password for <tomcat7>
        (RETURN if same as keystore password):
Re-enter new password:
```

3. Generate the certificate in CSR format using the following command. It will ask for the password and send it to the respective vendor for signed certificate creation.

```
[root@localhost conf]# keytool -certreq -alias tomcat7 -file csr.
   txt - keystore tomcat.jks

Enter keystore password:
```

4. Import the certificate to the following Tomcat key store. Copy the `tomcat7.jks` in the `TOMCAT_HOME/conf`.

```
[root@localhost conf] # keytool -import -trustcacerts -alias
   tomcat7 -file tomcat7packtpub.com.pb7 -tomcat7.jks
```

Once you have signed the certificate created now, it's time to make changes in the Tomcat configuration.

1. Open `server.xml` and change the settings, as in the following code snippet:

```
<Connector port="443" maxHttpHeaderSize="8192" maxThreads="150"
   minSpareThreads="25" maxSpareThreads="75" enableLookups="false"
   disableUploadTimeout="true" acceptCount="100" scheme="https"
   secure="true" SSLEnabled="true" clientAuth="false"
   sslProtocol="TLS" keyAlias="server" keystoreFile="tomcat7.jks"
   keypass="changeit" />
```

2. Save the `server.xml` and restart the Tomcat services.

4. Once the installation is done, the next step is to verify the SSL. You can access the application using the URL `https://yoursitename` or `https://localhost:8443`. Here, we have not created the signed certificate as it is a paid service, but we can use `www.gmail.com` as an example, which also uses SSL. Hit the URL, once the page is loaded, you will see the SSL icon. Click on it to view the certificate details, as shown in the following screenshot:

5. If you click on **Details**, it shows that your certificate is successfully installed, as shown in the following screenshot:

Summary

In this chapter, we have discussed the various policies of Tomcat 7 and their functionalities, such as the Catalina policy and System level policy. We have also discussed the different measures of enabling security and their benefits, such as SSL, best practices used in real-time industries to secure Tomcat 7 in the production environment by changing the configuration, and SSL implementation.

In the next chapter, we will discuss various real-time issues with reference to Tomcat and their components and solutions.

6
Logging in Tomcat 7

Logging services play a vital role in the life of the administrator and developer to manage the application from the phase of development to production issues. It's the logging services that help you to find the actual problem in the web application. Also, it plays an essential role in performance tuning for many applications.

In this chapter, we will discuss:

- Logging services in Tomcat 7
- JULI
- Log4j
- Log level
- Valve component
- Analysis of logs

JULI

Previous versions of Tomcat (until 5.x) use Apache common logging services for generating logs. A major disadvantage with this logging mechanism is that it can handle only a single JVM configuration and it makes it difficult to configure separate logging for each class loader for independent applications. In order to resolve this issue, Tomcat developers have introduced a separate API for the Tomcat 6 version, that comes with the capability of capturing each class loader activity in the Tomcat logs. It is based on the `java.util.logging` framework.

By default, Tomcat 7 uses its own **Java logging API** to implement logging services. This is also called **JULI**. This API can be found in TOMCAT_HOME/bin of the Tomcat 7 directory structures (tomcat-juli.jar). The following screenshot shows the directory structure of the bin directory where tomcat-juli.jar is placed. JULI also provides the feature for custom logging for each web application, and it also supports private per-application logging configurations. With the enhanced feature of separate class loader logging, it also helps in detecting memory issues while unloading the classes at runtime.

For more information on JULI and the class loading issue, please refer to http://tomcat.apache.org/tomcat-7.0-doc/logging.html and http://tomcat.apache.org/tomcat-7.0-doc/class-loader-howto.html respectively.

```
[root@localhost bin]# ls -ltrh
total 740K
-rwxr-xr-x 1 root root 1.6K Apr  1  2011 version.sh
-rw-r--r-- 1 root root 2.1K Apr  1  2011 version.bat
-rwxr-xr-x 1 root root 4.6K Apr  1  2011 tool-wrapper.sh
-rw-r--r-- 1 root root 3.6K Apr  1  2011 tool-wrapper.bat
-rw-r--r-- 1 root root 236K Apr  1  2011 tomcat-native.tar.gz
-rw-r--r-- 1 root root  34K Apr  1  2011 tomcat-juli.jar
-rw-r--r-- 1 root root 2.1K Apr  1  2011 startup.bat
-rwxr-xr-x 1 root root 1.6K Apr  1  2011 shutdown.sh
-rw-r--r-- 1 root root 2.1K Apr  1  2011 shutdown.bat
-rwxr-xr-x 1 root root 3.9K Apr  1  2011 setclasspath.sh
-rw-r--r-- 1 root root 3.3K Apr  1  2011 setclasspath.bat
-rwxr-xr-x 1 root root 1.6K Apr  1  2011 digest.sh
-rw-r--r-- 1 root root 2.1K Apr  1  2011 digest.bat
-rw-r--r-- 1 root root 1.4K Apr  1  2011 cpappend.bat
-rwxr-xr-x 1 root root 1.9K Apr  1  2011 configtest.sh
-rw-r--r-- 1 root root 195K Apr  1  2011 commons-daemon-native.tar.gz
-rw-r--r-- 1 root root  23K Apr  1  2011 commons-daemon.jar
-rw-r--r-- 1 root root 2.5K Apr  1  2011 catalina-tasks.xml
-rw-r--r-- 1 root root  12K Apr  1  2011 catalina.bat
-rw-r--r-- 1 root root  27K Apr  1  2011 bootstrap.jar
-rwxr-xr-x 1 root root 2.0K Jul 10  2011 startupbackup.sh
-rwxr-xr-x 1 root root 2.3K Jul 10  2011 startup.sh
-rwxr-xr-x 1 root root  19K Sep 25 10:33 catalina.sh
```

Loggers, appenders, and layouts

There are some important components of logging which we use at the time of implementing the logging mechanism for applications. Each term has its individual importance in tracking the events of the application. Let's discuss each term individually to find out their usage:

- **Loggers**: It can be defined as the logical name for the log file. This logical name is written in the application code. We can configure an independent logger for each application.

- **Appenders**: The process of generating logs is handled by appenders. There are many types of appenders, such as **FileAppender**, **ConsoleAppender**, **SocketAppender**, and so on, which are available in log4j. The following are some examples of appenders for log4j:

```
log4j.appender.CATALINA=org.apache.log4j.DailyRollingFileAppender
log4j.appender.CATALINA.File=${catalina.base}/logs/catalina.out
log4j.appender.CATALINA.Append=true
log4j.appender.CATALINA.Encoding=UTF-8
```

The previous four lines of appender define the DailyRollingFileAppender in log4j, where the filename is `catalina.out`. These logs will have UTF-8 encoding enabled.

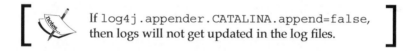

If `log4j.appender.CATALINA.append=false`, then logs will not get updated in the log files.

```
# Roll-over the log once per day
log4j.appender.CATALINA.DatePattern='.'dd-MM-yyyy'.log'
log4j.appender.CATALINA.layout = org.apache.log4j.PatternLayout
log4j.appender.CATALINA.layout.ConversionPattern = %d [%t] %-5p
  %c- %m%n
```

The previous three lines of code show the roll-over of the log once per day.

- **Layout**: It is defined as the format of logs displayed in the log file. The appender uses the layout to format the log files (also called patterns). The highlighted code shows the pattern for the access logs:

```
<Valve className="org.apache.catalina.valves.AccessLogValve"
  directory="logs" prefix="localhost_access_log." suffix=".txt"
  pattern="%h %l %u %t &quot;%r&quot; %s %b" resolveHosts="false"/>
```

 Loggers, appenders, and layouts together help the developer to capture the log message for the application event.

Types of logging in Tomcat 7

We can enable logging in Tomcat 7 in different ways, based on the requirement. There are a total of five types of logging that we can configure in Tomcat, such as application, server, console, and so on. The following figure shows the different types of logging for Tomcat 7. These methods are used in combination with each other based on the environment needs. For example, if you have issues where Tomcat services are not displayed, then the console logs are very helpful to identify the issue, as we can verify the real-time boot sequence. Let's discuss each logging method briefly:

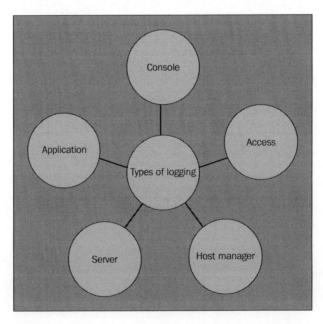

Application log

These logs are used to capture the application event while running the application transaction. These logs are very useful in order to identify the application level issues. For example, suppose your application performance is slow on a particular transition, then the details of that transition can only be traced in the application log. The biggest advantage of application logs is we can configure separate log levels and log files for each application, making it very easy for the administrators to troubleshoot the application.

> Log4j is used in 90 percent of cases for application log generation.

Server log

Server logs are identical to console logs. The only advantage of server logs is that they can be retrieved anytime, but console logs are not available after we log out from the console.

Console log

This log gives you the complete information of the Tomcat 7 startup and loader sequence. The log file is named as `catalina.out` and is found in TOMCAT_HOME/logs. This log file is very useful in checking the application deployment and server startup testing for any environment. This log is configured in the Tomcat file `catalina.sh`, which can be found in TOMCAT_HOME/bin.

```
CLASSPATH="$CLASSPATH""$CATALINA_HOME"/bin/bootstrap.jar

if [ -z "$CATALINA_BASE" ] ; then
  CATALINA_BASE="$CATALINA_HOME"
fi

if [ -z "$CATALINA_OUT" ] ; then
  CATALINA_OUT="$CATALINA_BASE"/logs/catalina.out
fi

if [ -z "$CATALINA_TMPDIR" ] ; then
  # Define the java.io.tmpdir to use for Catalina
  CATALINA_TMPDIR="$CATALINA_BASE"/temp
fi
```

The previous screenshot shows the definition for Tomcat logging. By default, the console logs are configured as INFO mode.

 There are different levels of logging in Tomcat such as WARN, INFO, CONFIG, and FINE. We will discuss each log level in detail in the section *Types of log levels in Tomcat 7* in this chapter.

```
[root@localhost logs]# ls -ltrh
total 172K
-rw-r--r-- 1 root root    0 May 16 21:03 manager.2011-05-16.log
-rw-r--r-- 1 root root    0 May 16 21:03 host-manager.2011-05-16.log
-rw-r--r-- 1 root root  714 May 16 21:19 localhost_access_log.2011-05-16.txt
-rw-r--r-- 1 root root  920 May 16 21:20 localhost.2011-05-16.log
-rw-r--r-- 1 root root 5.3K May 16 21:20 catalina.2011-05-16.log
-rw-r--r-- 1 root root    0 May 22 16:15 manager.2011-05-22.log
-rw-r--r-- 1 root root    0 May 22 16:15 host-manager.2011-05-22.log
-rw-r--r-- 1 root root    0 May 22 16:15 localhost_access_log.2011-05-22.txt
-rw-r--r-- 1 root root  460 May 22 16:19 localhost.2011-05-22.log
-rw-r--r-- 1 root root 2.9K May 22 16:19 catalina.2011-05-22.log
-rw-r--r-- 1 root root    0 Jun 23 02:25 manager.2011-06-23.log
-rw-r--r-- 1 root root    0 Jun 23 02:25 host-manager.2011-06-23.log
-rw-r--r-- 1 root root    0 Jun 23 02:26 localhost_access_log.2011-06-23.txt
-rw-r--r-- 1 root root  232 Jun 23 02:26 localhost.2011-06-23.log
-rw-r--r-- 1 root root 2.0K Jun 23 02:26 catalina.2011-06-23.log
-rw-r--r-- 1 root root    0 Jul 10 11:01 manager.2011-07-10.log
-rw-r--r-- 1 root root    0 Jul 10 11:01 host-manager.2011-07-10.log
-rw-r--r-- 1 root root    0 Jul 10 11:01 localhost_access_log.2011-07-10.txt
-rw-r--r-- 1 root root 1.6K Jul 10 15:22 localhost.2011-07-10.log
-rw-r--r-- 1 root root  30K Jul 10 15:22 catalina.out
-rw-r--r-- 1 root root  20K Jul 10 15:22 catalina.2011-07-10.log
[root@localhost logs]# pwd
/opt/apache-tomcat-7.0.12/logs
```

The previous screenshot shows the Tomcat log file location, after the start of the Tomcat services.

```
May 22, 2011 4:15:47 PM org.apache.catalina.core.StandardEngine startInternal
INFO: Starting Servlet Engine: Apache Tomcat/7.0.12
May 22, 2011 4:15:47 PM org.apache.catalina.startup.HostConfig deployDirectory
INFO: Deploying web application directory examples
May 22, 2011 4:15:48 PM org.apache.catalina.util.SessionIdGenerator createSecureRandom
INFO: Creation of SecureRandom instance for session ID generation using [SHA1PRNG] took [136] milliseconds.
May 22, 2011 4:15:48 PM org.apache.catalina.startup.HostConfig deployDirectory
INFO: Deploying web application directory host-manager
May 22, 2011 4:15:49 PM org.apache.catalina.startup.HostConfig deployDirectory
INFO: Deploying web application directory docs
May 22, 2011 4:15:49 PM org.apache.catalina.startup.HostConfig deployDirectory
INFO: Deploying web application directory ROOT
May 22, 2011 4:15:49 PM org.apache.catalina.startup.HostConfig deployDirectory
INFO: Deploying web application directory manager
May 22, 2011 4:15:49 PM org.apache.coyote.AbstractProtocolHandler start
INFO: Starting ProtocolHandler ["http-bio-8080"]
May 22, 2011 4:15:49 PM org.apache.coyote.AbstractProtocolHandler start
INFO: Starting ProtocolHandler ["ajp-bio-8009"]
May 22, 2011 4:15:49 PM org.apache.catalina.startup.Catalina start
INFO: Server startup in 1903 ms
```

The previous screenshot shows the output of the `catalina.out` file, where the Tomcat services are started in `1903 ms`.

Access log

Access logs are customized logs, which give information about the following:

- Who has accessed the application
- What components of the application are accessed
- Source IP and so on

These logs play a vital role in traffic analysis of many applications to analyze the bandwidth requirement and they also help in troubleshooting the application under a heavy load. These logs are configured in `server.xml` in `TOMCAT_HOME/conf`. The following screenshot shows the definition of the access logs. You can customize them according to the environment and your auditing requirements.

```
<!-- SingleSignOn valve, share authentication between web applications
     Documentation at: /docs/config/valve.html -->
<!--
<Valve className="org.apache.catalina.authenticator.SingleSignOn" />
-->

<!-- Access log processes all example.
     Documentation at: /docs/config/valve.html
     Note: The pattern used is equivalent to using pattern="common" -->
<Valve className="org.apache.catalina.valves.AccessLogValve" directory="logs"
       prefix="localhost_access_log." suffix=".txt"
       pattern="%h %l %u %t &quot;%r&quot; %s %b" resolveHosts="false"/>
```

Let's discuss the pattern format of the access logs and understand how we can customize the logging format:

```
<Valve className="org.apache.catalina.valves.AccessLogValve"
directory="logs" prefix="localhost_access_log." suffix=".txt"
pattern="%h %l %u %t &quot;%r&quot; %s %b" resolveHosts="false"/>
```

- **Class Name**: This parameter defines the class name used for the generation of logs. By default, Apache Tomcat 7 uses the `org.apache.catalina.valves.AccessLogValve` class for the access logs.

- **Directory**: This parameter defines the directory location for the log file. All the log files are generated in the log directory — `TOMCAT_HOME/logs` — but we can customize the log location based on our environment setup and then update the directory path in the definition of the access logs.

- **Prefix**: This parameter defines the prefix of the access log filename, that is, by default, the access log files are generated by the name `localhost_access_log.yy-mm-dd.txt`.

- **Suffix**: This parameter defines the file extension of the log file. Currently it is in `.txt` format.

- **Pattern**: This parameter defines the format of the log file. The pattern is a combination of values defined by the administrator, for example, `%h` = remote host address. The following screenshot shows the default log format for Tomcat 7. The access logs show the remote host address, date/time of the request, the method used for the response, URI mapping, and HTTP status code.

```
[root@localhost logs]# cat localhost_access_log.2012-01-24.txt
127.0.0.1 - - [24/Jan/2012:09:53:21 -0800] "GET / HTTP/1.1" 200 12079
127.0.0.1 - - [24/Jan/2012:09:53:22 -0800] "GET /tomcat.css HTTP/1.1" 304 -
127.0.0.1 - - [24/Jan/2012:09:53:22 -0800] "GET /favicon.ico HTTP/1.1" 304 -
127.0.0.1 - - [24/Jan/2012:09:53:23 -0800] "GET /asf-logo.png HTTP/1.1" 304 -
127.0.0.1 - - [24/Jan/2012:09:53:23 -0800] "GET /tomcat.png HTTP/1.1" 304 -
127.0.0.1 - - [24/Jan/2012:09:53:23 -0800] "GET /bg-nav.png HTTP/1.1" 304 -
127.0.0.1 - - [24/Jan/2012:09:53:23 -0800] "GET /bg-upper.png HTTP/1.1" 304 -
```

 In case you have installed the web traffic analysis tool for applications, then you have to change the access logs to a different format.

Host manager

These logs define the activity performed using the Tomcat Manager, such as the various tasks performed, the status of the application, the deployment of the application, and the lifecycle of Tomcat. These configurations are done on the `logging.properties`, which can be found in TOMCAT_HOME/conf.

```
2localhost.org.apache.juli.FileHandler.level = FINE
2localhost.org.apache.juli.FileHandler.directory = ${catalina.base}/logs
2localhost.org.apache.juli.FileHandler.prefix = localhost.

3manager.org.apache.juli.FileHandler.level = FINE
3manager.org.apache.juli.FileHandler.directory = ${catalina.base}/logs
3manager.org.apache.juli.FileHandler.prefix = manager.

4host-manager.org.apache.juli.FileHandler.level = FINE
4host-manager.org.apache.juli.FileHandler.directory = ${catalina.base}/logs
4host-manager.org.apache.juli.FileHandler.prefix = host-manager.

java.util.logging.ConsoleHandler.level = FINE
java.util.logging.ConsoleHandler.formatter = java.util.logging.SimpleFormatter
```

The previous screenshot shows the definition of the host, manager, and host-manager details. If you see the definitions, it defines the log location, log level, and the prefix of the filename.

In `logging.properties`, we are defining file handlers and appenders using JULI.

The log file for `manager` looks similar to the following:

```
28 Jun, 2011 3:36:23 AM org.apache.catalina.core.ApplicationContext log
INFO: HTMLManager: list: Listing contexts for virtual host 'localhost'
28 Jun, 2011 3:37:13 AM org.apache.catalina.core.ApplicationContext log
INFO: HTMLManager: list: Listing contexts for virtual host 'localhost'
28 Jun, 2011 3:37:42 AM org.apache.catalina.core.ApplicationContext log
INFO: HTMLManager: undeploy: Undeploying web application at '/sample'
28 Jun, 2011 3:37:43 AM org.apache.catalina.core.ApplicationContext log
INFO: HTMLManager: list: Listing contexts for virtual host 'localhost'
28 Jun, 2011 3:42:59 AM org.apache.catalina.core.ApplicationContext log
INFO: HTMLManager: list: Listing contexts for virtual host 'localhost'
28 Jun, 2011 3:43:01 AM org.apache.catalina.core.ApplicationContext log
INFO: HTMLManager: list: Listing contexts for virtual host 'localhost'
28 Jun, 2011 3:53:44 AM org.apache.catalina.core.ApplicationContext log
INFO: HTMLManager: list: Listing contexts for virtual host 'localhost'
```

Types of log levels in Tomcat 7

There are seven levels defined for Tomcat logging services (JULI). They can be set based on the application's requirement. The following figure shows the sequence of the log levels for JULI:

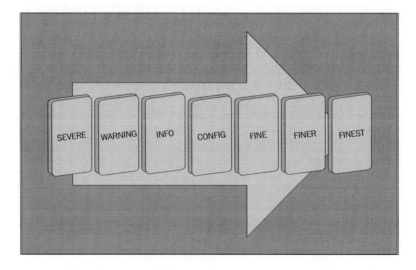

Every log level in JULI has its own functionality. The following table shows the functionality of each log level in JULI:

Log level	Description
SEVERE(highest)	Captures exception and Error
WARNING	Warning messages
INFO	Informational message, related to the server activity
CONFIG	Configuration message
FINE	Detailed activity of the server transaction (similar to debug)
FINER	More detailed logs than FINE
FINEST(least)	Entire flow of events (similar to trace)

For example, let's take an appender from logging.properties and find out the log level used; the first log appender for localhost is using FINE as the log level, as shown in the following code snippet:

```
localhost.org.apache.juli.FileHandler.level = FINE

localhost.org.apache.juli.FileHandler.directory = ${catalina.base}/logs

localhost.org.apache.juli.FileHandler.prefix = localhost.
```

The following code shows the default file handler configuration for logging in Tomcat 7 using JULI. The properties and log levels are mentioned:

```
############################################################
# Facility specific properties.
# Provides extra control for each logger.
############################################################

org.apache.catalina.core.ContainerBase.[Catalina].[localhost].level =
   INFO

org.apache.catalina.core.ContainerBase.[Catalina].[localhost].handlers =
   2localhost.org.apache.juli.FileHandler

org.apache.catalina.core.ContainerBase.[Catalina].[localhost].[/manager]
   .level = INFO

org.apache.catalina.core.ContainerBase.[Catalina].[localhost].[/manager]
   .handlers = 3manager.org.apache.juli.FileHandler

org.apache.catalina.core.ContainerBase.[Catalina].[localhost].[/host-
   manager].level = INFO

org.apache.catalina.core.ContainerBase.[Catalina].[localhost].[/host-
   manager].handlers = 4host-manager.org.apache.juli.FileHandler
```

Log4j

Log4j is the project run by The Apache Software Foundation. This project helps in enabling the logs at the various levels of the server and application.

The major advantage of log4j is manageability. It provides the developer a freedom to change the log level at the configuration file level. Also, you can enable/disable logs at the configuration level, so there is no need to change the code. We can customize the log pattern based on the application, separately. Log4j has six log levels. The following figure shows the different types of log levels in log4j:

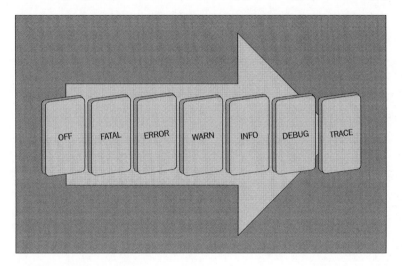

Log level for log4j

Every log level in log4j has its own functionality. The following table shows the functionality of each log level in log4j:

Log level	Description
OFF	This level is set when you want logging to be set as `false` (Stopped logging).
FATAL	This log level will print the severe errors that cause premature termination.
ERROR	This log level is used to capture runtime errors or unexpected conditions.
	Expect these to be immediately visible on a status console.
WARN	This level is used in the previous version.
	It gives you *almost* errors, other runtime situations that are undesirable or unexpected, but not necessarily *wrong*.
	Expect these to be immediately visible on a status console.

Log level	Description
INFO	This log level will define the interesting runtime events (startup/shutdown). It is best practice to put the logs at the INFO level.
DEBUG	Detailed information on the flow through the system is defined in this level.
TRACE	This log level captures all the events in the system and application.

How to use log4j

Following are the steps to be performed to use log4j:

1. Download **apache-log4j-1.2.X.tar.gz** from its official URL http://logging. apache.org/log4j/1.2/download.html, where **X** is the minor version.

2. Unzip the folder and place the log4j.jar in the lib for TOMCAT_HOME/lib and delete the juli*.jar from lib.

3. Delete the logging.properties from the TOMCAT_HOME/CONF.

4. Create a file log4j.properties in the TOMCAT_HOME/CONF and define the log appenders for the Tomcat instance. The following screenshot shows the appenders for catalina.out. Also, the highlighted code shows the roll-over of logs per day:

```
log4j.rootLogger=INFO, CATALINA

# Define all the appenders
log4j.appender.CATALINA=org.apache.log4j.DailyRollingFileAppender
log4j.appender.CATALINA.File=${catalina.base}/logs/catalina.
log4j.appender.CATALINA.Append=true
log4j.appender.CATALINA.Encoding=UTF-8
# Roll-over the log once per day
log4j.appender.CATALINA.DatePattern='.'dd-MM-yyyy'.log'
log4j.appender.CATALINA.layout = org.apache.log4j.PatternLayout
log4j.appender.CATALINA.layout.ConversionPattern = %d [%t] %-5p %c- %m%n

log4j.appender.LOCALHOST =org.apache.log4j.DailyRollingFileAppender
log4j.appender.LOCALHOST.File=${catalina.base}/logs/localhost.
log4j.appender.LOCALHOST.Append=true
log4j.appender.LOCALHOST.Encoding=UTF-8
log4j.appender.LOCALHOST.DatePattern='.'yyyy-MM-dd'.log'
log4j.appender.LOCALHOST.layout = org.apache.log4j.PatternLayout
log4j.appender.LOCALHOST.layout.ConversionPattern = %d [%t] %-5p %c- %m%
```

 You can customize the log rotation based on size, day, hour, and so on, using the previous log4j appenders marked in bold.

5. Restart the Tomcat services.

Important tip for the production environment

DEBUG and TRACE modes are ideal modes for troubleshooting, but we have to disable them after log analysis. For a production environment, the ideal mode is INFO (DEBUG and TRACE generate heavy logging and also affect the server performance).

Appenders should be enabled everyday in a production environment. This helps the administrator to perform a log analysis very easily (the file size is less).

Log level mapping

Until now, we have discussed the various log levels for JULI and log4j. Let us do a quick log level mapping for JULI and log4j. The following table shows the one-to-one mapping for log4j and JULI:

Log level in JULI	Log level in log4j
SEVERE	FATAL, ERROR
WARNING	WARN
INFO	INFO
CONFIG	NA
FINE	DEBUG
FINER	DEBUG
FINEST	TRACE

Values for Tomcat 7

Values are defined as identifiers which change the pattern of the string in the log. Suppose you want to know the IP address of a remote host, which has accessed the website, then you add the combination of the following values mentioned in the log appenders. For example, let's customize the access logs for Tomcat 7. By default, access logs for Tomcat are defined as follows:

```
<Valve className="org.apache.catalina.valves.AccessLogValve"
    directory="logs" prefix="localhost_access_log." suffix=".txt"
    pattern="%h %l %u %t &quot;%r&quot; %s %b" resolveHosts="false"/>
```

We want to change the log pattern to show the time taken to process the request. We have to add the %T in the patterns. The changed code is shown as follows:

```
<Valve className="org.apache.catalina.valves.AccessLogValve"
  directory="logs"
  prefix="localhost_access_log." suffix=".txt"
  pattern="%h %l %u %t %T &quot;%r&quot; %s %b" resolveHosts="false"/>
```

The following table shows the values used in Tomcat 7 for log pattern customization:

Values	Description
%a	Remote IP address
%A	Local IP address
%b	Bytes sent, excluding HTTP headers, or " if zero
%B	Bytes sent, excluding HTTP headers
%h	Remote hostname (or IP address if enableLookups for the connector is false)
%H	Request protocol
%l	Remote logical username from identd
%m	Request method (GET, POST, and so on)
%p	Local port on which this request was received
%q	Query string (prepended with a '?' if it exists)
%r	First line of the request (method and request URI)
%s	HTTP status code of the response
%S	User session ID
%t	Date and time, in Common Log format
%u	Remote user that was authenticated (if any)
%U	Requested URL path
%v	Local server name
%D	Time taken to process the request, in milliseconds
%T	Time taken to process the request, in seconds
%I	Current request thread name (can compare later with stack traces)

Log analysis

Log analysis is a very important and tricky issue, which needs to be handled with a lot of care. If you overlook a few lines, then you will never be able to find the root cause of the issue. Some of the best practices which need to be kept in consideration while doing the log analysis are mentioned as follows:

- Check the logs of the last 1 hour from the issue
- Always go to the first exception in the logs when the error has started
- Always keep in mind that issues are not caused due to malfunction of Tomcat, also check the other infrastructure resources

In non-DOS operating systems (Linux, Unix, Ubuntu, and so on), there are two utilities which are very useful in log analysis, grep and awk. Let's discuss grep and awk utilities briefly:

- **grep**: This utility prints the lines which match the string searched.

  ```
  grep Error catalina.out
  ```

  The previous command is an example of the grep command for searching the word "error" in the file catalina.out and displays the lines which contain the word "error".

- **awk**: This command is used for pattern scanning. Suppose we want to print 10 columns in the entire data file, then this command is very useful. The following screenshot shows the output of the command when run for the /opt directory:

  ```
  find "location of directory " -type f -size +10000k -exec ls -lh
     {} \; | awk '{ print $9 ": " $5 }'
  ```

  ```
  find "/opt" -type f -size +10000k -exec ls -lh {} \; | awk '{
     print $9 ": " $5 }'
  ```

```
[root@localhost conf]# find /opt -type f -size +10000k -exec ls -lh {} \; | awk '{ print $9 ": " $5 }'
/opt/httpd-2.2.19.tar: 36M
/opt/jdk1.6.0_24/src.zip: 19M
/opt/jdk1.6.0_24/lib/tools.jar: 13M
/opt/jdk1.6.0_24/lib/ct.sym: 15M
/opt/jdk1.6.0_24/jre/lib/rt.jar: 50M
/opt/jdk1.6.0_24/jre/lib/i386/client/classes.jsa: 15M
/opt/jdk-6u24-linux-i586.bin: 81M
```

Helpful commands for log analysis

Administrators are looking for shortcut commands to do their work efficiently. The following are some useful commands that I have collected during log analysis:

The following commands are used for searching big log files. Sometimes in a production environment, we get alerts for disk out of space. The following commands can be used:

- Finding large files and directories in Linux:

```
find "location of directory " type f -size +10000k -exec ls -lh {}
  \; | awk '{ print $9 ": " $5 }'
```

- Finding directories with a size over 100MB:

```
find / -type d -size +100000k
```

- Sort directories as per size using du:

```
du --max-depth=1 -m | sort -n -r
```

- Finding directory sizes:

```
du -sh folder_name

du -ch folder_name

du -csh folder_name
```

- The following command is used for truncating huge log files on the live system (log rotation can be done without recycle of services):

```
cat /dev/null > file_name
```

The following mentioned commands are used for searching the string in different files:

- Finding ERROR exception

```
grep ERROR log_file
```

- Last 200 lines in log file:

```
tail -200 log_file
```

- Current logs to be updated

```
tail -f log_file
```

Summary

In this chapter, we have discussed the different methods of enabling logs in Tomcat 7 using log4j and JULI. Also, we have discussed the best practices used for log analysis, tips, and tricks.

In the next chapter, we will discuss the real-time issues, which are faced by the web administrator, in managing and maintaining the application production environment. So, get ready for the real fun!

Troubleshooting in Tomcat

7

Every day, IT administrators face new problems with servers in the production environment. Administrators have to troubleshoot these issues to make sure that the applications work perfectly.

Troubleshooting is an art of solving critical issues in the environment. It comes with experience and the number of issues you have come across in your career. But there is a set of rules for fixing the issues. We will discuss the real-time issues, which may occur in the production environment. We will also discuss tips and tricks for resolving issues.

In this chapter, we will discuss:

- Common issues
- Third-party tools for thread dump analysis
- Tomcat specific issues related to the OS, JVM, and database
- How to troubleshoot a problem
- Best practices for the production environment

Common problem areas for web administrators

Web administrators always find issues with applications, not due to server failure of the Tomcat server, but because applications start malfunctioning due to other components as well. The following figure shows different components for a typical middleware environment:

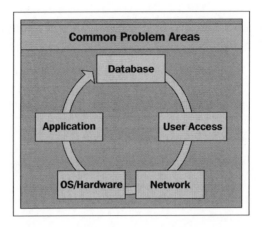

Let's briefly discuss the issues encountered by web administrators in real-time production support:

- **Application**: These issues occur when an application doesn't work correctly due to reasons such as class loader conflicts, application deployment conflicts, configuration parameters missing, and so on.

- **Database**: Database issues are very critical for the web administrator. It is very difficult to find the issues related to the DB. Some of them are; JNDI not found, broken pipe errors, and so on.

- **User Access**: Access issues can occur due to database or application mis-configuration. Some examples of these issues are; users are not able to access the application, login page doesn't appear, access denied, and so on.

- **Network**: This plays a vital role in the IT infrastructure. If the connectivity between the servers goes down, then the communication between the servers also goes down, and we face an interruption of services.

- **OS/Hardware**: The OS/hardware creates the lower layer where the application layer resides. If there are any issues with reference to the OS/hardware, it will affect the services of the Tomcat server.

How to troubleshoot a problem

We cannot troubleshoot any issue by just referring to the user comments or problem statement. In order to troubleshoot the issue, we have to narrow down the problem to its root level and fix the issue.

Many web administrators always ask this question; how do we know that the system has a particular problem?

The solution to these issues will be found, if you dig the problem in the correct path. Secondly, if you come across a number of problems in your career, then you can correlate them and solve the problem. If you ask me, practically it's impossible to teach troubleshooting, as it comes from your own experience and your interest to solve the problem. Here, we discuss one of the common problems, *application slowness*, that occurs in every environment and the web administrator has to face this problem in his/her career.

Slowness issue in applications

Let's take a real-time situation where users complain about the performance of the application. The application comprises of an enterprise setup, which is a combination of the Apache HTTP server as a frontend, Tomcat 7 is used as a servlet container, and the Oracle database running as a backend database server.

Issue:

Let's discuss one of the common issues of the middleware application, which make it very difficult for the administrator to solve. This issue is called *slowness of application*, where users complain that the application is running slow. It's a very critical problem from the administrator's point of view, as slowness can be caused by any component of the web application, such as the OS, DB, web server, network, and so on.

Until and unless we find out which particular component is causing the problem, the slowness will persist and from the user's point of view, the application will not run in a stable manner. The following figure shows the typical web infrastructure request flow for a web application:

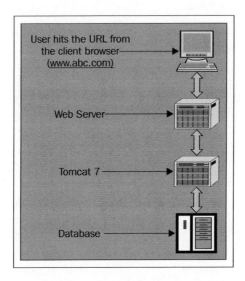

How to solve slowness issues in Tomcat 7

Slowness in the application can be caused by any component, so it is best practice to start troubleshooting from the user end.

User end troubleshooting

Perform the following steps to troubleshoot:

1. Try to access the application from the user's browser and check how much time it takes to load the application page.

2. Check the ping response of the server from the user side, for example, abc. com, using the command ping. If you get an appropriate response, it means the connectivity for the application server and user machine is working fine.

```
ping abc.com
```

```
C:\Users\user>ping abc.com

Pinging abc.com [199.181.132.250] with 32 bytes of data:

Reply from 199.181.132.250: bytes=32 time=349ms TTL=232
Reply from 199.181.132.250: bytes=32 time=289ms TTL=230
Reply from 199.181.132.250: bytes=32 time=296ms TTL=232
Reply from 199.181.132.250: bytes=32 time=294ms TTL=230

Ping statistics for 199.181.132.250:
    Packets: Sent = 4, Received = 4, Lost = 0 (0% loss),
Approximate round trip times in milli-seconds:
    Minimum = 289ms, Maximum = 349ms, Average = 307ms
```

- The previous screenshot indicates the `ping` response for `abc.com`. There are some important points we have to keep in mind during ping status monitoring, which are mentioned as follows:

  - The packet sent and received should have an equal count. In the previous screenshot we can see it's 4. If the count is less, it means that there is some issue within the network.

  - There should be no packet loss. Also, the average response time should not be high.

Many external sites disable the `ping` response for their nodes. This doesn't mean the system is down. In that case, try the telnet port, by using the command `telnet URL port`.

Windows 7, by default, does not come with telnet, we need to install it.

The previous screenshot shows the `ping` response for the server working appropriately. That means there are no issues from the user end in terms of the system and network.

Web server troubleshooting

Once we know that there are no issues at the user end, we will move to the next level in the application, that is web server. Now, we have to dig down in the server to check if there are any issues.

Web server issues are more often related to the load of the server, user threads, or mounting problems. Let us see how to solve the issue.

1. Check whether the web server process is running or not. If it is running, check how many processes are running by using the following command. This command will show the number of processes and their status.

    ```
    ps -aef |grep httpd
    ```

    The previous command shows the number of the processes running for the Apache httpd server. If the processes are greater than 50, it means that there is some issue with the web server such as a high CPU utilization, high user traffic, high disk I/O, and so on.

2. Then, check the CPU utilization and memory status of the system to see if any Apache processes are consuming a high CPU usage by using the following command:

    ```
    top|head
    ```

    The previous command will display the process which consumes the highest CPU usage and load average of the machine. The following screenshot shows the output of the previous command. If the load average is high or Apache process has a high CPU utilization, then it is one of the reasons for slowness in the application, otherwise we can proceed to the next level.

 In such cases, as mentioned earlier, you have to kill all Apache processes and then recycle the Apache instance.

```
[root@localhost ~]# top|head
top - 09:01:39 up  1:42,  3 users,  load average: 1.99, 2.09, 1.74
Tasks: 117 total,   3 running, 113 sleeping,   0 stopped,   1 zombie
Cpu(s):  1.1%us, 19.9%sy,  2.5%ni, 73.5%id,  2.5%wa,  0.1%hi,  0.5%si,  0.0%st
Mem:   1571836k total,   604168k used,   967668k free,    85108k buffers
Swap:  2040212k total,        0k used,  2040212k free,   388400k cached

  PID USER      PR  NI  VIRT  RES  SHR S %CPU %MEM    TIME+  COMMAND
 6765 root      39  19  4664 1400 1016 S  3.5  0.1  1:03.79 makewhatis
27389 root      15   0  2156 1004  740 R  1.8  0.1  0:00.04 top
    1 root      15   0  2032  676  576 S  0.0  0.0  0:01.90 init
[root@localhost ~]# []
```

3. The next step is to check the Apache logs and search for errors in the error and access logs. The following screenshot shows the system has started successfully:

```
[Tue Jul 26 02:48:01 2011] [notice] Apache/2.2.19 (Win32) configured -- resuming normal operations
[Tue Jul 26 02:48:01 2011] [notice] Server built: May 20 2011 17:39:35
[Tue Jul 26 02:48:01 2011] [notice] Parent: Created child process 2860
httpd.exe: Could not reliably determine the server's fully qualified domain name, using 10.0.0.3 for ServerName
httpd.exe: Could not reliably determine the server's fully qualified domain name, using 10.0.0.3 for ServerName
[Tue Jul 26 02:48:01 2011] [notice] Child  2860: Child process is running
[Tue Jul 26 02:48:01 2011] [notice] Child 2860: Acquired the start mutex.
[Tue Jul 26 02:48:01 2011] [notice] Child 2860: Starting 64 worker threads.
[Tue Jul 26 02:48:01 2011] [notice] Child 2860: Starting thread to listen on port 80.
```

httpd.exe: Could not reliably determine the server's fully qualified domain name, using 10.0.0.3 for ServerName.

The previous message is a notification message (info) in `apache error_log`. The log in the previous screenshot shows that " the Apache HTTP server could not find a fully qualified domain". This means that in the `httpd.conf`, we have missed defining the server name with a fully-qualified domain, for example, we have defined the localhost as the server name; instead of that, we have to define `localhost@localdomain.com`.

Also, there are two commands which are useful for searching the error in the logs. They are as follows:

tail -f log file |grep ERROR

The previous command is used when you want to search the error in the logs.

grep " 500 " access_log

The previous command is used to search error codes in the logs.

 In case logs are not generated for Apache, it may be due to the hard drive running out of space.

4. One of the major reasons for the hard drive running out of space on the server mount, where application logs are mounted, is improper log rotation. Use the `df` command to check the mount space, where `df` = disk free and switch `-h` = human readable. The syntax to use the `df` command is as follows and the output is shown in the following screenshot:

df -h

```
[root@localhost opt]# df -h
Filesystem           Size  Used Avail Use% Mounted on
/dev/sda2            3.8G  2.4G  1.3G  66% /
/dev/sda1             46M  9.2M   35M  22% /boot
tmpfs                768M     0  768M   0% /dev/shm
/dev/sda3             14G  778M   13G   6% /home
[root@localhost opt]#
```

If any mount is running greater than 95 percent, then reduce the disk utilization, otherwise the system may cause a disruption of services.

If we don't find any error in the previously mentioned components, than we can conclude that there are no issues with the web server.

Tomcat 7 troubleshooting

In Java-based applications, slowness is caused due to many issues. Some of them are due to the JVM memory, improper application deployment, incorrect DB configuration, and so on. Let's discuss some basic troubleshooting steps for Tomcat 7:

1. Check the Java processes for Tomcat and the load average for the instance machine:

   ```
   ps -ef |grep java
   ```

   ```
   [root@localhost bin]# ps -ef |grep java
   root     10638     1 15 10:45 pts/2    00:00:04 /opt/jdk1.6.0_24/bin/java -Djava.util.logging.config.file=/opt/apache-tomcat-7.0.12/conf/logging.properties -
   Xms128m -Xmx512m -XX:MaxPermSize=256m -Dorg.jboss.resolver.warning=true -Dsun.rmi.dgc.client.gcInterval=3600000 -Dsun.rmi.dgc.server.gcInterval=3600000 -Djav
   a.util.logging.manager=org.apache.juli.ClassLoaderLogManager -Djava.endorsed.dirs=/opt/apache-tomcat-7.0.12/endorsed -classpath /opt/apache-tomcat-7.0.12/bin
   /bootstrap.jar:/opt/apache-tomcat-7.0.12/bin/tomcat-juli.jar -Dcatalina.base=/opt/apache-tomcat-7.0.12 -Dcatalina.home=/opt/apache-tomcat-7.0.12 -Djava.io.tm
   pdir=/opt/apache-tomcat-7.0.12/temp org.apache.catalina.startup.Bootstrap start
   root     10707 24708  0 10:46 pts/2    00:00:00 grep java
   [root@localhost bin]#
   ```

   The previous screenshot shows the Java processes running in the machine. The previous command checks all the Java processes running in the system and the load average for the Tomcat instance. The load average gives us some important clues. In case you find the load average is very high, then check which process has a high CPU usage and find out the reason for using a high CPU. Also, it shows the RAM and Swap usage.

   The following screenshot shows the output of the head command on the Tomcat server:

   ```
   top|head
   ```

   ```
   [root@localhost bin]# top|head
   top - 10:54:56 up  3:35,  3 users,  load average: 0.00, 0.02, 0.01
   Tasks: 111 total,   1 running, 109 sleeping,   0 stopped,   1 zombie
   Cpu(s):  0.6%us, 12.2%sy,  1.3%ni, 84.1%id,  1.3%wa,  0.1%hi,  0.4%si,  0.0%st
   Mem:   1571836k total,   683860k used,   887976k free,    86100k buffers
   Swap:  2040212k total,        0k used,  2040212k free,   426956k cached

     PID USER      PR  NI  VIRT  RES  SHR S %CPU %MEM    TIME+  COMMAND
       1 root      15   0  2032  676  576 S  0.0  0.0   0:01.95 init
       2 root      RT   0     0    0    0 S  0.0  0.0   0:00.00 migration/0
       3 root      39  19     0    0    0 S  0.0  0.0   0:00.00 ksoftirqd/0
   ```

The `head` command displays the content from the first line of a file or output. It is very frequently used with –n switch where n= the number of lines to display. By default, it displays 10 lines if –n is not used.

2. Then check the Tomcat logs which can be found in `TOMCAT_HOME/logs`, and search for the exception in the log files, mainly in `catalina.out`, `localhost.yyyy-mm-dd.log` using the following command:

    grep INFO catalina.out

```
Sep 12, 2011 10:45:47 AM org.apache.catalina.startup.HostConfig deployDirectory
INFO: Deploying web application directory examples
Sep 12, 2011 10:45:49 AM org.apache.catalina.startup.HostConfig deployDirectory
INFO: Deploying web application directory host-manager
Sep 12, 2011 10:45:49 AM org.apache.catalina.startup.HostConfig deployDirectory
INFO: Deploying web application directory docs
Sep 12, 2011 10:45:49 AM org.apache.catalina.startup.HostConfig deployDirectory
INFO: Deploying web application directory ROOT
Sep 12, 2011 10:45:49 AM org.apache.catalina.startup.HostConfig deployDirectory
INFO: Deploying web application directory manager
Sep 12, 2011 10:45:49 AM org.apache.coyote.AbstractProtocolHandler start
INFO: Starting ProtocolHandler ["http-bio-8080"]
Sep 12, 2011 10:45:49 AM org.apache.coyote.AbstractProtocolHandler start
INFO: Starting ProtocolHandler ["ajp-bio-8009"]
Sep 12, 2011 10:45:49 AM org.apache.catalina.startup.Catalina start
INFO: Server startup in 3133 ms
```

The previous screenshot shows the Tomcat startup in the logs. If there are any errors in the logs, they can be checked using the following command:

    grep ERROR catalina.out

Troubleshooting at the database level

As a web administrator, you don't have access to the database servers. But a web administrator can connect to the DB server externally, without logging into a physical machine, as the administrator has the connection string (credentials for accessing the database). For example, you can do the telnet on the port where the DB server is running, and check whether the services are running or not.

Telnet DB server IP port

If the telnet is successful, then you can verify the following processes:

- **Number of database connections**: We can always ask our DBA to check the number of connections on the database. If the connections count is high, then we can work with the DBA to reduce the connections on the server.

- **SQL query optimization**: We can check with the DBA to see which queries consume more time to execute in the database and ask our developers to optimize the query. This really helps in improving the performance of the application.

- **Load balancing database across multiple servers**: Another important point which may cause slowness in the application is the load balancing of the database across multiple servers. If the load balancing is not configured correctly, then it may cause slowness in the application. If there is a delay in the network between the two database servers, then sync may not happen appropriately.

JVM analysis in the Tomcat instance

There are some chances where the JVM is over utilized in the application. To view the memory allocation for the JVM instance, you can use the command-line utility, `jmap`. This command comes with JDK 1.6. It's a Java utility, which determines the entire memory allocation of the Tomcat instance.

```
[root@localhost logs]# jmap -heap  "TOMCAT INSTANCE PID "
```

Let us discuss how the previous command performs. The `jmap` command internally collects the JVM memory details, `-heap` is the switch that tells `jmap` to collect and display the heap memory footprint, TOMCAT INSTANCE PID is the process ID of the Tomcat instance for which process `jmap` has to fetch the memory details.

```
[root@localhost logs]# jmap -heap  10638
```

The following screenshot shows the output of the `jmap` command for the previous process ID:

How to find the process ID

We can find the process ID using the following command:

```
ps -ef |grep "tomcat instance name " |awk -F" "
  '{print $2}'|head -1
```

This command can be described as, `ps -ef |grep "tomcat instance name "` will find all the processes running for the Tomcat instance. `awk -F" " '{print $2}'` awk prints the process ID of a particular process and `head -1` will display the first process ID.

The `jmap` command is present in JAVA_HOME/bin and if you set the JAVA _HOME/bin in the path, then you can execute the command from anywhere.

```
Mark Sweep Compact GC

Heap Configuration:
   MinHeapFreeRatio = 40
   MaxHeapFreeRatio = 70
   MaxHeapSize      = 134217728 (128.0MB)
   NewSize          = 1048576 (1.0MB)
   MaxNewSize       = 4294901760 (4095.9375MB)
   OldSize          = 4194304 (4.0MB)
   NewRatio         = 2
   SurvivorRatio    = 8
   PermSize         = 16777216 (16.0MB)
   MaxPermSize      = 268435456 (256.0MB)

Heap Usage:
New Generation (Eden + 1 Survivor Space):
   capacity = 40239104 (38.375MB)
   used     = 22928384 (21.8662109375MB)
   free     = 17310720 (16.5087890625MB)
   56.98035423452769% used
Eden Space:
   capacity = 35782656 (34.125MB)
   used     = 22928384 (21.8662109375MB)
   free     = 12854272 (12.2587890625MB)
   64.07680860805861% used
From Space:
   capacity = 4456448 (4.25MB)
   used     = 0 (0.0MB)
   free     = 4456448 (4.25MB)
   0.0% used
To Space:
   capacity = 4456448 (4.25MB)
   used     = 0 (0.0MB)
   free     = 4456448 (4.25MB)
   0.0% used
tenured generation:
   capacity = 89522176 (85.375MB)
   used     = 1666064 (1.5888824462890625MB)
   free     = 87856112 (83.78611755371094MB)
   1.8610628946284773% used
Perm Generation:
   capacity = 16777216 (16.0MB)
   used     = 11317504 (10.793212890625MB)
   free     = 5459712 (5.206787109375MB)
   67.4575805640625% used
```

The previous utility gives the entire footprint of the JVM memory and its allocation for the Tomcat instance. The JVM memory comprises of the following components:

- Heap configuration
- Heap usage
- From space
- To space
- Tenured generation
- Perm generation
- Eden space

Out of memory issues such as perm generation and max heap are very commonly known issues in the production environment. Check the memory to see whether any of the previous components are utilizing more than 95 percent. If so, then we have to increase the respective parameter.

Now it comes to the place where we can determine which JVM component is creating the issue for the Tomcat instance. If the memory is working fine, then it is time to generate a thread dump to drill the application-level issue.

How to obtain a thread dump in Tomcat 7

The thread dump is a way through which we can determine the application-level thread status for any Java process. There are many ways to obtain a thread dump in Tomcat; here we will discuss two different ways which are widely used in the IT environment.

Thread dump using Kill command

This command generates and redirects the thread dump in `catalina.out` log. But, the limitation to this command is it works in a non-DOS environment such as Linux, Unix, and so on.

```
Kill -3 java process id
```

For example:

```
Kill -3 10638
```

```
Full thread dump Java HotSpot(TM) Client VM (19.1-b02 mixed mode, sharing):

""ajp-bio-8009"-AsyncTimeout" daemon prio=10 tid=0x0919b800 nid=0x29cf waiting on condition [0xb4816000]
   java.lang.Thread.State: TIMED_WAITING (sleeping)
        at java.lang.Thread.sleep(Native Method)
        at org.apache.tomcat.util.net.JIoEndpoint$AsyncTimeout.run(JIoEndpoint.java:143)
        at java.lang.Thread.run(Thread.java:662)

""ajp-bio-8009"-Acceptor-0" daemon prio=10 tid=0x0919a400 nid=0x29ce runnable [0xb4867000]
   java.lang.Thread.State: RUNNABLE
        at java.net.PlainSocketImpl.socketAccept(Native Method)
        at java.net.PlainSocketImpl.accept(PlainSocketImpl.java:408)
        - locked <0x6e16cc80> (a java.net.SocksSocketImpl)
        at java.net.ServerSocket.implAccept(ServerSocket.java:462)
        at java.net.ServerSocket.accept(ServerSocket.java:430)
        at org.apache.tomcat.util.net.DefaultServerSocketFactory.acceptSocket(DefaultServerSocketFactory.java:59)
        at org.apache.tomcat.util.net.JIoEndpoint$Acceptor.run(JIoEndpoint.java:211)
        at java.lang.Thread.run(Thread.java:662)

""http-bio-8080"-AsyncTimeout" daemon prio=10 tid=0x09196000 nid=0x29cd waiting on condition [0xb495a000]
   java.lang.Thread.State: TIMED_WAITING (sleeping)
        at java.lang.Thread.sleep(Native Method)
        at org.apache.tomcat.util.net.JIoEndpoint$AsyncTimeout.run(JIoEndpoint.java:143)
        at java.lang.Thread.run(Thread.java:662)

""http-bio-8080"-Acceptor-0" daemon prio=10 tid=0x09197c00 nid=0x29cc runnable [0xb4b8000]
   java.lang.Thread.State: RUNNABLE
        at java.net.PlainSocketImpl.socketAccept(Native Method)
        at java.net.PlainSocketImpl.accept(PlainSocketImpl.java:408)
        - locked <0x6e16cec0> (a java.net.SocksSocketImpl)
        at java.net.ServerSocket.implAccept(ServerSocket.java:462)
        at java.net.ServerSocket.accept(ServerSocket.java:430)
        at org.apache.tomcat.util.net.DefaultServerSocketFactory.acceptSocket(DefaultServerSocketFactory.java:59)
        at org.apache.tomcat.util.net.JIoEndpoint$Acceptor.run(JIoEndpoint.java:211)
        at java.lang.Thread.run(Thread.java:662)

"ContainerBackgroundProcessor[StandardEngine[Catalina]]" daemon prio=10 tid=0x09196400 nid=0x29cb waiting on condition [0xb4909000]
   java.lang.Thread.State: TIMED_WAITING (sleeping)
        at java.lang.Thread.sleep(Native Method)
        at org.apache.catalina.core.ContainerBase$ContainerBackgroundProcessor.run(ContainerBase.java:1369)
        at java.lang.Thread.run(Thread.java:662)
```

The previous screenshot shows the output of the thread dump command in
`catalina.out` logs. We can see that the highlighted section shows the `http-
bio-8080- Acceptor` thread status, which is currently in a runnable state, which
means that the thread is alive and performing its functionality for the application.

```
Heap
 def new generation   total 39424K, used 11208K [0x63550000, 0x66010000, 0x6dff0000)
  eden space 35072K,   31% used [0x63550000, 0x640423f0, 0x65790000)
  from space 4352K,    0% used [0x65bd0000, 0x65bd0000, 0x66010000)
  to   space 4352K,    0% used [0x65790000, 0x65790000, 0x65bd0000)
 tenured generation   total 87424K, used 3212K [0x6dff0000, 0x73550000, 0x83550000)
   the space 87424K,   3% used [0x6dff0000, 0x6e3133f0, 0x6e313400, 0x73550000)
 compacting perm gen  total 12288K, used 6484K [0x83550000, 0x84150000, 0x93550000)
   the space 12288K,   52% used [0x83550000, 0x83ba5298, 0x83ba5400, 0x84150000)
    ro space 10240K,   61% used [0x93550000, 0x93b78a38, 0x93b78c00, 0x93f50000)
    rw space 12288K,   60% used [0x93f50000, 0x94688ec0, 0x94689000, 0x94b50000)
```

Once the thread generation is complete, it then collects the memory dump for the Java
processes. The previous screenshot shows the memory status at the time of the thread
dump. This memory dump gives us the complete footprint of the memory used.

Thread dump using jstack

There is another way of generating a thread dump, that is using the Java command-
line utility called `jstack`, which comes with JDK 1.5 or later versions. `jstack` prints
the Java stack thread for a Java process. This utility is very useful in a production
environment, where we have not redirected the thread output in the server logs. The
major advantage of this utility is that it can be used with any J2EE server. There are
some switches which are commonly used with the `jstack` command, as mentioned
in the following table:

Options	Description
-f	Generates a Java stack forcefully. Majorly used when the process is in the hang state
-l	Long listing (displays the additional information on locks)
-m	Mixed mode Java stack generation

The following command syntax generates a Java stack for a Java process and
redirects the output in a text file:

```
jstack -f Pid  > threaddump.txt
```

For example:

```
jstack -f 10638 > threaddump.txt
```

JStack on a 64 bit OS: If you are using a 64 bit operating system, then you have to run the `jstack -J-d64 -m pid` command to generate the thread dump.

JStack on Windows: On the Windows system, only one switch will work, and that is, `jstack [-l] pid`.

How to analyze the thread dump for Tomcat instance

The thread-dump analysis is tricky to understand. It gives a deep insight of application-related issues to the IT administrators. The following approach is applicable to do the thread-dump analysis. The steps are mentioned as follows:

1. Obtain the thread dumps six times for the Java process ID with an interval of 10 seconds, using the command `kill -3` or `jstack`.

2. Then compare all the six thread dumps to find the long running threads.

3. Find all the threads in the stuck state and try to find the reason for all the stuck threads for the application and server-level threads.

If the stuck thread is at the application level, then the issue is related to the application code and if the thread is stuck at the server level, then it may be a server or application-level issue.

There are two open source tools which are widely used for the thread dump analysis; Java **Thread Dump Analyzer (TDA)** and **Samurai**.

For a thread dump analyzer, check the link `http://java.net/projects/tda`.

For Samurai, check the link `http://yusuke.homeip.net/samurai/en/index.html`.

Thread dump analysis using Samurai

In the previous section, *How to analyze the thread dump for a Tomcat instance,* we have discussed the various steps for the thread-dump analysis. Let's do a real-time analysis using a Samurai tool.

It's a GUI-based tool, which has the capability to segregate the thread dump and verbose GC from the log file and display it on a user-friendly screen. Let's start the analysis process:

1. Run the Samurai thread dump analyzer online using the link `http://yusuke.homeip.net/samurai/en/index.html`.

2. Once the Samurai console is open, upload the logs to the Samurai tool.

3. The Samurai tool internally separates the logs and visualizes the thread dump and memory dashboard. The following screenshot shows the GC verbose utilization displayed by Samurai:

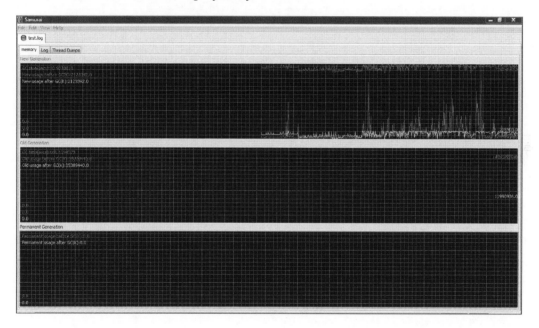

4. Now, click on the **Thread Dumps** tab, it will display the graphical status of the thread dump. The following screenshot shows the thread status. Also, on the left-hand corner, we can find the description of the symbol used for the thread dumps:

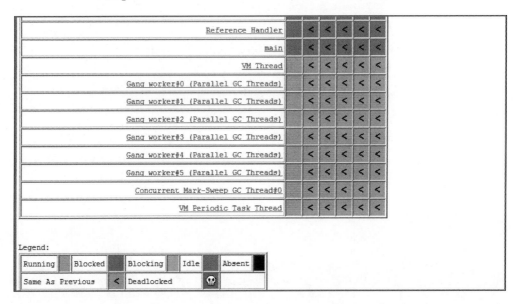

5. Now that we have the complete information, compare long threads manually and find the issue.

Thread dump analysis using the Thread Dump Analyzer

There is another very powerful tool, and very commonly used by the web administrator, known as Thread Dump Analyzer. This tool is capable of generating a summary for the thread dump. Following are the advantages of using this analyzer:

-   Long running threads can be compared among multiple thread dumps
-   It visualizes each thread separately
-   It generates a summary for each thread dump

Let's start the analysis process using the Thread Dump Analyzer:

1. Run the TDA online using the link `http://java.net/projects/tda` and click on **TDA Webstart**.

2. Once the TDA console is open, upload the logs to the TDA console. It will segregate the thread dumps, display the thread dumps in ascending order of the thread dump generation, and the summary of the first thread dump. The following screenshot shows the multiple thread dumps on the upper frame and summary for the first thread dump:

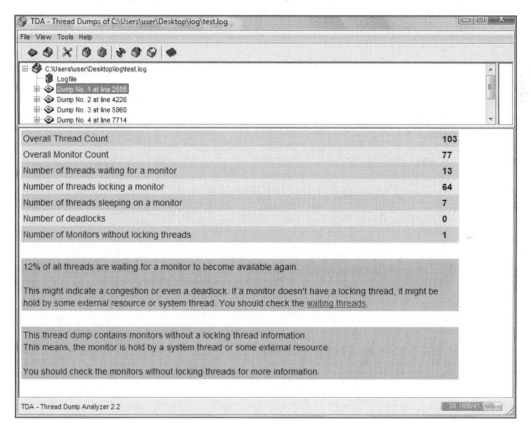

3. Now, compare the long running threads by selecting multiple thread dumps on the TDA console. Click on the long thread detection icon in the console tab, a pop-up window will appear on the screen. Click on **Start Detection**. The following screenshot shows multiple thread dumps selected on the TDA console and the pop-up window shows the long thread detection button:

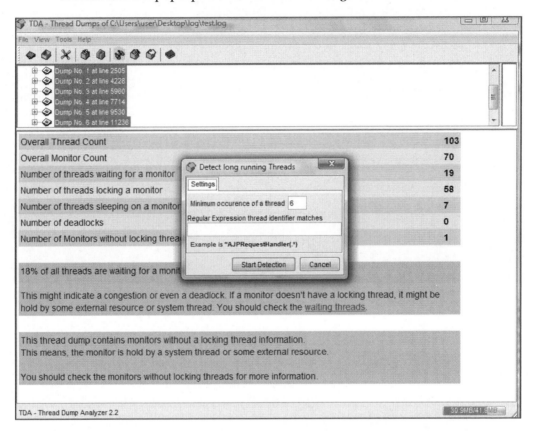

4. It generates the long running threads summary. Based on the summary, you can detect the problem. The following screenshot shows the complete summary of long running threads. The table displays the name of the thread, type, process ID, thread ID, native ID, thread status, and the address range:

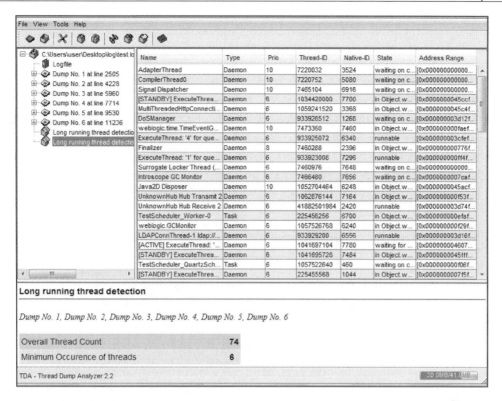

Name	Type	Prio	Thread-ID	Native-ID	State	Address Range
AdapterThread	Daemon	10	7220032	3524	waiting on c...	[0x000000000000...
CompilerThread0	Daemon	10	7220752	5080	waiting on c...	[0x000000000000...
Signal Dispatcher	Daemon	10	7465104	6916	waiting on c...	[0x000000000000...
[STANDBY] ExecuteThrea...	Daemon	6	1034420000	7700	in Object.w...	[0x0000000045ccf...
MultiThreadedHttpConnecti...	Daemon	6	1059241520	3368	in Object.w...	[0x0000000045c4f...
DoSManager	Daemon	6	933928512	1268	waiting on c...	[0x000000003d12f...
weblogic.time.TimeEventG...	Daemon	10	7473360	7460	in Object.w...	[0x000000000faef...
ExecuteThread: '4' for que...	Daemon	6	933925072	6340	runnable	[0x000000003cfef...
Finalizer	Daemon	8	7460288	2396	in Object.w...	[0x000000000776f...
ExecuteThread: '1' for que...	Daemon	6	933923008	7296	runnable	[0x000000000ff4f...
Surrogate Locker Thread (...	Daemon	6	7460976	7648	waiting on c...	[0x000000000000...
Introscope GC Monitor	Daemon	6	7466480	7656	waiting on c...	[0x0000000007caf...
Java2D Disposer	Daemon	10	1052704464	6248	in Object.w...	[0x0000000045acf...
UnknownHub Hub Transmit 2	Daemon	6	1062876144	7164	in Object.w...	[0x000000000f53f...
UnknownHub Hub Receive 2	Daemon	6	41882501984	2420	runnable	[0x000000003d74f...
TestScheduler_Worker-0	Task	6	225456256	6700	in Object.w...	[0x000000000efaf...
weblogic.GCMonitor	Daemon	6	1057526768	6240	in Object.w...	[0x000000000f29f...
LDAPConnThread-1 ldap://...	Daemon	6	933929200	6556	runnable	[0x000000003d16f...
[ACTIVE] ExecuteThread: '...	Daemon	6	1041697104	7780	waiting for ...	[0x000000004607...
[STANDBY] ExecuteThrea...	Daemon	6	1041695728	7484	in Object.w...	[0x0000000045fff...
TestScheduler_QuartzSch...	Task	6	1057522640	460	waiting on c...	[0x000000000f06f...
[STANDBY] ExecuteThrea...	Daemon	6	225455568	1044	in Object.w...	[0x0000000007f5f...

Long running thread detection

Dump No. 1, Dump No. 2, Dump No. 3, Dump No. 4, Dump No. 5, Dump No. 6

Overall Thread Count	74
Minimum Occurence of threads	6

TDA - Thread Dump Analyzer 2.2

Thread states can be classified into five types. The following figure shows the different thread states:

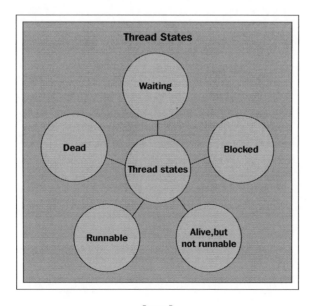

- **Runnable**: A thread goes in the runnable state once the `start()` method is invoked.

- **Waiting**: A thread goes in the waiting state when it waits for a resource to get allocated or another thread to execute its function.

- **Blocked**: A thread goes in the blocked state when it waits for the monitor lock.

- **Alive but not runnable**: A thread in this state is still alive but not runnable, it might return to the runnable state later, if that method is invoked again.

- **Dead**: A thread goes in the dead state once its operation is complete, or when its operation is terminated abnormally. If any thread comes to this state, it cannot ever run again. It's also called a deadlock state.

Dead threads are critical threads for the instance, as they cause slowness in the application. They can be released as part of the garbage collection and the system will generate new threads causing memory leaks.

Till now we have discussed the troubleshooting steps performed for any issue. If you have performed these, there is a 99 percent chance that the issue may be resolved.

Errors and their solutions

There are many issues which occur in the production environment and the web administrator has to dig the logs. It's always difficult for the administrator to understand what those exceptions mean and why they are generated in the application. The best way to understand the exception is to go to the logs and check for the first exception which will give you the exact idea of the issue.

Errors can be classified into three major types based on different components of the enterprise application:

- Application
- JVM (memory)
- Database

Let's discuss some of the exceptions and their solutions that help in making the environment stable.

JVM (memory) issues

Nowadays, applications are very resource-intensive; Tomcat instances run out of memory due to these issues. Administrators have to work very hard to fine tune the Tomcat 7 instances and make the environment very stable to run critical web applications on the Internet.

Out of Memory exception

In an enterprise environment, out of memory issues are encountered on a regular basis due to a high memory requirement of applications and the administrator has to tune the JVM. Failure of this causes an Out of Memory exception for the Tomcat instance.

Exception:

```
SEVERE: Servlet.service() for servlet jsp threw exception
java.lang.OutOfMemoryError: Java heap space
```

Reason:

This error may often occur while running an application, which requires high memory-intensive resources. Hence, it causes the Out of Memory exception on the server and leads to an interruption of services.

Solution:

You have to increase the maximum heap size for the Tomcat system. It's important to note that you can only allocate 70 percent of physical memory as JVM memory and 30 percent is reserved for the OS. Check the JVM configuration using the command `jmap` and then increase it in the configuration.

You have to add the following Java parameters in the startup script of Tomcat, which can be found in TOMCAT_HOME/bin, to increase the JVM allocation based on the memory requirement and recycle the Tomcat instance.

```
JAVA_OPTS="-Xms512m -Xmx1048m
```

OutOfMemoryError: PermGen space

Tomcat administrators often face the problem with the application's permanent object generation, as every application has different requirements of object generation. Hence, application slowness also results in the generation of OutOfMemoryError: PermGen space exception in catalina.out.

Exception:

```
MemoryError: PermGen space
java.lang.OutOfMemoryError: PermGen space
```

Reason:

The permanent generation is unique because it holds metadata describing user classes. Applications with a large code base can quickly fill up this segment of the heap which causes `java.lang.OutOfMemoryError: PermGen`, no matter how high your `-Xmx` and how much memory you have on the machine.

 Java code methods and classes are stored in the permanent generation.

Solution:

The following parameter should be added to the startup script of Tomcat 7. The parameter will increase the permanent generation space at the time of startup of Tomcat 7.

```
-XX:MaxPermSize=(MemoryValue)m
```

For example:

```
-XX:MaxPermSize=128m
```

Stack over flow exception

We have come across this issue in many applications. This exception is mainly caused due to recursive class loading (improper coding). This issue also causes performance degradation for the application: we observe that the application was working fine an hour ago but then it becomes unresponsive. This is a key indication of the stack overflow exception. The following screenshot shows the error in the logs:

Exception:

```
        at java.lang.Thread.run(Thread.java:534)
----- Root Cause -----
java.lang.StackOverflowError
```

```
javax.servlet.ServletException: Invoker service() exception
    at org.apache.catalina.servlets.InvokerServlet.serveRequest(InvokerServlet.java:524)
    at
    at org.apache.catalina.core.StandardPipeline$StandardPipelineValveContext.invokeNext(StandardPipeline.java:643)
    at LocaWebValve.invoke(LocaWebValve.java:101)
    at org.apache.catalina.core.StandardPipeline$StandardPipelineValveContext.invokeNext(StandardPipeline.java:641)
    at org.apache.catalina.core.StandardPipeline.invoke(StandardPipeline.java:480)
    at org.apache.catalina.core.ContainerBase.invoke(ContainerBase.java:995)
    at org.apache.ajp.tomcat4.Ajp13Processor.process(Ajp13Processor.java:457)
    at org.apache.ajp.tomcat4.Ajp13Processor.run(Ajp13Processor.java:576)
    at java.lang.Thread.run(Thread.java:534)
------- Root Cause --------
java.lang.StackOverflowError
```

Reason:

The exception thrown when the execution stack overflows is because it contains too many nested method calls.

Solution:

You have to increase the value of the `-xss` parameter in the startup file of Tomcat.

```
-Xss=(memory value in k)
```

For example:

```
-Xss=128k
```

By default, the stack overflow exception comes with the value of 64 k followed by the recycle.

Database-related issues

Until now we have discussed various JVM-level issues. Now it's time to discuss common database-related issues.

Broken pipe exception

The broken pipe exception is one of the most common issues reported in the production environment. What does this exception mean? It means that the database connectivity from the J2EE container is terminated. Possible causes for this issue are frequent network disconnects, Ethernet failure on the database, or the J2EE server-level container.

The following screenshot shows the error in the logs:

Exception:

`at java.lang.Thread.run(Thread.java:619)`

`Caused by: ClientAbortException:  java.net.SocketException: Broken pipe`

```
        at
org.apache.catalina.core.StandardContextValve.invoke(StandardContextValv
e.java:175)

        at
org.apache.catalina.core.StandardHostValve.invoke(StandardHostValve.java
:128)

        at
org.apache.catalina.valves.ErrorReportValve.invoke(ErrorReportValve.java
:102)

        at
org.apache.catalina.core.StandardEngineValve.invoke(StandardEngineValve.
java:109)

        at
org.apache.catalina.connector.CoyoteAdapter.service(CoyoteAdapter.java:2
86)

        at
org.apache.coyote.http11.Http11Processor.process(Http11Processor.java:84
4)

        at
org.apache.coyote.http11.Http11Protocol$Http11ConnectionHandler.process(
Http11Protocol.java:583)

        at
org.apache.tomcat.util.net.JIoEndpoint$Worker.run(JIoEndpoint.java:447)

        at java.lang.Thread.run(Thread.java:619)

Caused by: ClientAbortException:  java.net.SocketException: Broken pipe
```

Reason:

This issue is caused due to a connectivity loss between Tomcat 7 and the database.

Solution:

Recycle the Tomcat instance to restore the connectivity.

Timeout waiting for an idle object

Many times, when we click on the application for any transaction, the application displays a blank page after a while. It seems that the application server does not respond but the truth may differ. In many cases, the actual culprit is the database. What happens is the application server sends the request to the database and waits for the response, but the connection is abnormally terminated at the server causing a connection timeout exception. The following screenshot shows the errors in the logs:

Exception:

```
at org.apache.commons.dbcp.PoolingDataSource.getConnection
   (PoolingDataSource.java:104)

Caused by: java.util.NoSuchElementException: Timeout waiting for idle
   object
```

```
.  [ERROR 2010-05-05 23:57:58,839] Sernks in avlet.service() for servlet action threw exception
.  org.springframework.transaction.CannotCreateTransactionException: Could not open JDBC Connection for transaction:
.  nested exception is org.apache.commons.dbcp.SQLNestedException: Cannot get a connection, pool error Timeout waiting for idle object
.
.  Caused by: org.apache.commons.dbcp.SQLNestedException: Cannot get a connection, pool error Timeout waiting for idle object
.
.         at org.apache.commons.dbcp.PoolingDataSource.getConnection(PoolingDataSource.java:104)
Caused by: java.util.NoSuchElementException: Timeout waiting for idle object
```

Reason:

This issue is caused due to connection pooling for Tomcat.

Solution:

Change the connection idle values for Tomcat, these settings are in `server.xml`, followed by the recycle.

Database connectivity exception

This kind of issue is often reported in an enterprise environment, where installation of a new application is in process or the migration of an application is in process. It's an issue with an incorrect configuration with JNDI in Tomcat 7.

Exception:

```
java.lang.RuntimeException: Error initializing application.
   Error Unable to load any specified brand or the default brand:
   net.project.persistence.PersistenceException: Unable to load brand
   from database.
```

The previous error often indicates that the database could not be accessed.

```
Please check your database configuration or contact your system
    administrator: java.sql.SQLException: Error looking up data source
    for name: jdbc/abc
```

Reason:

Tomcat 7 is unable to connect to the database due to an incorrect JNDI name or the JNDI name doesn't exist.

Solution:

Work with the database administrator to get the correct JNDI name and configure it correctly, followed by a recycle.

Web server benchmarking

Now we know how to troubleshoot problems and find potential solutions in the systems. There is one more point left to discuss, **Web server benchmarking**. Without discussing this topic, troubleshooting in Tomcat 7 cannot be marked as complete. It's a process through which we gauge the performance of a web server, also known as **Load testing**. In this process, we run the server virtually on a heavy load and estimate the real-time performance. This process is very useful if we want to do capacity planning for the web server. There are many tools available for performing load testing on the server such as **ApacheBench (ab)**, **JMeter**, **LoadRunner**, **OpenSTA**, and so on. Let's discuss the commonly used open source tools such as ApacheBench and JMeter. If we do the benchmarking of the server before the go live stage, then we will face less issues in production support. Also, it helps in improving the performance and designing the scalable environment architecture.

ApacheBench

ApacheBench is a command-line tool for web server benchmarking. It comes under the Apache HTTP server and is very useful when we want to generate only HTTP threads. It's a single thread process.

JMeter

JMeter is one of the widely used open source tools used for load testing. This tool is developed under the Apache Jakarta project. It is capable of generating traffic for JDBC, web services, HTTP, HTTPS, and JMS services. It's a desktop software, which does not support all features of browsers. Following are the advantages of JMeter:

- Portable (can be run on any platform)
- Supports multitasking that allows the administrator to test multiple processes

 For more information on JMeter and ApacheBench, visit `http://jmeter.apache.org/` and `http://httpd.apache.org/docs/2.0/programs/ab.html` respectively.

Summary

In this chapter, we have discussed different issues faced by the application and web administrators in a real-time environment, how to avoid these issues in the production environment using different techniques with errors and their solutions, thread dump analysis and tools used for analysis, memory issues, steps for troubleshooting real-time problems, and web server benchmarking.

By the end of this chapter, the reader will be quite confident to work on the issues that are faced in a real-time environment and I am confident that, by now, they would have resolved some of the major issues in their environments. If not, then they are planning to fix the issues. In the next chapter, we will discuss different ways of managing and monitoring Tomcat 7.

8
Monitoring and Management of Tomcat 7

Monitoring plays a vital role in an IT administrator's life. It makes the life of a web/infrastructure engineer predictable. When I started my career in web infrastructure support, I always wondered, how does my boss know that a process is 90 percent utilized for a particular system or how does he know that a particular process will die after about 90 minutes from now, without logging into the application? Later, I found out that they have set up a monitoring system using various third-party tools available in the market for servers and application monitoring.

In this chapter, we will discuss:

- How to monitor Tomcat 7
- Management of applications using the Tomcat Manager
- A third-party utility used for monitoring Tomcat 7

Before we learn how to monitor Tomcat 7, let us understand why monitoring is actually required for any system, as we have configured the systems well for the user.

The answer to this question is very tricky. In a real-time environment, the system may break down due to many reasons such as a network glitch, sudden CPU spike, JVM crash, and so on. There are some revenue-generating applications, for example, if bank sites go down, then there will be a huge revenue loss, also administrators will not know unless users start complaining about the issues. This will also have a bad impact on the business. If monitoring systems were set up on the server, the web administrator would get a notification stating that the following systems are going down, and he/she would take the necessary actions to fix the problem. Hence, it minimizes the impact on the application downtime.

IT administrators support thousand of servers, it's practically impossible to validate the system every day. Hence, monitoring is very helpful.

Different ways of monitoring

In today's world, with increasing infrastructure, it becomes very difficult for administrators to manage servers. In order to identify the issue beforehand, and to minimize the downtime, monitors are configured on the system. We can configure multi-level monitoring on the systems, based on the infrastructure requirements for example, the OS, Web, Application, and Database level servers and individual application level. There are different ways of configuring multi-level monitoring. The following figure shows different ways to configure monitoring for any infrastructure:

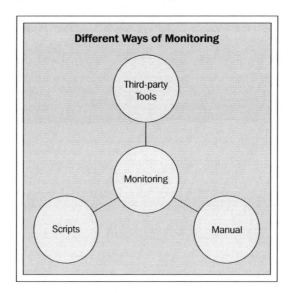

Monitoring can be mainly done in three ways on a system, which are as follows:

- **Third-party tools**
  - ○ Monitoring setups are configured using third-party tools present in the market, such as Wily, SiteScope, Nagios, and so on.
  - ○ These kind of monitoring tools are used in an enterprise infrastructure setup, where there are more than 100 servers with different infrastructure components (domains) such as web, application, database, filesystem servers, and so on.

- **Scripts**
  - ° Scripts are used in monitoring, where a specific use case needs to be monitored, such as the results of how many users are logged in for a particular interval of time or application-specific user roles.
  - ° Used everywhere in small and big IT organizations.

- **Manual**
  - ° This process is used when any application's performance is slow for a particular module.
  - ° Mostly used at the time of troubleshooting and where the number of systems are less than three.

Monitoring setup for a web application and database server

In the previous section, we have discussed the types of monitors, but still we don't know which monitors are configured on these systems. Let's prepare a table for the different infrastructure system monitors and why they are configured. The following table shows the basic monitors, which are normally configured for web application and database servers:

Monitored component	Benefit	Web server	Application server	Database server
CPU	Proactive measure to identify system issues	Yes	Yes	Yes
Physical Memory (RAM)	Proactive measure to identify system issues	Yes	Yes	Yes
JVM	Proactive measure to identify system issues	No	Yes	Yes
HTTP connection	Helps us identify the performance of the web server	Yes	Yes (only if HTTP services are running)	No
AJP connection	Helps us find out the connectivity of the web/application server	Yes	Yes	No
Database connection count	Helps us identify the performance of the database server	No	No	Yes

Monitored component	Benefit	Web server	Application server	Database server
Connection Idle	Helps us identify the issues of the database server	No	No	Yes
Disk space	Proactive measure to identify system issues (Disk out of space)	Yes	Yes	Yes
Error code in logs	Helps us identify potential issues on systems	No	Yes	Yes

Tomcat Manager in Tomcat 7

The Tomcat Manager is a default tool for managing operations of Apache Tomcat 7. It provides freedom to the IT administrators to remotely manage the application and monitor the systems. Following are the advantages of the Tomcat Manager:

- Allow remote deploy, rollback, start, and stop features for the administrator.
- Provide detailed monitoring status for the application and server.
- Administrators need not stay in the office 24x7. In case of any issues, he/she can log in to the Tomcat Manager to resolve the issue. In short, we can say remote administration of Tomcat becomes very easy for administrators.

It's not recommended to open the Tomcat Manager from the Internet. In case you have to do so, then we have to enforce strong security policies on Tomcat 7 or we can configure the **Virtual Private Network** (**VPN**) for the administrators.

Perform the following steps to access Tomcat Manager:

1. You can access the Tomcat Manager using the URL `http://localhost:8080/`. The following screenshot shows the main page for Tomcat 7 with **Manager App** highlighted.

2. Click on **Manager App**, it will prompt for the username and password. Provide the credential given in `tomcat_user.xml`, where `tomcat_user.xml` can be found in `TOMCAT_HOME/CONF`.

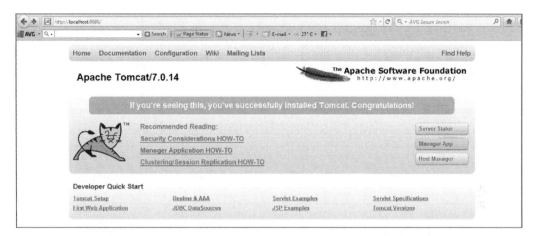

3. The Tomcat Manager console is displayed. If you look at the console, it gives you the complete picture of the application's deployment, server status, diagnostics, server information, and so on. The following screenshot shows the application's status and the different deployment-related tasks performed during application support:

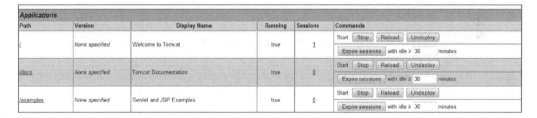

The following screenshot shows the other features of the Tomcat 7 Manager such as:

- Deployment of a new application
- Diagnostic (memory or connection leak)
- Server information

Deploy					
Deploy directory or WAR file located on server					

Context Path (required):

XML Configuration file URL

WAR or Directory URL

Deploy

WAR file to deploy

Select WAR file to upload   Browse...

Deploy

Diagnostics

Check to see if a web application has caused a memory leak on stop, reload or undeploy

Find leaks   This diagnostic check will trigger a full garbage collection. Use it with extreme caution on production systems.

Server Information

Tomcat Version	JVM Version	JVM Vendor	OS Name	OS Version	OS Architecture
Apache Tomcat/7.0.14	1.6.0_24-b07	Sun Microsystems Inc.	Windows Vista	6.0	x86

Monitoring in Tomcat 7

Monitoring in Tomcat 7 can be done using the Tomcat Manager. By default, the Tomcat Manager provides the status of the server with a detailed description of requests and their status. This information is very useful to administrators at the time of troubleshooting. Apart from this, the administrator need not log in to the machine for collecting this information. It takes a minimum of 30 minutes to collect the entire information of the application, if you are checking the server status manually, but using the Tomcat Manager, you are getting it online. That's truly amazing and a great help for IT administrators.

Let's discuss the various components used for monitoring that are available in the Tomcat Manager.

Summary of the Server Status of Tomcat 7

The basic synopsis of Tomcat 7 includes the details of the JVM, HTTP, and the HTTPS connection, which can be accessed using the URL `http://localhost:8080/manager/status`. The following screenshot shows the synopsis of Tomcat 7:

JVM

Free memory: 8.36 MB Total memory: 15.56 MB Max memory: 247.50 MB

"ajp-bio-8009"

Max threads: 200 Current thread count: 0 Current thread busy: 0
Max processing time: 0 ms Processing time: 0.0 s Request count: 0 Error count: 0 Bytes received: 0.00 MB Bytes sent: 0.00 MB

Stage	Time	B Sent	B Recv	Client	VHost	Request

P: Parse and prepare request S: Service F: Finishing R: Ready K: Keepalive

"http-bio-8080"

Max threads: 200 Current thread count: 10 Current thread busy: 1
Max processing time: 1008 ms Processing time: 3.635 s Request count: 31 Error count: 3 Bytes received: 0.00 MB Bytes sent: 0.30 MB

Stage	Time	B Sent	B Recv	Client	VHost	Request
R	?	?	?	?	?	?
R	?	?	?	?	?	?
R	?	?	?	?	?	?
S	2056 ms	0 KB	0 KB	0:0:0:0:0:0:0.1	localhost	GET /manager/status HTTP/1.1

P: Parse and prepare request S: Service F: Finishing R: Ready K: Keepalive

The displayed synopsis of Tomcat 7 contains the details of the JVM, HTTP connection, and the AJP connection summary. The details of the output summary for each component are as follows:

- JVM
  - **Free memory**
  - **Used memory**
  - **Total memory**

- Connections on the HTTP port
  - **Max threads**
  - **Current thread count**
  - **Current thread busy**
  - **Max processing time** (ms)
  - **Processing time** (s)
  - **Request count**
  - **Error count**
  - **Bytes received** (MB)
  - **Bytes sent** (MB)

- Connections on the AJP

  ◦ **Max threads**

  ◦ **Current thread count**

  ◦ **Current thread busy**

  ◦ **Max processing time** (ms)

  ◦ **Processing time** (s)

  ◦ **Request count**

  ◦ **Error count**

  ◦ **Bytes received** (MB)

  ◦ **Bytes sent** (MB)

Complete Server Status of Tomcat 7

This page gives the complete report of Tomcat 7's status. It includes all the parameters which are part of the **Server Status**. In addition to that, it displays the detailed application list, application response time, servlet response time, and so on. It can be accessed using the URL `http://localhost:8080/manager/status/all`. Let's discuss each component of the dashboard briefly.

Application List

This gives us the list of all applications hosted in Tomcat 7 and their URL mapping for the application's access. The following screenshot shows the application list deployment in the Tomcat 7 instance:

Application list

localhost/sample
localhost/
localhost/manager
localhost/docs
localhost/host-manager
localhost/examples

The following points gives the details of the applications hosted in Tomcat:

- **Application details**: Once we click on the application list, it displays the complete summary of the application including its internal deployment component. The following screenshot shows the internal components with their statuses such as the status of the application response, servlet response, and the JSP responses:

```
localhost/sample
Start time: Sun Sep 25 22:39:10 IST 2011 Startup time: 32 ms TLD scan time: 78 ms
Active sessions: 0 Session count: 0 Max active sessions: 0 Rejected session creations: 0 Expired sessions: 0 Longest session alive time: 0 s Average session alive time: 0 s Processing time: 0 ms
JSPs loaded: 0 JSPs reloaded: 0

HelloServlet [ /hello ]
Processing time: 0.0 s Max time: 0 ms Request count: 0 Error count: 0 Load time: 0 ms Classloading time: 0 ms

jsp [ *.jsp , *.jspx ]
Processing time: 0.0 s Max time: 0 ms Request count: 0 Error count: 0 Load time: 124 ms Classloading time: 0 ms
```

- **Application response**: Application response for a deployed application gives us the current state of the application. For example, the previous screenshot shows the following parameters with reference to the current behavior of the sample application:
  - ○ **Start time**
  - ○ **Startup time** (ms)
  - ○ **TLD scan time** (ms)
  - ○ **Active sessions**
  - ○ **Session count**
  - ○ **Max active sessions**
  - ○ **Rejected session creations**
  - ○ **Expired sessions**
  - ○ **Longest session alive time** (s)
  - ○ **Average session alive time** (s)
  - ○ **Processing time** (ms)
  - ○ **JSPs loaded**
  - ○ **JSPs reloaded**
- **Servlet details**: In this section, the dashboard displays the response time of the servlet deployed for a sample application with the following parameters:
  - ○ **Processing time** (s)
  - ○ **Max time** (ms)
  - ○ **Request count**
  - ○ **Error count**
  - ○ **Load time** (ms)
  - ○ **Classloading time** (ms)

- **JSP**: In this section, the dashboard displays the response time of the JSP deployed for a sample application with the following parameters:

    ° **Processing time** (s)

    ° **Max time** (ms)

    ° **Request count**

    ° **Error count**

    ° **Load time** (ms)

    ° **Classloading time** (ms)

JVM

In this section, the dashboard displays the JVM memory utilization for the Tomcat instance. The first column in the following screenshot shows the JVM memory utilization for the sample application with the following parameters:

- **Free memory**
- **Used memory**
- **Total memory**

Connections on the HTTP port (8080)

In this section, the dashboard displays the HTTP connection status for the Tomcat instance. The second column in the following screenshot shows the HTTP connection status for the application sample with the following parameters:

- **Max threads**
- **Current thread count**
- **Current thread busy**
- **Max processing time** (ms)
- **Processing time** (s)
- **Request count**
- **Error count**
- **Bytes received** (MB)
- **Bytes sent** (MB)

Connections on the AJP

In this section, the dashboard displays the AJP connection status for the Tomcat instance. The third column in the following screenshot shows the status of AJP connection for the application sample with the following parameters:

- **Max threads**
- **Current thread count**
- **Current thread busy**
- **Max processing time** (ms)
- **Processing time** (s)
- **Request count**
- **Error count**
- **Bytes received** (MB)
- **Bytes sent** (MB)

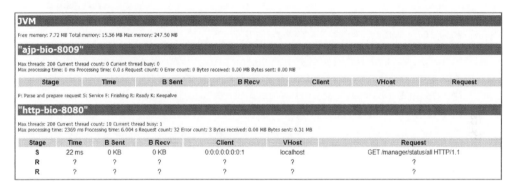

JConsole configuration on Tomcat 7

JConsole is one of the best monitoring utilities that comes with JDK 1.5 or later. The full form of the JConsole is the **Java Monitoring and Management Console**. It's a graphical tool, which gives complete details of the application and server performance. It gives us the following information about the application hosted in Tomcat 7:

- Detect low memory
- Enable or disable the GC and class loading verbose tracing
- Detect deadlocks
- Control the log level of any loggers in an application
- Access the OS resources—Sun's platform extension
- Manage an application's **Managed Beans (MBeans)**

Remote JMX enabling

In order to use the JConsole for Tomcat 7 monitoring, we have to enable the **Java Management Extension (JMX)** on Tomcat 7. By doing this, we can monitor the Tomcat 7 server details from our desktop machine also, or in simple terms, we can monitor the server status remotely without logging into the server machine. It gives great flexibility to the administrator to work from any location and troubleshoot the problem. In order to enable it in Tomcat 7, we have to add the CATALINA_OPTS parameter in catalina. sh. By default, the following values are added to enable the details:

```
CATALINA_OPTS=-Dcom.sun.management.jmxremote \
 -Dcom.sun.management.jmxremote.port=%my.jmx.port% \
 -Dcom.sun.management.jmxremote.ssl=false \
 -Dcom.sun.management.jmxremote.authenticate=false
```

Let's do the real-time configuration on Tomcat 7 and understand the meaning of each parameter:

```
CATALINA_OPTS="-Djava.awt.headless=true -Xmx128M -server
 -Dcom.sun.management.jmxremote -Dcom.sun.management.jmxremote.
 port=8086 -Dcom.sun.management.jmxremote.authenticate=false
 -Dcom.sun.management.jmxremote.ssl=false"
```

* -Djava.awt.headless: It is a system configuration option that helps the graphics rendering program to accept the graphics console and redirects the program to work in the command-line mode. It is very useful while connecting to the remote server.

* -Dcom.sun.management.jmxremote: This JMX allows the host to connect to the system.

* -Dcom.sun.management.jmxremote.port: It defines the port where your **Remote Method Invocation (RMI)** is connected.

* -Dcom.sun.management.jmxremote.authenticate: It defines the authentication mechanism for the connection.

* -Dcom.sun.management.jmxremote.ssl: It defines the protocol used for communication. If it is set to false, then, by default, it uses the HTTP protocol.

How to connect to the JConsole

Once Tomcat 7 configurations are done, it's time to connect to Tomcat 7 through the JConsole remotely using the command `jconsole`, as follows. It will open the GUI interface. We have to provide the IP address and port for the server where we want to connect; in our case, it's `localhost` and `8086`. The following screenshot shows the default console for the JConsole:

```
[root@localhost bin] # jconsole
```

[

`jconsole` can be found in JAVA_HOME/bin.

If we have included JAVA_HOME/bin in the path, then we can execute this command from anywhere in the system.
]

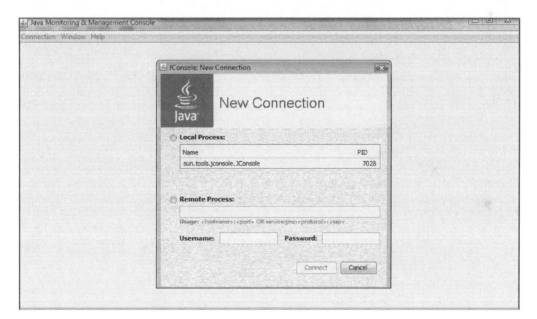

The following screenshot shows the JConsole connecting to Tomcat 7 using the port 8086:

 To connect to remote servers, we have to enable the firewall to allow the JConsole port on the server.

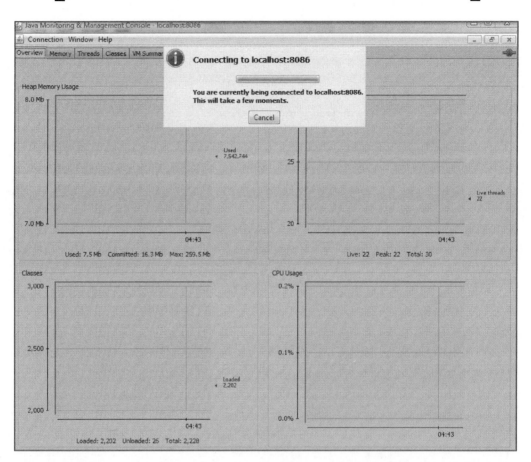

Once the system is connected, it gives the complete overview of the system such as the CPU, memory, thread, and classes. The following screenshot shows the details. We can also do a deep analysis for the following components of Java-based applications:

- Memory
- Thread
- Classes
- MBeans

The advantages of using this tool are:

- Online analysis of the application
- Customized report for the analysis
- Deadlock can be retrieved in the systems

Different tabs for the JConsole and their features

We will now discuss the different components of monitoring for the JConsole.

Memory overview

It's necessary for web administrators to analyze the memory status for Tomcat 7 to avoid future issues with the server. The following screenshot shows the real-time heap memory utilization for Tomcat 7. This tab provides the following features:

- Graphical presentation of memory with their JVM footprints
- Customization of the Memory chart based on the requirement analysis
- Ability to perform the GC

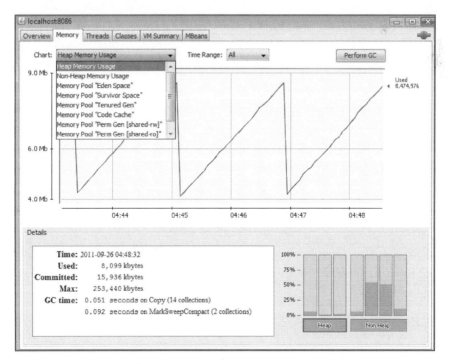

Threads overview

This tab gives the complete picture of the server threads and the web application hosted in Tomcat 7, for a particular instance. The following screenshot shows the live status of the threads utilization, and the **Deadlock Detection** button is highlighted. In real-time, this thread analysis tool is a very handy tool for the administrators. Following are the features offered by the **Threads** tab:

- Graphical presentation of threads and their picture
- Individual thread analysis with their status
- Deadlock detection

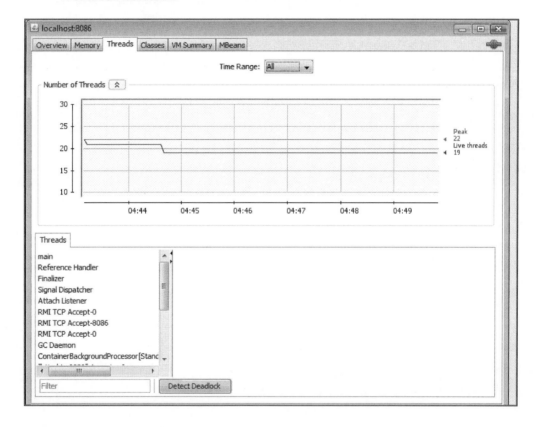

VM Summary and Overview

These two tabs are very important for an administrator. In practice, it's not possible for the administrator to view each and every component of the application every time. What the administrator does is, he/she checks for the overall performance of the system. If any anomalies are found, they will drill down the component. Following are the features of these tabs:

- Complete summary of the instances (**Heap Memory Usage, Threads, CPU Usage, Classes**)

- VM argument summary

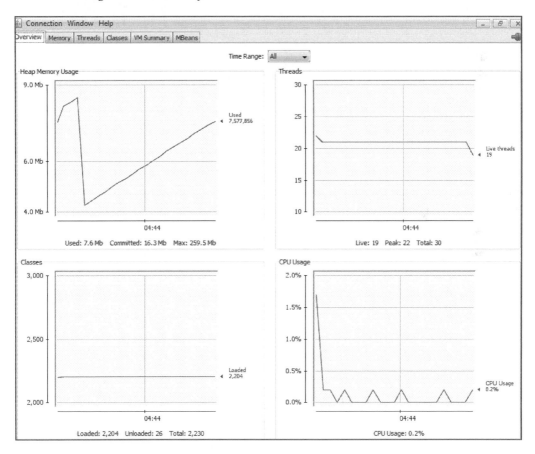

The previous screenshot shows the real-time status of Tomcat 7. It consists of four graphs displaying the real-time utilization of the heap, threads, classes and CPU usage for the Tomcat 7 instance. On the other hand, the following screenshot shows the complete summary of the Tomcat instance:

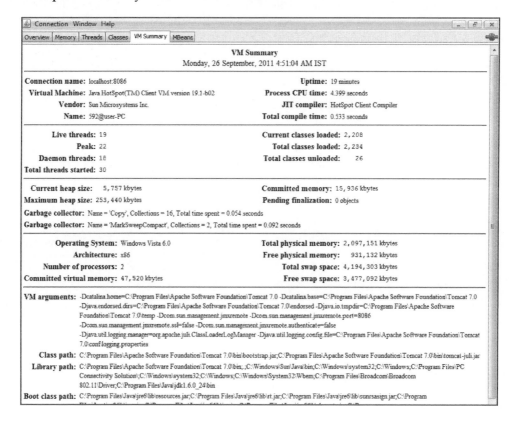

MBeans

This tab gives you the complete picture of **Managed Beans (MBeans)** deployed in the Tomcat instance. It includes both Tomcat and application-level MBeans. The following screenshot shows the attributes of **MBeans**. It's very useful if a particular MBean is the source for an issue. Following are the advantages of the **MBeans** tab:

- All parameters used in one tab
- Easy-to-deploy, rollback, and invoke
- We can create a user at the database level using MBeans
- We can create notifications for events using MBeans
- Configuration for resources can be done dynamically

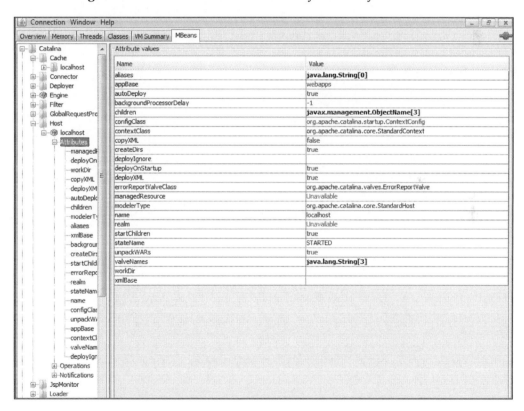

Types of MBeans

There are four types of MBeans. The following figure shows the different types of MBeans. Let's discuss each MBean briefly:

- **Standard MBeans**: A standard MBean is a combination of an MBean interface and a class, where the interface defines the entire list of attributes and operations, while the class provides the functionalities for communication for a remote interface. It is one of the simplest MBeans.

- **Dynamic MBeans**: A dynamic MBean implements a separate interface (a specific method) and can be invoked at runtime.

- **Open MBeans**: It is a composition of Dynamic MBeans and the universal dataset used for manageability.

- **Model MBeans**: It is a composition of Dynamic MBeans with complete access to configurable parameters at runtime and self-described methods. This MBean requires classes.

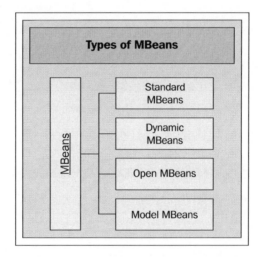

Let's take an example of the Connectors deployed in Tomcat 7, where we can configure and perform operations on the Connectors remotely using MBeans. By default, the HTTP and AJP Connectors are configured. In our example, we have the HTTPS Connector also configured. The following screenshot shows the three Connectors—HTTP, AJP, and HTTPS:

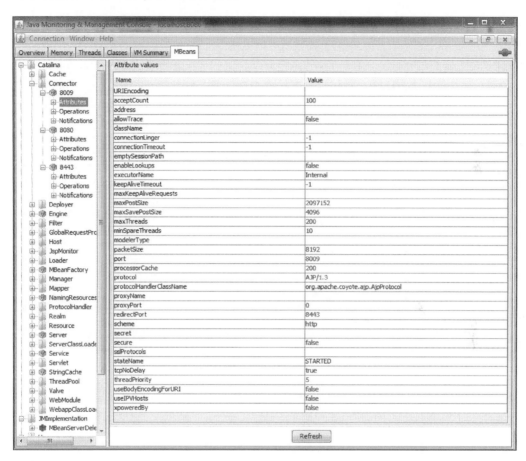

If we observe the **Connector** folder, we can view the three sublevels for each Connector. Following are the functions of each section:

- **Attributes**: This section contains information about the different parameters loaded in the memory during the startup of the Tomcat instance. In short, we can say that information of the configured parameter is loaded at runtime.

- **Operations**: The functionality of this mode is to perform runtime operations for MBeans. Following are the different operations we can perform:
  - Destroy
  - Start
  - Stop
  - Init
  - Resume
  - Pause

The following screenshot shows the **pause** operation successfully invoked for the HTTP Connector for Tomcat 7:

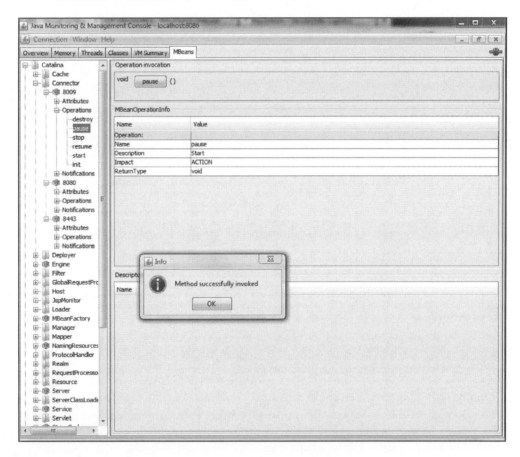

- **Nofitications**: It is used to configure notifications for an event such as the state of MBeans, deadlock, and so on. To enable notifications, we have to subscribe to it.

 For more information on monitoring, please refer to the link `http://java.sun.com/developer/technicalArticles/J2SE/monitoring/`.

Summary

In this chapter, we have discussed the various processes of monitoring in Tomcat 7 and their components using the Tomcat Manager and JConsole, such as different ways of monitoring, how monitoring is done in Tomcat 7, JConsole, and how it is used. In the next chapter, we will discuss the high availability setup for Tomcat 7 using clustering, load balancing, high availability concepts, architecture design, scalability, and so on.

Clustering in Tomcat 7

9

I would like to start this topic with a story. There were two teams; A and B, in an IT organization, managing different systems. Both teams consisted of highly qualified experts in middleware. One day, the CEO of that organization called a meeting for both teams, stating that they had to manage two different middleware environments, one middleware environment was individually assigned to teams A and B. Each team had to follow their own approaches to fix the environmental issues. After 3 months, each client performed a process review and the results surprised the higher management. Team A had maintained 50 percent uptime for the application and Team B had maintained 99 percent uptime for the application hosted in their environment. While comparing the approaches followed by each team, it was found that Team B had followed a high availability architecture using clustering while Team A had followed a single-server architecture.

In mid-year, the management announced the financial appraisal; Team A received no appraisal and, on the contrary, Team B members received high bonuses with promotions. Today, it's your chance to decide whether you want to join Team A or B. If you want to join Team B and follow a high availability architecture, read this chapter carefully.

In this chapter, we discuss:

- High availability architecture and its advantages
- Different types of high availability architectures including load balancing and clustering
- Approaches used by IT industries while building a high availability architecture in an enterprise setup
- How to do Apache Tomcat clustering
- Various clustering architectures
- How to solve common problems in clustering

What is a cluster?

The cluster is a group of servers or computers connected together, which may perform similar functionality in the system. These systems are normally connected to each other through high speed Ethernet. Cluster systems are used where quick processing or system availability is required. Some of the examples where clusters are highly used are the financial sector, banking, security areas, and so on. The following figure shows the J2EE containers clustered in the environment:

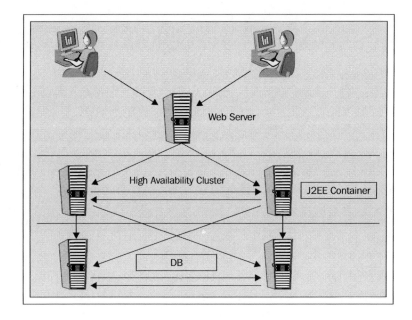

 Cluster topology varies from environment to environment, based on the application requirements.

Benefits of clustering

There are many advantages of clustering in a middleware environment. It also depends on which cluster techniques we are using. We will discuss the various advantages of clustering:

- **Scalability**: It gives freedom to the system architect to accommodate future enhancements for applications and servers. Suppose the web application currently has 100 concurrent users, and at the time of an event, you are expecting 500 concurrent users. What would you do to make sure that the system runs as expected? Clustering is one of the best solutions.

- **High availability**: High availability systems are implemented in environments that need to be up 99.99 percent, such as banking, financial sectors, and so on where entire transactions need to be recorded on the systems. They cannot afford to have their websites down for a minute. Hence, they implement a high availability system to make sure the system will not be down at any time.

- **High performance**: One of the major advantages of clustering is that it boosts up the system performance by n times where, n = number of systems. For example, if you are running the system with a single server and the system supports 100 concurrent users, then just by adding another server system you can support 200 concurrent users. Also, if you want to decrease the response time for the application, you can use the JVM performance tuning.

- **Cloud computing**: Clustering is also very useful in a cloud computing environment. It is used while setting the grid computing architecture for cloud computing to improve performance.

Disadvantages of clustering

Until now, we have discussed how useful clustering is for a web environment. Let's discuss the disadvantages of clustering:

- **Cost**: It plays a major role in the implementation of a new environment. If we want to setup web clustering, then we need more servers. This, again, increases the cost of the project.

- **Monitoring**: With an increase in the number of servers, the monitoring of servers will also increase, making it difficult for the web administrator to manage the servers.

Clustering architecture

In this topic, we will discuss the various architectures of clustering used by IT industries. These architectures may vary on each implementation, depending on the application and business requirements. There are basically two types of clustering architectures implemented in a real-time IT infrastructure:

- Vertical clustering
- Horizontal clustering

By default, Apache Tomcat 7 supports both horizontal and vertical clustering. In the next section, we will discuss the implementation of both types of clustering in Apache Tomcat 7. Before that, let's discuss clustering architectures, where they can be implemented, and their advantages.

Vertical clustering

Vertical clustering consists of a single hardware with multiple instances running, using shared resources from the system. This kind of setup is mainly done in development and quality systems for the developer to test the functionality of the application. Also, vertical clustering can be implemented in production in certain cases, where there is a resource crunch for the hardware. It uses the concept of a shared resource such as CPU, RAM, and so on. The following figure shows the pictorial presentation of vertical clustering:

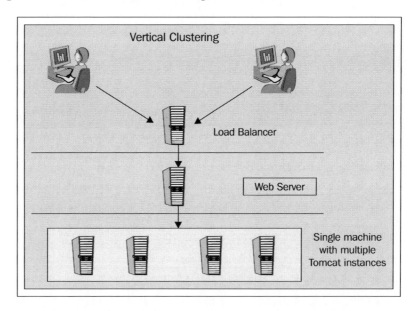

Every architecture has its pros and cons. Let's discuss some of the pros and cons of vertical clustering.

Advantages of vertical clustering

Following are the advantages of vertical clustering:

- No network bandwidth issue, as instances are hosted on a single machine
- Hardware is shared by different Tomcat instances

- Addition of physical hardware is not required
- Single JVM can be shared by multiple instances

Disadvantages of vertical clustering

Following are the disadvantages of vertical clustering:

- No failover in case of hardware issues
- More maintenance issues
- High-end hardware used for implementation
- High cost

Horizontal clustering

In this type of clustering method, instances are configured separately on each physical machine and connected through high speed Ethernet. It's a very popular implementation technique in the production environment. Resources of one machine are not shared with the other machine. Also, failover can be done in the case of hardware failure. The following figure shows the horizontal clustering for different Apache Tomcat instances using separate physical hardware:

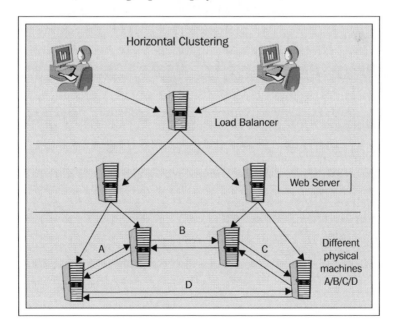

Let's discuss some of the pros and cons of horizontal clustering:

Advantages of horizontal clustering

Following are the advantages of horizontal clustering:

- Failover is possible in the case of hardware failure
- A low-end system can be used, as a single instance runs for each physical or VM instance
- Low maintenance issues

Disadvantages of horizontal clustering

Following are the disadvantages of horizontal clustering:

- Network bandwidth issues
- Network connectivity issues between machines
- Each instance requires a separate physical hardware component

 Horizontal clustering is the most preferred method in a production environment.

Vertical clustering in Apache Tomcat 7

In the previous topics, we have discussed the different types of cluster architecture, supported by Apache Tomcat 7. It's time to take a real-time challenge to implement clustering. Let's start with vertical clustering.

For vertical clustering, we have to configure at least two instances of Apache Tomcat and the complete process consists of three stages. Let's discuss and implement the steps for vertical cluster in Tomcat 7:

1. Installation of the Tomcat instance.
2. Configuration of the cluster.
3. Apache HTTP web server configuration for the vertical cluster.

Installation of the Tomcat instance

The installation of Apache Tomcat 7 can be done in three easy steps:

1. Download and unzip the software in the required directory.

2. Install the JDK and set the `JAVA_HOME`.

3. Copy the Apache Tomcat source code in two different directories, for example, `/opt/tomcatX` (where X= instance number) and verify that the files are properly copied on both instances, using the following command:

   ```
   [root@localhost opt]# ls -l apache-tomcat*
   ```

   The following screenshot shows the output of the previous command:

```
apache-tomcat1:
total 160
drwxr-xr-x 2 root root  4096 Oct  8 14:15 bin
drwxr-xr-x 3 root root  4096 Oct  8 13:59 conf
drwxr-xr-x 2 root root  4096 May 22 15:08 lib
-rw-r--r-- 1 root root 57851 Apr  1  2011 LICENSE
drwxr-xr-x 2 root root  4096 Oct 11 15:30 logs
-rw-r--r-- 1 root root  1230 Apr  1  2011 NOTICE
-rw-r--r-- 1 root root  9031 Apr  1  2011 RELEASE-NOTES
-rw-r--r-- 1 root root  6860 Apr  1  2011 RUNNING.txt
drwxr-xr-x 3 root root  4096 Oct  8 13:59 temp
drwxr-xr-x 7 root root  4096 Apr  1  2011 webapps
drwxr-xr-x 3 root root  4096 May 16 21:03 work

apache-tomcat2:
total 116
drwxr-xr-x 2 root root  4096 Oct  8 13:54 bin
drwxr-xr-x 3 root root  4096 Oct  8 13:56 conf
drwxr-xr-x 2 root root  4096 May 22 15:08 lib
-rw-r--r-- 1 root root 57851 Apr  1  2011 LICENSE
drwxr-xr-x 2 root root  4096 Oct 11 15:30 logs
-rw-r--r-- 1 root root  1230 Apr  1  2011 NOTICE
-rw-r--r-- 1 root root  9031 Apr  1  2011 RELEASE-NOTES
-rw-r--r-- 1 root root  6860 Apr  1  2011 RUNNING.txt
drwxr-xr-x 3 root root  4096 Oct  8 13:57 temp
drwxr-xr-x 7 root root  4096 Apr  1  2011 webapps
drwxr-xr-x 3 root root  4096 May 16 21:03 work
```

Configuration of a vertical cluster

This section is the most critical section for vertical clustering, as all the configurations are done in this section and a simple error can make the cluster non-functioning. So, be careful while carrying out the configuration. Let's do the step-by-step configuration on each node.

Configuration of instance 1

For the first instance; node 1, we can use the default configuration, such as Connector, AJP, or shutdown port in `server.xml`. Let's discuss each component where the configuration needs to be done and why it is used:

1. **Shutdown port**: The following screenshot shows the configuration for the `shutdown` port for the Tomcat instance. While running multiple instances, if by any chance, you have skipped configuring the `shutdown` port, then the Tomcat instance will be unable to start it.

```
-->
<Server port="8006" shutdown="SHUTDOWN">
  <!-- Security listener. Documentation at /docs/config/listeners.html
  <Listener className="org.apache.catalina.security.SecurityListener" />
  -->
  <!--APR library loader. Documentation at /docs/apr.html -->
```

2. **Connector port**: The following screenshot shows the `Connector port` configuration for Tomcat 7. This port is used to access the Tomcat instance, for example, normally we access the Tomcat instance by using `http://localhost:8080`, the 8080 port is called the Connector port. While running multiple instances, if you have skipped configuring this port, then the Tomcat instance will be unable to start it and you will get the `Port already in use` exception.

```
<!-- A "Connector" represents an endpoint by which requests are received
     and responses are returned. Documentation at :
     Java HTTP Connector: /docs/config/http.html (blocking & non-blocking)
     Java AJP  Connector: /docs/config/ajp.html
     APR (HTTP/AJP) Connector: /docs/apr.html
     Define a non-SSL HTTP/1.1 Connector on port 8080
-->
<Connector port="8080" protocol="HTTP/1.1"
           connectionTimeout="20000"
           redirectPort="8443" />
<!-- A "Connector" using the shared thread pool-->
<!--
```

3. **AJP port**: The following screenshot shows the AJP port configuration for Tomcat 7. This port is used for AJP communication between the Apache HTTP server and the Tomcat instance. While running multiple instances, if you have skipped to configuring port, then the Tomcat instance will be unable to start it and you will get the `Port already in use` exception.

```
<!-- Define an AJP 1.3 Connector on port 8009 -->
<Connector port="8009" protocol="AJP/1.3" redirectPort="8443" />
```

4. **Cluster attributes**: Enable the cluster attributes for clustering in `server.xml` and the following screenshot shows the cluster class used for clustering:

```
<!--For clustering, please take a look at documentation at:
    /docs/cluster-howto.html  (simple how to)
    /docs/config/cluster.html (reference documentation) -->

<Cluster className="org.apache.catalina.ha.tcp.SimpleTcpCluster"/>
```

5. **Configuration test**: Run the `configtest.sh` script from `TOMCAT_HOME/bin` to check the configuration. The following screenshot shows the output for the following `config.sh` command:

   [root@localhost bin]# ./configtest.sh

```
[root@localhost bin]# ./configtest.sh
Using CATALINA_BASE:   /opt/apache-tomcat1
Using CATALINA_HOME:   /opt/apache-tomcat1
Using CATALINA_TMPDIR: /opt/apache-tomcat1/temp
Using JRE_HOME:        /opt/jdk1.6.0_24
Using CLASSPATH:       /opt/apache-tomcat1/bin/bootstrap.jar:/opt/apache-tomcat1/bin/tomcat-juli.jar
Oct 11, 2011 4:55:58 PM org.apache.catalina.core.AprLifecycleListener init
INFO: The APR based Apache Tomcat Native library which allows optimal performance in production environments was not found on the java.library.path: /opt/jdk
1.6.0_24/jre/lib/i386/server:/opt/jdk1.6.0_24/jre/lib/i386:/opt/jdk1.6.0_24/jre/../lib/i386:/usr/java/packages/lib/i386:/lib/i386:/usr/lib
Oct 11, 2011 4:56:01 PM org.apache.coyote.AbstractProtocolHandler init
INFO: Initializing ProtocolHandler ["http-bio-8080"]
Oct 11, 2011 4:56:01 PM org.apache.coyote.AbstractProtocolHandler init
INFO: Initializing ProtocolHandler ["ajp-bio-8009"]
Oct 11, 2011 4:56:01 PM org.apache.catalina.startup.Catalina load
INFO: Initialization processed in 8569 ms
```

6. **Tomcat instance startup**: Start the instance 1 configuration using the script `startup.sh`. The following screenshot shows the output for the following `startup.sh` script:

   [root@localhost bin]# ./startup.sh

```
[root@localhost bin]# ./startup.sh
Using CATALINA_BASE:   /opt/apache-tomcat1
Using CATALINA_HOME:   /opt/apache-tomcat1
Using CATALINA_TMPDIR: /opt/apache-tomcat1/temp
Using JRE_HOME:        /opt/jdk1.6.0_24
Using CLASSPATH:       /opt/apache-tomcat1/bin/bootstrap.jar:/opt/apache-tomcat1/bin/tomcat-juli.jar
```

Check the Tomcat instance process using the following mentioned command. The following screenshot shows the output for the `ps` command:

```
[root@localhost bin]# ps -ef |grep java
```

```
[root@localhost bin]# ps -ef |grep java
root       11766     1 11 17:00 pts/3    00:00:17 /opt/jdk1.6.0_24/bin/java -Djava
m -Xmx512m -XX:MaxPermSize=256m -Dorg.jboss.resolver.warning=true -Dsun.rmi.dgc.
.logging.manager=org.apache.juli.ClassLoaderLogManager -Djava.awt.headless=true
e.port=7091 -Dcom.sun.management.jmxremote.authenticate=false -Dcom.sun.manageme
sspath /opt/apache-tomcat1/bin/bootstrap.jar:/opt/apache-tomcat1/bin/tomcat-juli
-Djava.io.tmpdir=/opt/apache-tomcat1/temp org.apache.catalina.startup.Bootstrap
root       11902 10149  0 17:02 pts/3    00:00:00 grep java
[root@localhost bin]# []
```

Configuration of instance 2

We cannot use the default configuration on node 2. There will be port conflicts as we are running the instance with single a IP on the same physical machine. Let's configure instance 2 step-by-step:

1. Change the `shutdown` port for instance 2 in `server.xml` (increment it by 1). The following screenshot shows the configuration:

```
-->
<Server port="8007" shutdown="SHUTDOWN">
  <!-- Security listener. Documentation at /docs/config/listeners.html
  <Listener className="org.apache.catalina.security.SecurityListener" />
```

2. Change the Connector and redirect the port for instance 2 in `server.xml` (increment it by 1). The following screenshot shows the configuration:

```
    -->
    <Connector port="8081" protocol="HTTP/1.1"
               connectionTimeout="20000"
               redirectPort="8444" />
    <!-- A "Connector" using the shared thread pool-->
```

3. Change the AJP and redirect the port for instance 2 in `server.xml` (increment it by 1). The following screenshot shows the configuration:

```
  <!-- Define an AJP 1.3 Connector on port 8009 -->
  <Connector port="8010" protocol="AJP/1.3" redirectPort="8444" />
```

4. Enable the cluster attributes for clustering in `server.xml`. The following screenshot shows the configuration:

```
<!--For clustering, please take a look at documentation at:
    /docs/cluster-howto.html   (simple how to)
    /docs/config/cluster.html (reference documentation) -->

<Cluster className="org.apache.catalina.ha.tcp.SimpleTcpCluster"/>
```

5. Save `server.xml`.

6. Run the `configtest.sh` script from TOMCAT_HOME/bin to check the configuration. The following screenshot shows the output for the following `startup.sh` script:

[root@localhost bin]# ./configtest.sh

```
[root@localhost bin]# ./configtest.sh
Using CATALINA_BASE:   /opt/apache-tomcat2
Using CATALINA_HOME:   /opt/apache-tomcat2
Using CATALINA_TMPDIR: /opt/apache-tomcat2/temp
Using JRE_HOME:        /opt/jdk1.6.0_24
Using CLASSPATH:       /opt/apache-tomcat2/bin/bootstrap.jar:/opt/apache-tomcat2
Oct 11, 2011 5:21:07 PM org.apache.catalina.core.AprLifecycleListener init
INFO: The APR based Apache Tomcat Native library which allows optimal performanc
1.6.0_24/jre/lib/i386/server:/opt/jdk1.6.0_24/jre/lib/i386:/opt/jdk1.6.0_24/jre/
Oct 11, 2011 5:21:13 PM org.apache.coyote.AbstractProtocolHandler init
INFO: Initializing ProtocolHandler ["http-bio-8081"]
Oct 11, 2011 5:21:14 PM org.apache.coyote.AbstractProtocolHandler init
INFO: Initializing ProtocolHandler ["ajp-bio-8010"]
Oct 11, 2011 5:21:14 PM org.apache.catalina.startup.Catalina load
INFO: Initialization processed in 14385 ms
```

7. Start the configuration of instance 2 using the script `startup.sh`. The following screenshot shows the output for the following `startup.sh` script:

[root@localhost bin]# ./startup.sh

```
[root@localhost bin]# ./startup.sh
Using CATALINA_BASE:   /opt/apache-tomcat2
Using CATALINA_HOME:   /opt/apache-tomcat2
Using CATALINA_TMPDIR: /opt/apache-tomcat2/temp
Using JRE_HOME:        /opt/jdk1.6.0_24
Using CLASSPATH:       /opt/apache-tomcat2/bin/bootstrap.jar:/opt/apache-tomcat2
/bin/tomcat-juli.jar
[root@localhost bin]#
```

8. Check the Tomcat instance process. The following screenshot shows the output for the `ps` command:

```
[root@localhost bin]# ps -ef |grep java
```

```
[root@localhost bin]# ps -ef |grep java
root     11766    1  1 17:00 pts/3    00:00:25 /opt/jdk1.6.0_24/bin/java -Djava.util.logging.config.file=/opt/apache-tomcat1/conf/logging.properties -Xms128
m -Xmx512m -XX:MaxPermSize=256m -Dorg.jboss.resolver.warning=true -Dsun.rmi.dgc.client.gcInterval=3600000 -Dsun.rmi.dgc.server.gcInterval=3600000 -Djava.util
.logging.manager=org.apache.juli.ClassLoaderLogManager -Djava.awt.headless=true -Xmx128M -server -Dcom.sun.management.jmxremote -Dcom.sun.management.jmxremot
e.port=7091 -Dcom.sun.management.jmxremote.authenticate=false -Dcom.sun.management.jmxremote.ssl=false -Djava.endorsed.dirs=/opt/apache-tomcat1/endorsed -cla
sspath /opt/apache-tomcat1/bin/bootstrap.jar:/opt/apache-tomcat1/bin/tomcat-juli.jar -Dcatalina.base=/opt/apache-tomcat1 -Dcatalina.home=/opt/apache-tomcat1
-Djava.io.tmpdir=/opt/apache-tomcat1/temp org.apache.catalina.startup.Bootstrap start
root     12535    1 29 17:23 pts/3    00:00:17 /opt/jdk1.6.0_24/bin/java -Djava.util.logging.config.file=/opt/apache-tomcat2/conf/logging.properties -Xms128
m -Xmx512m -XX:MaxPermSize=256m -Dorg.jboss.resolver.warning=true -Dsun.rmi.dgc.client.gcInterval=3600000 -Dsun.rmi.dgc.server.gcInterval=3600000 -Djava.util
.logging.manager=org.apache.juli.ClassLoaderLogManager -Djava.awt.headless=true -Xmx128M -server -Dcom.sun.management.jmxremote -Dcom.sun.management.jmxremot
e.port=7092 -Dcom.sun.management.jmxremote.authenticate=false -Dcom.sun.management.jmxremote.ssl=false -Djava.endorsed.dirs=/opt/apache-tomcat2/endorsed -cla
sspath /opt/apache-tomcat2/bin/bootstrap.jar:/opt/apache-tomcat2/bin/tomcat-juli.jar -Dcatalina.base=/opt/apache-tomcat2 -Dcatalina.home=/opt/apache-tomcat2
-Djava.io.tmpdir=/opt/apache-tomcat2/temp org.apache.catalina.startup.Bootstrap start
root     12596 10199  0 17:24 pts/3    00:00:00 grep java
```

9. Now, check `catalina.out` for both the nodes.

The logs for node 1 are similar to the following:

```
Oct 11, 2011 5:00:24 PM org.apache.catalina.ha.tcp.
SimpleTcpCluster
startInternal
INFO: Cluster is about to start
Oct 11, 2011 5:00:24 PM
org.apache.catalina.tribes.transport.ReceiverBase bind
INFO: Receiver Server Socket bound to:/127.0.0.1:4000
Oct 11, 2011 5:00:24 PM
org.apache.catalina.tribes.membership.McastServiceImpl setupSocket
# Instance node 1 started on port 4000
INFO: Setting cluster mcast soTimeout to 500
Oct 11, 2011 5:00:24 PM
INFO: Sleeping for 1000 milliseconds to establish cluster
membership,
start level:8
Oct 11, 2011 5:00:26 PM
org.apache.catalina.tribes.membership.McastServiceImpl
waitForMembers
# waiting for other member to join the cluster
org.apache.catalina.ha.session.JvmRouteBinderValve startInternal
INFO: JvmRouteBinderValve started
Oct 11, 2011 5:00:37 PM org.apache.coyote.AbstractProtocolHandler
start
INFO: Starting ProtocolHandler ["http-bio-8080"]
Oct 11, 2011 5:00:37 PM org.apache.coyote.AbstractProtocolHandler
start
INFO: Starting ProtocolHandler ["ajp-bio-8009"]
Oct 11, 2011 5:00:37 PM org.apache.catalina.startup.Catalina start
INFO: Server startup in 13807 ms
Oct 11, 2011 5:23:42 PM org.apache.catalina.tribes.io.BufferPool
getBufferPool
```

```
INFO: Created a buffer pool with max size:104857600 bytes of
type:org.apache.catalina.tribes.io.BufferPool15Impl
Oct 11, 2011 5:23:43 PM org.apache.catalina.ha.tcp.
SimpleTcpCluster
memberAdded
INFO: Replication member
added:org.apache.catalina.tribes.membership.MemberImpl
[tcp://{127, 0, 0, 1}:4001,{127, 0, 0, 1},4001, alive=1043,
securePort=-1, UDP Port=-1, id={33 91 -59 78 -34 -52 73 -9 -99 124
-53 34 69 21 -40 -82 }, payload={}, command={}, domain={}, ]
#Instance 2 joined the cluster node.
```

The logs for node 2 are similar to the following:

```
INFO: Starting Servlet Engine: Apache Tomcat/7.0.12
Oct 11, 2011 5:23:41 PM org.apache.catalina.ha.tcp.
SimpleTcpCluster
startInternal
INFO: Cluster is about to start
Oct 11, 2011 5:23:42 PM org.apache.catalina.tribes.transport.
ReceiverBase bind
INFO: Receiver Server Socket bound to:/127.0.0.1:4001
Oct 11, 2011 5:23:42 PM
org.apache.catalina.tribes.membership.McastServiceImpl setupSocket
# Instance node 2 started on port 4001
INFO: Setting cluster mcast soTimeout to 500
Oct 11, 2011 5:23:42 PM
org.apache.catalina.tribes.membership.McastServiceImpl
waitForMembers
INFO: Sleeping for 1000 milliseconds to establish cluster
membership,
start level:4
Oct 11, 2011 5:23:43 PM org.apache.catalina.ha.tcp.
SimpleTcpCluster
memberAdded
INFO: Replication member
added:org.apache.catalina.tribes.membership.MemberImpl
[tcp://{127, 0, 0, 1}:4000,{127, 0, 0, 1},4000, alive=1398024,
securePort=-1, UDP Port=-1, id={28 42 60 -68 -99 126 64 -35 -118
-97 7 84 26 20 90 24 }, payload={}, command={}, domain={}, ]
# Instance 1 joined the cluster node 2.
```

Apache web server configuration for vertical clustering

Until now, we have done the Tomcat-level configuration to configure vertical clustering in the Tomcat instance. It's time to integrate the Apache web server to Tomcat 7. Let's enable the integration by performing the following steps:

1. We have to create a new file called mod_jk.conf in the conf directory of APACHE_HOME/conf using the following commands:

    ```
    [root@localhost apache-2.0]# cd /opt/apache-2.2.19/conf
    vi mod-jk.conf
    ```

    The contents of mod_jk include the following lines of code:

    ```
    LoadModulejk_module modules/mod_jk.so
    JkWorkersFile conf/workers.properties
    JkLogFile logs/mod_jk.log
    JkLogLevel info
    JkMount /sample/* loadbalancer
    JkMount /* loadbalancer
    ```

2. Create a new file named as workers.properties in conf using the following command:

    ```
    [root@localhost conf]# vi workers.properties
    ```

    worker.list lists all the nodes in Tomcat through which Apache communicates using the AJP protocol. In our example, it has two nodes, as shown in the following line of code:

    ```
    worker.list=tomcatnode1, tomcatnode2, loadbalancer
    ```

    Define the worker.list for the entire nodes in the cluster:

    ```
    worker.tomcatnode1.port=8009
    worker.tomcatnode1.host=localhost
    worker.tomcatnode1.type=ajp13
    worker.tomcatnode1.lbfactor=1
    ```

    The previous lines of code define the tomcatnode1 properties. The highlighted code shows the AJP port and hostname of tomcatnode1, which is essential for vertical clustering:

    ```
    worker.tomcatnode2.port=8010
    worker.tomcatnode2.host=localhost
    worker.tomcatnode2.type=ajp13
    worker.tomcatnode2.lbfactor=1
    ```

The previous lines of code define the `tomcatnode2` properties. The highlighted code shows the AJP port and hostname of `tomcatnode2`. This is essential for vertical clustering.

```
worker.loadbalancer.type=lb
worker.loadbalancer.balanced_workers=tomcatnode1, tomcatnode2
worker.loadbalancer.sticky_session=1
```

The previous lines of code define the load balancing properties for `mod_jk`.

3. The last step is to include the `mod_jk.conf` in the main configuration file of `httpd`, that is `httpd.conf` and reload the Apache services:

    [root@localhostconf]# vi httpd.conf

 Include `conf/mod_jk.conf`. in the end of the `httpd.conf`.

Horizontal clustering in Apache Tomcat 7

For horizontal clustering, we have to configure at least two instances of Apache Tomcat on two different physical or virtual systems. These physical machines can be on the same physical network. It also helps in providing a high-speed bandwidth to the system.

If you want to configure clustering on different networks, then you have to open the firewall between the two networks for the AJP port and the clustering port.

There are prerequisites for configuring horizontal clustering. The following are the details:

*   Time sync between the two servers
*   Proper network connectivity between the two servers
*   Firewall ports between the two servers (if you are connecting from a different network)

In order to configure horizontal clustering, you have to perform the following steps:

1. Installation of the Tomcat instance
2. Configuration of the cluster
3. Apache HTTP web server configuration for the horizontal cluster

Installation of the Tomcat instance

We have already discussed the installation of Tomcat in the previous section.The steps for installation will remain the same here and, hence, we are skipping the installation. Let's move to step 2.

Configuration of the cluster

This section is the most critical section for horizontal clustering, as all the configurations are done in this section and a simple error can make the cluster not work. So, be careful before carrying out the configuration. Let's do the step-by-step configuration on each node.

Configuration of instance 1

For the first instance, we can use the default configuration such as the Connector, AJP, or shutdown port in `server.xml`. Let's discuss each component where configuration needs to be done and why it is used:

1. **Shutdown port**: The following screenshot shows the configuration for the shutdown port for the Tomcat instance. While running multiple instances, if you have skipped configuring the port, then the Tomcat instance will be unable to initiate it.

```
-->
<Server port="8006" shutdown="SHUTDOWN">
  <!-- Security listener. Documentation at /docs/config/listeners.html
  <Listener className="org.apache.catalina.security.SecurityListener" />
  -->
  <!--APR library loader. Documentation at /docs/apr.html -->
```

2. **Connector port**: The following screenshot shows the configuration of the `Connector port`. This port is used to access the Tomcat instance, for example, normally you access the Tomcat instance by using `http://localhost:8080`. The 8080 port is called the connector port. While running multiple instances, if you have skipped configuring the port, then the Tomcat instance will be unable to start it and you will get the `Port already in use` exception.

```
<!-- A "Connector" represents an endpoint by which requests are received
     and responses are returned. Documentation at :
     Java HTTP Connector: /docs/config/http.html (blocking & non-blocking)
     Java AJP  Connector: /docs/config/ajp.html
     APR (HTTP/AJP) Connector: /docs/apr.html
     Define a non-SSL HTTP/1.1 Connector on port 8080
-->
<Connector port="8080" protocol="HTTP/1.1"
        connectionTimeout="20000"
        redirectPort="8443" />
<!-- A "Connector" using the shared thread pool-->
<!--
```

3. **AJP port**: The following screenshot shows the AJP port configuration for
    Tomcat. This port is used for AJP communication between the Apache HTTP
    and the Tomcat instance. While running multiple instances, if you have
    skipped configuring this port, then the Tomcat instance will be unable to
    start and you will get a `Port already in use` exception.

```
<!-- Define an AJP 1.3 Connector on port 8009 -->
<Connector port="8009" protocol="AJP/1.3" redirectPort="8443" />
```

4. **Cluster attributes**: Enable the cluster attributes for clustering in `server.xml`.
    The following screenshot shows the cluster class used for clustering:

```
<!--For clustering, please take a look at documentation at:
     /docs/cluster-howto.html  (simple how to)
     /docs/config/cluster.html (reference documentation) -->

<Cluster className="org.apache.catalina.ha.tcp.SimpleTcpCluster"/>
```

In horizontal clustering every machine has a separate IP. We have to
configure the broadcast address and port for the instance to connect with
each other and create a cluster session. Add the following code to `server.`
`xml` to enable broadcast setting and replication:

```
<Cluster className="org.apache.catalina.ha.tcp.SimpleTcpCluster"
  channelSendOptions="6">
  <Manager className="org.apache.catalina.ha.session.
    BackupManager" expireSessionsOnShutdown="false"
    notifyListenersOnReplication="true" mapSendOptions="6"/>
  <Channel className="org.apache.catalina.tribes.group.
    GroupChannel">
    <Membership className=
      "org.apache.catalina.tribes.membership.McastService"
      address="228.0.0.4" port="54446" frequency="500"
      dropTime="3500"/>
```

```
      <Receiver className=
        "org.apache.catalina.tribes.transport.nio.NioReceiver"
        address="auto" port="6000" selectorTimeout="100"
        maxThreads="6"/>
      <Sender className=
        "org.apache.catalina.tribes.transport.
        ReplicationTransmitter">
        <Transport className=
          "org.apache.catalina.tribes.transport.nio.
          PooledParallelSender"/>
      </Sender>
    </Channel>
    <Deployer className="org.apache.catalina.ha.deploy.
      FarmWarDeployer" tempDir="/opt/apachetomcat1/tomcat7-temp/"
      deployDir="/opt/apachetomcat1/tomcat7-deploy/"
      watchDir="/opt/apachetomcat1/tomcat7-listen/"
      watchEnabled="false"/>
    <ClusterListener className=
      "org.apache.catalina.ha.session.ClusterSessionListener"/>
  </Cluster>
```

The first highlighted code section shows the multicast IP. Multicast creates a communication change for these two instances. The second highlighted section shows the deployment properties for the cluster instances.

5. **Configuration test**: Run the `configtest.sh` script from TOMCAT_HOME/bin to check the configuration. The following screenshot shows the output for the following `config.sh` command:

   ```
   [root@localhost bin]# ./configtest.sh
   ```

```
[root@localhost bin]# ./configtest.sh
Using CATALINA_BASE:    /opt/apache-tomcat1
Using CATALINA_HOME:    /opt/apache-tomcat1
Using CATALINA_TMPDIR:  /opt/apache-tomcat1/temp
Using JRE_HOME:         /opt/jdk1.6.0_24
Using CLASSPATH:        /opt/apache-tomcat1/bin/bootstrap.jar:/opt/apache-tomcat1/bin/tomcat-juli.jar
Oct 11, 2011 4:55:58 PM org.apache.catalina.core.AprLifecycleListener init
INFO: The APR based Apache Tomcat Native library which allows optimal performance in production environments was not found on the java.library.path: /opt/jdk
1.6.0_24/jre/lib/i386/server:/opt/jdk1.6.0_24/jre/lib/i386:/opt/jdk1.6.0_24/jre/../lib/i386:/usr/java/packages/lib/i386:/lib/i386:/lib:/usr/lib
Oct 11, 2011 4:56:01 PM org.apache.coyote.AbstractProtocolHandler init
INFO: Initializing ProtocolHandler ["http-bio-8080"]
Oct 11, 2011 4:56:01 PM org.apache.coyote.AbstractProtocolHandler init
INFO: Initializing ProtocolHandler ["ajp-bio-8009"]
Oct 11, 2011 4:56:01 PM org.apache.catalina.startup.Catalina load
INFO: Initialization processed in 8569 ms
```

6. **Host entry**: Add the instance IP in the host files (/etc/hosts). The following screenshot shows the output for /etc/hosts file:

```
# Do not remove the following line, or various programs
# that require network functionality will fail.
127.0.0.1               localhost.localdomain localhost
::1             localhost6.localdomain6 localhost6
192.168.1.15    tomcat1
192.168.1.16    tomcat2
~
```

7. **Tomcat instance startup**: Start the instance 1 configuration using the script `startup.sh`. The following screenshot shows the output for the following `startup.sh` script:

[root@localhost bin]# ./startup.sh

```
[root@localhost bin]$ ./startup.sh
Using CATALINA_BASE:    /opt/apache-tomcat1
Using CATALINA_HOME:    /opt/apache-tomcat1
Using CATALINA_TMPDIR:  /opt/apache-tomcat1/temp
Using JRE_HOME:         /opt/jdk1.6.0_24
Using CLASSPATH:        /opt/apache-tomcat1/bin/bootstrap.jar:/opt/apache-tomcat1/bin/tomcat-juli.jar
```

Check the Tomcat instance process using the following mentioned command. The following screenshot displays the output for the following `ps` command:

[root@localhost bin]# ps -ef |grep java

```
[root@localhost bin]$ ps -ef |grep java
root      11766    1 11 17:00 pts/3    00:00:17 /opt/jdk1.6.0_24/bin/java -Djava
m -Xmx512m -XX:MaxPermSize=256m -Dorg.jboss.resolver.warning=true -Dsun.rmi.dgc.
.logging.manager=org.apache.juli.ClassLoaderLogManager -Djava.awt.headless=true
e.port=7091 -Dcom.sun.management.jmxremote.authenticate=false -Dcom.sun.manageme
sspath /opt/apache-tomcat1/bin/bootstrap.jar:/opt/apache-tomcat1/bin/tomcat-juli
-Djava.io.tmpdir=/opt/apache-tomcat1/temp org.apache.catalina.startup.Bootstrap
root      11902 10149  0 17:02 pts/3    00:00:00 grep java
[root@localhost bin]$ []
```

Configuration of instance 2

In order to start the configuration of instance 2, install Tomcat on the other machine and perform the same steps as performed on node 1.

Check `catalina.out` for both the nodes. The following mentioned logs show the activity performed during the startup of the Tomcat instance with the cluster instance. It also gives us complete visibility of the clustering functionality.

```
Oct 11, 2011 5:00:24 PM org.apache.catalina.ha.tcp.SimpleTcpCluster
startInternal
INFO: Cluster is about to start
Oct 11, 2011 5:00:24 PM org.apache.catalina.tribes.transport.
ReceiverBase
bind
INFO: Receiver Server Socket bound to:/192.168.1.15:4000
Oct 11, 2011 5:00:24 PM
org.apache.catalina.tribes.membership.McastServiceImpl setupSocket
# Instance node 1 started on port 4000
to establish cluster membership, start level:4
Oct 11, 2011 5:00:25 PM
org.apache.catalina.tribes.membership.McastServiceImpl waitForMembers
```

```
INFO: Done sleeping, membership established, start level:4
Oct 11, 2011 5:00:25 PM
org.apache.catalina.tribes.membership.McastServiceImpl waitForMembers
INFO: Sleeping for 1000 milliseconds to establish cluster membership,
start
level:8
Oct 11, 2011 5:00:26 PM
org.apache.catalina.tribes.membership.McastServiceImpl waitForMembers
# waiting for other member to join the cluster
INFO: Server startup in 13807 ms
Oct 11, 2011 5:23:42 PM org.apache.catalina.tribes.io.BufferPool
getBufferPool
INFO: Created a buffer pool with max size:104857600 bytes of
type:org.apache.catalina.tribes.io.BufferPool15Impl
Oct 11, 2011 5:23:43 PM org.apache.catalina.ha.tcp.SimpleTcpCluster
memberAdded
```
INFO: Replication member
added:org.apache.catalina.tribes.membership.MemberImpl
[tcp://{192.168.1.16, 0, 0, 1}:4001,{192, 168, 1, 16},4001,
alive=1043, securePort=-1, UDP Port=-1, id={33 91 -59 78 -34 -52
73 -9 -99 124 -53 34 69 21 -40 -82 }, payload={}, command={},
domain={},]
```
#Instance 2 joined the cluster node
```

The following are the logs for node 2:

INFO: Starting Servlet Engine: Apache Tomcat/7.0.12
Oct 11, 2011 5:23:41 PM org.apache.catalina.ha.tcp.SimpleTcpCluster
startInternal
INFO: Cluster is about to start
Oct 11, 2011 5:23:42 PM
org.apache.catalina.tribes.transport.ReceiverBase bind
INFO: Receiver Server Socket bound to:/192.198.1.16:4001
Oct 11, 2011 5:23:42 PM
org.apache.catalina.tribes.membership.McastServiceImpl setupSocket
```
# Instance node 1 started on port 4001
INFO: Setting cluster mcast soTimeout to 500
Oct 11, 2011 5:23:42 PM
org.apache.catalina.tribes.membership.McastServiceImpl waitForMembers
INFO: Sleeping for 1000 milliseconds to establish cluster membership,
start
level:4
```
Oct 11, 2011 5:23:43 PM org.apache.catalina.ha.tcp.SimpleTcpCluster
memberAdded
INFO: Replication member
added:org.apache.catalina.tribes.membership.MemberImpl
[tcp://{192,168, 1, 15}:4000,{127, 0, 0, 1},4000, alive=1398024,
securePort=-1, UDP Port=-1, id={28 42 60 -68 -99 126 64 -35 -118 -
97 7 84 26 20 90 24 }, payload={}, command={}, domain={},]
```
# Instance 1 joined the cluster node 2.
```

In the previously mentioned code, four sections are highlighted. Let's discuss each section briefly:

- The first section shows that `tomcatnode1` is started and ready to receive the cluster message on port 4000.

  ```
  INFO: Receiver Server Socket bound to:/192.168.1.15:4000
  ```

- The second section shows that `tomcatnode2` had joined the cluster, and node 1 is getting the notification.

  ```
  added:org.apache.catalina.tribes.membership.MemberImpl[tcp://
  {192.168.1.16, 0, 0, 1}:4001,{192, 168, 1, 16},4001, alive=1043
  ```

- The third section shows that `tomcatnode2` is started and ready to receive the cluster message on port 4000.

  ```
  INFO: Receiver Server Socket bound to:/192.198.1.16:4001
  ```

- The fourth section shows that `tomcatnode1` had joined the cluster, and node 2 is getting the notification.

  ```
  added:org.apache.catalina.tribes.membership.MemberImpl[tcp://
  {192,168, 1, 15}:4000,{127, 0, 0, 1},4000, alive=1398024
  ```

Apache web server configuration for horizontal clustering

We have done the Tomcat level configuration to configure horizontal clustering on the Tomcat instance. It's time to integrate the Apache web server to Tomcat 7. Let's enable the integration by performing the following steps:

1. We have to create a new file called `mod_jk.conf` in the `conf` directory of `APACHE_HOME/conf` using the following commands:

   ```
   [root@localhost apache-2.0]# cd /opt/apache-2.2.19/conf
   vi mod-jk.conf
   ```

   The following mentioned code defines the configuration parameters for `mod_jk.conf`:

   ```
   LoadModule jk_module modules/mod_jk.so
   JkWorkersFile conf/workers.properties
   JkLogFile logs/mod_jk.log
   JkLogLevel info
   JkMount /sample/* loadbalancer
   JkMount /* loadbalancer
   ```

2. Create a new file named `workers.properties` in the `conf` directory using the following command:

```
[root@localhost conf]# vi workers.properties
```

```
worker.list=tomcatnode1, tomcatnode2, loadbalancer
```

Define the `worker.list` for the entire nodes in the cluster:

```
worker.tomcatnode1.port=8009
worker.tomcatnode1.host=192.168.1.15
worker.tomcatnode1.type=ajp13
worker.tomcatnode1.lbfactor=1
```

The previous lines of code define the `tomcatnode1` properties. The highlighted code shows the IP address of `tomcatnode1`. This is essential for horizontal clustering.

```
worker.tomcatnode2.port=8009
worker.tomcatnode2.host=192.168.1.16
worker.tomcatnode2.type=ajp13
worker.tomcatnode2.lbfactor=1
```

The previous lines of code define the `tomcatnode2` properties. The highlighted code shows the IP address of `tomcatnode2`. This is essential for horizontal clustering.

```
worker.loadbalancer.type=lb
worker.loadbalancer.balanced_workers=tomcatnode1, tomcatnode2
worker.loadbalancer.sticky_session=1
```

The previous lines of code define the load balancing properties for `mod_jk`.

 The only difference in the Apache configuration for `workers.properties` for horizontal and vertical clustering is vertical hosting. (`worker.tomcatnode2.host` is configured as localhost, whereas in horizontal clustering `worker.tomcatnode2.host` is configured with the IP address of a different machine.)

3. The last step is to include the `mod_jk.conf` in the main configuration file of `httpd`, that is `httpd.conf` and reload the Apache services using the following command:

```
[root@localhost conf]# vi httpd.conf
```

 Include `conf/mod_jk.conf` in the end of `httpd.conf`.

Testing of the clustered instance

To perform cluster testing, we are going to take you through a sequence of events. In the following event, we only plan to use two Tomcat instances—tomcatnode1 and tomcatnode2. We will cover the following sequence of events:

1. Start tomcatnode1.

2. Start tomcatnode2 (wait for node 1 to start completely).

3. Node 1 crashes.

4. Node 2 takes over the user session of node 1 to node 2.

5. Start node 1 (wait for node 1 to start completely).

6. Node 2 and node 1 are in running state.

Now we have a good scenario with us, we will walk through how the entire process works:

1. **Start instance 1**: tomcatnode1 starts up using the standard startup sequence. When the host object is created, a cluster object is associated with it. Tomcat asks the cluster class (in this case SimpleTcpCluster) to create a manager for the cluster and the cluster class will start up a membership service.

    The membership service is a mechanism in the cluster instance through the cluster domain, which adds the member node in the cluster. In simple terms, it is a service through which members are able to join the cluster.

2. **Start instance 2**: When Tomcat instance 2 starts up, it follows the same sequence as tomcatnode2 with one difference. The cluster is started and will establish a connection (tomcatnode1, tomcatnode2). tomcatnode2 will now send a request to the server that already exists in the cluster, which is now tomcatinstance2.

    In case the Tomcat instance does not respond within an interval of 60 seconds, then Tomcat instance 2 will update the cluster, and generate the entry in the logs.

3. **Node 1 crashes**: Once the Tomcat instance crashes, the cluster manager will send a notification to all the members, in our case it's `tomcatnode2`. The entire session of node 1 will be replicated to node 2, but the user will not see any issues while browsing the website.

4. **Node 2 will take over the user session of node 1 to node 2**: `tomcatnode2` will process the request as with any other request. User requests are served with node 2.

5. **Start instance 1**: Upon start up, tomcatnode1 first joins the cluster, and then contacts tomcatnode2 for the current state of all the users in the session. It starts serving the user requests and shares the load for node 2.

6. **Node 2 and node 1 are in running state**: Now both the instances are in running state. Node 2 will continue to serve the user requests and once the request is served, it will terminate the user session.

If the previous mentioned test is working, it means clustering is working fine.

Monitoring of Tomcat clustering

Once the cluster is up and working, the next stage is to set up the monitoring of the clustering. This can be done in the following ways:

- Various monitoring tools
- Scripts
- Manual

Following are the steps to manually monitor the clusters:

1. Check the Tomcat process using the following command:
   ```
   root@localhost bin]# ps -ef |grep java
   ```

2. Check the logs to verify the connectivity of the cluster.
3. Verify the URL for both cluster members.

Summary

In this chapter, we have discussed the clustering of Tomcat 7 and its implementation techniques. We have discussed clustering architecture, horizontal and vertical clusters and their benefits, the implementation of horizontal and vertical clustering on Tomcat 7, and the verification of clusters.

In the next chapter, we will discuss the most awaited topic of Tomcat 7, that is, Tomcat 6 upgrade to Tomcat 7 and different techniques used during the upgrade.

10
Tomcat Upgrade

Technological changes and innovations happen at a very rapid pace. In order to accommodate the current technology requirements and serve the user with the latest technology, an upgrade of the systems is needed. The new version of the systems comes with the latest features and bug fixes, making them more stable and reliable.

In this chapter, we will discuss:

- The life cycle of the upgrade process
- Best practices followed by the IT industry
- How to upgrade Tomcat 6 to Tomcat 7

Every organization follows their process to upgrade the servers, based on the criticality of the system. Normally, evaluation of a product is done by the Technical Architect. Based on the application's criticality, the architect defines the architecture, which needs to be followed to upgrade the application. Upgrades in production can be done only after a successful upgrade on the development server(s).

Different types of environment

There are basically four types of environments for any system in an IT industry, based on their architecture. The following figure shows the different environments created in most industries:

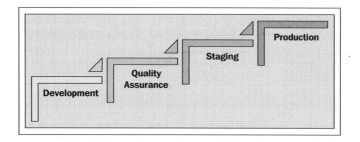

Development environment

It can be defined as the combination of software and hardware, which is required for a team to build the code and deploy it. In simple words, it is a complete package required to build the code and deploy it.

The following points describe why we need a development environment and its advantages:

- Consolidation: For example, by looking at the infrastructure needs of the development environment as a whole, you might find that you only need a single web/application server to deploy the application.

- Estimation of resources: Resources are required to support the development activities and test the development environment, before it is made available on any production infrastructure in support of a business project.

Quality Assurance environment

This environment is mainly used for the integration of the development module and followed by the functional testing undertaken by the Quality Assurance team. If the QA team finds any issues with the functionality of the application, they notify the developers to resolve the issue.

Staging environment

This environment is a replica of the production environment. It is mainly used for performance testing to simulate the real-time issues during the user load.

Production environment

This can be defined as the real environment that is available to the users to perform their operations in the application. For example, banking sites, where you perform your money transactions can be called a production environment.

Life cycle of the upgrade

In this topic, we will discuss the various steps performed during the upgrade. The life cycle consists of the end-to-end processes involved in the upgrade. Normally, upgrades are initiated from the development environment followed by the QA/stage/production environment. The following screenshot shows the basic sequence of steps followed in the upgrade for any system in the IT industry:

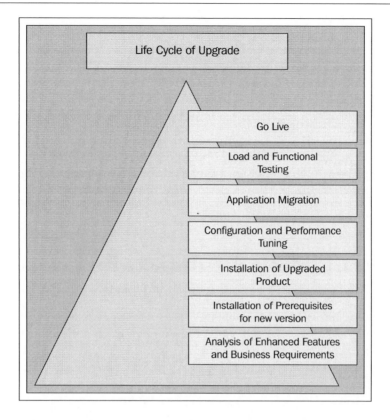

1. **Analysis of Enhanced Features and Business Requirements**: This step plays a very crucial role in the upgrade process. In this process, the standing committee (technical architect, business owner, and functional owner) decides which features are essential for the new version and how they are useful in supporting the business requirement.

2. **Installation of Prerequisites for new version**: By following the previous process, the infrastructure team makes sure that the entire software is available for the installation and their dependencies are also present.

3. **Installation of Upgraded Product**: In this process, the installation of a new version of products will be done by the infrastructure engineer.

4. **Configuration and Performance Tuning**: Once the installation is complete, it's time to do the configuration and performance tuning for the new product.

5. **Application Migration**: After the configuration is done for Tomcat 7, the upgrade is still incomplete. Now, the most tedious part of the migration starts here, that is, application migration from the current environment to the new system.

Before migrating the application from the current environment to the new environment, you need to confirm whether the new version is supported by the application or not. If not, confirm what are the workarounds provided by the vendors.

6. **Load and Functional Testing**: After the application migration is complete, you have to perform the load and functional testing on the upgraded system, in order to make sure that the application is working as excepted, and also that the new features, which are embedded through the upgrade process, are working according to the business requirement.

7. Go live for the new environment.

Tomcat upgrade from 6 to 7

Until now, we have discussed various theoretical processes of the upgrade. Now it's time to have some fun, which every administrator wants in his/her career.

In this topic, we will discuss the most waited topic of the book, that is the Tomcat upgrade. It's always a wish for the web administrator to perform the upgrade from its previous major version to the new version. It also changes the perception of the administrator from day-to-day maintenance issues to the architecture-level integration. If you are involved in the upgrade activity for the product, then you are the first person in the organization who is working on that product, which gives you better visibility among other people. But before performing the upgrade, let's discuss what new features/updates are offered by Tomcat 7 as compared to Tomcat 6. Following are the features:

- Servlet 3.0
    - Asynchronous support
    - Dynamic configuration
    - Extended Servlet API
    - Simpler, faster, more developer-friendly
    - Simplified embedding
    - Improved logging

- System improvement
    - No more memory leaks
    - Security improvement

Now we know what are the advantages of using Tomcat 7, let's start the upgrade from Tomcat 6 to Tomcat 7. In order to initiate the upgrade process, the first thing that comes to mind is, on which hardware do we have to perform the upgrade? There are basically two ways to perform the upgrade:

- On the same system where Tomcat 6 is already running: This approach is used when we have high-end servers, which have enough RAM and CPU to handle the load generated by the new version.

- On a separate system: In today's IT infrastructure, this approach is very common due to increasing trends of virtualization. Here, low-end servers are created, which can only handle the load for the new version of Tomcat 7.

 The major advantage of this approach is that you can run your current operation in parallel during the upgrade, and there is no impact to the current environment.

We will take the second approach for the upgrade since this is the most common approach used in any IT industry.

Prerequisites for Tomcat 7

By default, Tomcat 6 runs on JDK 1.5 and Tomcat 7 requires JDK 1.6, so the major prerequisite for the Tomcat 7 upgrade is the installation of JDK 1.6. In *Chapter 1, Installation of Tomcat 7*, we have discussed the detailed steps of the Java installation. Hence, we will move on to the next installation step.

In case you have to install Tomcat 7 on the same system where Tomcat 6 is running, then you must be thinking how is it possible to set the two different JAVA_HOME or Path? In that case, you have to install Tomcat with a different user and set the JAVA_HOME in the user profile. Also, the same user should have sudo access to run the Tomcat service.

Installation of Tomcat 7 for the upgrade

Once you are done with the installation and configuration of JDK 1.6 on the system, it's time to install Tomcat 7 on the machine. Perform the following steps:

1. Download the latest stable version from the Tomcat official site, http://tomcat.apache.org/download-70.cgi. Once the download is complete, save it in the /opt location.

2. Unzip the Tomcat 7 source, that is `apache-tomcat-7.0.12.zip`, using the following command:

```
[root@localhost opt]# unzip apache-tomcat-7.0.12.zip
```

3. After you unzip `apache-tomcat-7.0.12.zip`, it will create a folder named `apache-tomcat-7.0.12` in the `opt` directory.

4. Go to the `bin` directory of `apache-tomcat-7.0.12` using the following command:

```
[root@localhost opt]# cd apache-tomcat-7.0.12/bin/
```

5. Run the following command. If you miss executing the following command, then Tomcat will not start at the time of starting the services. The reason is that, the package comes with read/write permissions but no execute permissions are given to the package. We have to manually update the permissions.

```
[root@localhost bin]# chmod 0755 *.sh
```

```
[root@localhost bin]# pwd
```

```
/opt/apache-tomcat-7.0.12/bin
```

 `chmod 0755 file` is equivalent to `u=rwx (4+2+1),go=rx (4+1 & 4+1)`. The `0` specifies no special modes.

6. Start the Tomcat services and validate the Tomcat setup.

If you are doing the installation on the same machine, you have to change the default connector port for Tomcat 7, or you will receive the `Port already in use` exception and the services will not begin. To change the default connector port, you have to edit `server.xml`.

Configuration of Tomcat 7

You must be pondering as to whether we are installing or upgrading Tomcat. After reading this section, you will understand the actual upgrade. We will discuss the various configurations needed to be done with reference to Tomcat 7. It should also perform the same functionality as Tomcat 6, with the integration of new features. Let's discuss the configuration in a sequential manner.

JVM configuration

JVM plays a vital role in the performance and maintenance of the J2EE container. It is very important that we should accommodate the old environment's JVM parameters and add the new enhanced features, which are introduced with the new Java SDK version, while upgrading from Tomcat 6 to Tomcat 7. We have to customize the environment, based on the application's requirement. There are many things we have to keep in mind, while configuring JVM. Some of them are mentioned as follows:

- How many applications are currently running on Tomcat 6
- The number of concurrent users
- The current configuration
- Upgrade to 64 bit from 32 bit

Let's do a comparison on the default memory allocation for Tomcat 6 and Tomcat 7. You will find that there are not many significant changes done with reference to memory allocation. But, in practice, when we upgrade the system, we define more JVM memory as compared to the previous version. The reason is that, it has to support the current application and also the enhanced features of the latest version.

```
using thread-local object allocation.
Mark Sweep Compact GC

Heap Configuration:
   MinHeapFreeRatio = 40
   MaxHeapFreeRatio = 70
   MaxHeapSize      = 268435456 (256.0MB)
   NewSize          = 1048576 (1.0MB)
   MaxNewSize       = 4294901760 (4095.9375MB)
   OldSize          = 4194304 (4.0MB)
   NewRatio         = 2
   SurvivorRatio    = 8
   PermSize         = 12582912 (12.0MB)
   MaxPermSize      = 67108864 (64.0MB)
```

The previous screenshot shows the memory structure for Tomcat 6 and the internal division of its components. The following screenshot shows the memory allocation for Tomcat 7. If you compare the systems, you will find that there are not many differences in the architecture of the memory scheme, but in a real-time production environment, this configuration varies from system to system.

```
Heap Configuration:
   MinHeapFreeRatio = 40
   MaxHeapFreeRatio = 70
   MaxHeapSize      = 134217728 (128.0MB)
   NewSize          = 1048576 (1.0MB)
   MaxNewSize       = 4294901760 (4095.9375MB)
   OldSize          = 4194304 (4.0MB)
   NewRatio         = 2
   SurvivorRatio    = 8
   PermSize         = 16777216 (16.0MB)
   MaxPermSize      = 67108864 (64.0MB)
```

If you are upgrading the system from 32 bit to 64 bit, then the memory allocation will be 30 percent more than the current allocated memory on the system.

While doing the upgrade, you have to enable the same configuration parameters with reference to the old version, also, you have to enable the entire customized configuration to the environment. In order to provide support for the application, it helps in maintaining the performance of the Tomcat server. Let's take an example of the Tomcat 6 configuration and implement it with reference to Tomcat 7, as shown in the following lines of code:

```
JAVA_OPTS="-Xms128m -Xmx512m -XX:MaxPermSize=256m
-Dsun.rmi.dgc.client.gcInterval=3600000
-Dsun.rmi.dgc.server.gcInterval=3600000"
```

Now, if you want to do the same configuration with Tomcat 7, then you have to increase the configuration based on the availability of the resource and application requirement as shown in the following lines of code:

```
JAVA_OPTS="-Xms1024m –Xmx1024m -XX:MaxPermSize=256m
  -Dsun.rmi.dgc.client.gcInterval=3600000
  -Dsun.rmi.dgc.server.gcInterval=3600000"
```

The memory leak issue is completely resolved in Tomcat 7. If we increase the JVM memory, then the application will utilize the memory more intensively. Also, this will not cause any issues with the system over a period of time, as compared to the previous version of Tomcat, where we have to recycle Tomcat at regular intervals.

Database connection settings

Database response is very critical in application performance tuning. An insignificant error will also have a big impact on the application. But, if you do the configuration correctly, it will lead to a miracle (we will see the performance results exceeding the benchmark) in the application's performance. Let us compare the datasource configuration between Tomcat 6 and Tomcat 7. The highlighted code in the following lines of code show the difference in configuration for Tomcat 6 and 7:

Tomcat 6:

```
<Resource name="jdbc/myoracle" auth="Container"
  type="javax.sql.DataSource" driverClassName="oracle.jdbc.OracleDriver
  "url="jdbc:oracle:thin:@192.168.0.1:1521:mysid"username="scott"
  password="tiger" maxActive="20" maxIdle="10" maxWait="-1"/>
```

Tomcat 7:

```
<Resource name="jdbc/myoracle" auth="Container"
  type="javax.sql.DataSource" driverClassName="oracle.jdbc.
  OracleDriver" url="jdbc:oracle:thin:@192.168.2.1:1521:mysid"
  username="scott" password="tiger" maxActive="50"
  maxIdle="10" maxWait="-1"/>
```

Tomcat 6 and 7 are connected to different DB servers, but they are connected to the same database using the same username and password. The reason is that, at the time of the upgrade, it's recommended to use the new instances of the database. The advantage of this approach is, if the database crashes, then the current application will have no impact and you can do the upgrade in parallel. Also, you can try different configuration parameters to improve the performance.

> If you are upgrading the environment, it's recommended to use the latest JDBC driver for connecting the database.

Application migration

Application migration is very difficult and a tricky task in the upgrade life cycle. We cannot deploy the application directly. Some of the applications are not compatible with the new version of Tomcat 7 and also with JDK 1.6. In such a situation, we have to build and compile the application in the new version. It is a tricky issue when it comes to application deployment. We cannot directly point the errors without running the application in either TRACE or DEBUG mode. If we analyze the application logs carefully, we will find exceptions such as Path not found and Class not found.

> It's always recommended to check the compatible matrix of the third-party application JAR for the new version of the application.

Following are the steps for application migration:

1. Application recompilation on the JDK supported for Tomcat 7.
2. Upgrade the third-party JAR to the latest version.
3. Deployment of the new application.
4. Testing of the newly deployed application.

Alias configuration

In the current environment, you might have configured many virtual hosts. But you cannot use the same URL for the application, as they point to the old environment. To resolve this issue, you have to configure the dummy URL in the new Tomcat 7 environment for testing purposes. This will help us perform the pre-go live task for the environment.

Following are the steps for Alias configuration:

- **Creation of dummy URL**: By creating the dummy URL, the administrator can check the basic functionality for the application.

- **User testing using dummy URL**: By performing user testing on the new environment, the functional team can verify the application's functionality.

- **Creating CNAME from the current production environment to the new dummy URL**: By creating the **Canonical Name(CNAME)**, we are pointing the old application URL to the new environment.

- **Configuration of the virtual host on Tomcat 7**: By creating the virtual host in Tomcat 7, we let Tomcat know where the application content will be redirected.

The previous processes are followed during the upgrade of Tomcat 6 to Tomcat 7.

ITIL process implementation

Until now, we have discussed the technical process of Tomcat and its configuration. Now it's time to understand the **Information Technology Infrastructure Library (ITIL)** process followed during the upgrade process and its use in different sections of the upgrade, based on the features and implementation methods.

Availability management

It can be defined as the process which allows the organization to make sure its services support at minimal cost to the environment. It consists of the following features:

- **Reliability**: It's a process through which IT components are measured, based on the **Statement of Work (SOW)**.

- **Maintainability**: It's a process through which we manage the entire system without any unplanned downtime.

- **Security**: This service is associated to data. It always refers to the confidentiality, integrity, and availability of that data. The term availability means the entire system service available to the environment.

Capacity management

This support refers to the optimum and cost-effective provision of IT services by helping organizations match their IT resources to their business demands. It is also useful in estimating the project cost for any project or revenue usage for the environment.

Process	Environment
Application sizing	Stage environment
Capacity planning	Development environment or before the project begins
Performance management	Stage environment

Service Transition

Service Transition (ST) is related to the service delivery and often consists of various processes before the go live. Following is the list of ITIL processes in ST:

Process	Environment (used)
Transition planning and support	Post go live support in production
Change management	Before go live in production
Service asset and configuration management	Before go live in production
Release and deployment management	Before go live in production
Service validation and testing	Before go live in production
Change evaluation	Before go live in production
Knowledge management	Development/QA/stage/production

Summary

In this chapter, we have discussed the various strategies used in the upgrade of Tomcat 6 to Tomcat 7 and the various steps followed during the upgrade process such as the life cycle of the upgrade, the upgrade configuration of Tomcat 7, and the DataSource configuration.

In the next chapter, we will discuss the various advanced-level configurations of Tomcat 7 and how they are used in the real-time IT industry such as virtual hosting, multiple instances of Tomcat 7, multiple application deployment, environment configuration, and so on.

11
Advanced Configuration for Apache Tomcat 7

In the previous chapters, we have discussed various topics for Tomcat 7 such as clustering, load balancing and so on. But, in practice, there are some different configurations needed to perform on the system, apart from the Tomcat internal configuration, in order to manage the systems. In this chapter, we will discuss the advanced topics for Tomcat 7, used in real-world industries, to create the web infrastructure and support multiple web applications.

In this chapter, we will discuss the following topics:

- Virtual hosting
- Running multiple applications on a single Tomcat server
- Multiple Tomcat environments such as Development, QA, Stage, and Production
- Tuning cache
- Optimization of Tomcat

Virtual hosting

It's a method through which you can host multiple domain names on the same web server or on a single IP. The concept is called shared hosting, where one server is used to host multiple websites. For example, if you want to host abc.com and xyz.com, and later you want to add one more website on the same web server, that can be achieved by virtual hosting. Basically, there are two types of virtual hosting:

- Name-based virtual hosting
- IP-based virtual hosting

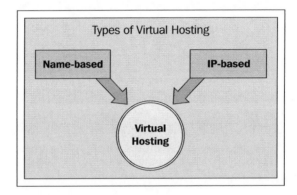

Name-based virtual hosting

It's a method through which you can host multiple domains on a single IP. It uses the concept of shared services. In practice, web hosting companies follow this approach to host multiple sites for a low cost. For example, we have multiple sites such as www.abc.com, www.xyz.com, and www.xzy.com, and we want to configure it on the single web server using a single IP, then name-based virtual hosting is used. Following are the advantages of name-based virtual hosting:

- Putting more than one website on a server using a single IP address
- Easy to configure
- Shared SSL certificates

In case you want to implement a named-based virtual host on the web server, then you have to complete the following prerequisites before doing the configuration.

For example, if you want to host the previous mentioned sites on the web server, then we have to perform the following mentioned methods to configure the **Domain Name Server (DNS)**. Let us assume the web server name is `webserver1.yxz.com` and is hosted on the IP 192.168.0.1. You have to add the following records in your DNS server:

Alias	Resource record	Domain
webserver1.yxz.com	A	192.168.0.1
www.xyz.com	C	webserver1.yxz.com
www.xzy.com	C	webserver1.yxz.com
www.abc.com	C	webserver1.yxz.com

Once these records are created, you can configure the virtual server in the web server configuration.

 A = Address record, used to map the hostname with an IP address.
C= CNAME is used to create multiple aliases for a single hostname.

IP-based virtual hosting

It's a method through which you can host multiple websites on the same server using a different IP. This approach follows the concept of a Dedicated Environment. Here, you can also configure multiple websites on a single server, but the only difference is the domain is configured on a different network interface.

Following are the advantages of IP-based virtual hosting:

- Hosting more than one website on a single server using different network interface addresses (different IP address)
- Dedicated network interface
- Dedicated SSL certificates

In case you want to implement IP-based virtual hosting on the web server, then you have to complete the following prerequisites before doing the configuration.

For example, if you want to host the previously mentioned sites on the web server, then the DNS will be configured in the following manner. Let us assume the web server name `webserver1.yxz.com` is hosted on the IP 192.168.0.1. All the other domains are configured on a different IP (192.168.0.2, 192.168.0.3, and 192.168.0.4), as shown in the following table:

Alias	Record	Domain
`webserver1.yxz.com`	A	192.168.0.1
`www.xyz.com`	A	192.168.0.2
`www.xzy.com`	A	192.168.0.3
`www.abc.com`	A	192.168.0.4

Once these records are created, you can configure the virtual server in the web server configuration.

Virtual hosting in Tomcat 7

Tomcat 7 supports name-based virtual hosting. This approach is very useful in hosting multiple web applications on the single instance of Tomcat 7. It also gives more privileges to the administrator to separate the applications from each other and their access control restrictions. You cannot understand the real concept of virtual hosting unless you implement it. So why wait, let's do the real-life implementation for virtual hosting in Tomcat 7.

For example, if you want to host the previously mentioned sites on the web server, then the DNS will be configured in the following manner. Let us assume the web server name is `webserver1.yxz.com` and is hosted on the IP 192.168.0.1. To implement the previous scenario, the following steps need to be performed:

1. Configure the domain names in the DNS server and reload the DNS services so that it can be replicated on the server. Following are the DNS records with the address and CNAME:

Alias	Record	Domain
`webserver1.yxz.com`	A	192.168.0.1
`www.xyz.com`	C	`webserver1.yxz.com`
`www.xzy.com`	C	`webserver1.yxz.com`
`www.abc.com`	C	`webserver1.yxz.com`

2. For implementing virtual hosting, you have to edit `server.xml`, which is present in `TOMCAT_HOME/conf`. The following entries need to be added for the virtual host, as shown in the following screenshot:

```
<Host name="www.xyz.com" appBase="../Webapps">
  <Context path="" docBase="."/>
</Host>
```

```
        </Host>
<!-- Setting for virtual hosting -->
<Host name="www.xyz.com" appBase="../Webapps">
        <Context path="" docBase="."/>
        </Host>

<Host name="www.xzy.com" appBase="../Webapps">
        <Context path="" docBase="."/>
        </Host>

<Host name="www.abc.com" appBase="../Webapps">
        <Context path="" docBase="."/>
        </Host>


        </Engine>
```

3. Once configuration is done, add the new DNS in the `hosts` file found in `/etc/hosts` in Linux, and `C:\Windows\System32\drivers\etc\` in Windows. The following screenshot shows the addition of a different hostname and IP address in the `hosts` file:

```
127.0.0.1                 localhost.localdomain localhost
::1             localhost6.localdomain6 localhost6
# Below are the entries for tomcat virtual host
192.168.0.1     webserver1.yxz.com
192.168.0.1             www.xyz.com
192.168.0.1             www.xzy.com
192.168.0.1             www.abc.com
```

4. Save the configuration, followed by the recycle, and check the logs if any errors persist.

5. Check the URLs www.xyz.com, www.xzy.com, www.abc.com in the browser.

Hostname aliases

There is one more important feature that comes with Tomcat 7 called **Host name aliases**. It's a very good feature that gives freedom to the administrator for multiple sites on the same network

For example, if you have a website which needs to be accessed through a subdomain by different users, then host aliases are created. It's also called **Sub domain aliases** for the main domain. It is not possible to implement aliases in the previous versions of Tomcat. In case we want to implement aliases for any website, we have to use Apache, IIS, or a separate web server before Tomcat as a front-end server.

The following mentioned code describes how to set the alias for a particular site:

```
<Host name="www.xyz.com" appBase="../Webapps">
  <Context path="" docBase="."/>
  <Alias>tomcatalias.com</Alias>
</Host>
```

Followed by recycle, once the system is up, you can browse the same application with different names.

Multiple applications hosting on a single Tomcat 7 instance

Once we are done with virtual hosting, a few potential problems may arise such as multiple application hosting, security, and deployment of multiple applications on a single instance of Tomcat 7. Configuration of multiple domains on one single instance of Tomcat 7 is a bit tricky. If we give the applications one document root, then all applications can be accessed by all developers. The solution is to implement a separate document root for each domain. This way, we can implement a separate security on each application that is hosted in the Tomcat instance. Let us implement the solution by creating multiple document roots in Tomcat 7. To do so, we have to edit the `server.xml` to enable multiple document roots in the server, as shown in the following code snippet:

```
<Host name="www.xyz.com" appBase="../home/tomcatuser1">
  <Context path="" docBase="/home/tomcatuser1/data"/>
  <Alias>tomcatalias.com</Alias>
</Host>
```

If we implement the separate document root on every application, then we can implement user security for the application at the OS level. By making these changes, we can give every developer different rights to access the code, based on their role. Also, every developer can access the code and deploy the code separately.

```
<Host name="www.xyz.com" appBase="../home/tomcatuser1">
        <Context path="" docBase="/home/tomcatuser1/data"/>
<Alias>tomcatalias.com</Alias>

    </Host>

<Host name="www.xyz.com" appBase="../home/tomcatuser2">
        <Context path="" docBase="/home/tomcatuser2/data"/>
<Alias>tomcatalias1.com</Alias>

    </Host>

<Host name="www.xyz.com" appBase="../home/tomcatuser3">
        <Context path="" docBase="/home/tomcatuser3/data"/>
<Alias>tomcatalias2.com</Alias>
```

Multiple Tomcat environments— Development/QA/Stage/Production

Information technology organizations follow a set of environments to manage their applications. These environments are based on their functionality and usage. Support available for any environment depends on the environment's functionality. Based on the functionality, the production environment has a high priority and development the least priority, as shown in the following figure:

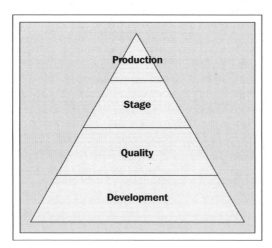

The following table compares the different environments and their functionalities with respect to different tasks performed during creation and management of the web infrastructure:

Task	Development	QA	Stage	Production
Auto deployment	Yes	Yes	No	No
Single machine	Yes	No	No	No
Clustering	No	Yes	Yes	Yes
Developer access	Yes	Yes	No	No
High-end machine	No	No	Yes	Yes
Change control	No	No	No	Yes
Performance testing	No	No	Yes	No
Functional testing	No	Yes	No	No

Tuning cache

When we are running multiple applications on Tomcat 7, it is always recommended to utilize the resource correctly. In order to do so, we need to optimize the tuning parameter. Every time the server receives a request, it consumes the amount of CPU and memory in the system. In order to resolve this problem, we generate cache on the server from the first request. One of the best examples used for caching in major web hosting organizations is to generate cache for the static content.

The following code shows the configuration for adding Expires and Cache-Control: max-age= headers to images, CSS, and JavaScript. This code is added in web.xml, which is present in TOMCAT_HOME/CONF.

```
<filter>
  <filter-name>ExpiresFilter</filter-name>
  <filter-class>org.apache.catalina.filters.ExpiresFilter</filter-
class>
  <init-param>
    <param-name>ExpiresByType image</param-name>
    <param-value>access plus 15 minutes</param-value>
  </init-param>
  <init-param>
    <param-name>ExpiresByType text/css</param-name>
    <param-value>access plus 15 minutes</param-value>
  </init-param>
  <init-param>
```

```
      <param-name>ExpiresByType text/javascript</param-name>
      <param-value>access plus 15 minutes</param-value>
   </init-param>
  </filter>
  <filter-mapping>
    <filter-name>ExpiresFilter</filter-name>
    <url-pattern>/*</url-pattern>
    <dispatcher>REQUEST</dispatcher>
  </filter-mapping>
```

Optimization of Tomcat 7

In *Chapter 3*, *Performance Tuning*, we have discussed various optimization methods for Tomcat at the software level, but until now, we have not done any system-level configurations. We will now discuss the various optimization methods, which are required for system administrators to make their work more successful. One of the most important things required is to run the Tomcat services as a non-privileged user.

Running Tomcat 7 as a non privileged user

It is not recommended way to run Tomcat as the root, because of security reasons and IT compliance policies. To resolve this issue, you have to run Tomcat as a non-privileged user. To implement this, you have to perform the following changes in the user permission. Let us assume tomcatuser1 will run the Tomcat server as a non-privileged user.

```
# groupadd tomcatuser1
# useradd -g tomcatuser1 -d /opt/apache-tomcat1
# chown -R tomcatuser1:tomcatuser1 /opt/apache-tomcat1
```

Once you change the permission at the OS level, it's time to set tomcat to run as a service. Now, copy the startup scripts in /etc/init.d using the following commands:

```
cp /opt/apache-tomcat1/bin/startup.sh /etc/init.d/tomcat
cd /etc/rc5.d
sudo ln -s ../init.d/tomcat S71tomcat
```

You have now created tomcat as a service. But before running the service, you have to change the permission to make it executable, then run the service as tomcat using the following command:

```
chown    0755   /etc/init.d/tomcat
```

Now we are ready to run tomcat as a service.

Summary

In this chapter, we have discussed the advanced configuration of Tomcat 7 and optimization parameters, key points covered in the environment such as virtual hosting, features of Development/QA/Stage/Production, Tomcat as a service, and running Tomcat as a non privileged user.

With this chapter, we have completed the journey of Tomcat 7. In this book, I have tried to complete major issues, which the web administrators and IT administrators face in day-to-day environments. I hope by reading the topics, you have gained enough confidence in running Tomcat 7 in real-time environments.

Best of luck!

Tanuj Khare

Index

Symbols

%a 158
%A 87, 158
%b 158
%B 87, 158
%C 87
%D 87, 158
%h 158
%H 158
%I 158
%l 158
%m 158
%p 158
%q 158
%r 158
%s 158
%S 158
%t 158
%T 87, 158
%u 158
%U 158
%v 158
.rar files 60
.war files 60
-Xms parameter 86
-Xmx parameter 86
-Xss parameter 86
-XX:-CITime parameter 86
-XX:-HeapDumpOnOutOfMemoryError 86
-XX:MaxPermSize=64m parameter 86
-XX:-PrintClassHistogram parameter 87
-XX:+ScavengeBeforeFullGC parameter 86
--XX:-UseParallelGC parameter 86

A

access log
  about 151
  pattern format 151
AJP 74
ApacheBench (ab) 188
Apache Extension Tool. *See* APXS
Apache HTTP
  installation 93
Apache HTTP installation, on Linux
  steps 100-104
Apache HTTP installation, on Windows
  Apache service, monitoring 99
  steps 94-98
Apache HTTP server 91
  about 92
  features 92
Apache Jserv protocol
  about 109
  mod_jk, comparing with mod_proxy 117
  mod_jk, configuring 109-116
  mod_jk, installing 109-115
  mod_proxy, comparing with mod_jk 117
Apache JServ Protocol. *See* AJP
Apache monitor console 32
Apache Monitor tool 99
Apache Portable Runtime. *See* APR
Apache Portable Runtime Utility (APR-util) 104
Apache Tomcat. *See* Tomcat
Apache Tomcat 7
  about 10
  aliases 11

enhancements 10, 11, 13
features 10, 11, 13
improved Logging 11
Servlet 3.0 10
web application memory leak detection 10
Apache Tomcat 7 installation
about 27
errors 37
on Linux environment 31, 32
on Windows environment 27-31
services setup 32
status, verifying 36
troubleshooting 37
Apache Tomcat integration
common issues 121, 122
troubleshooting 121, 122
Apache Tomcat version 7.0 7
appenders
about 147
ConsoleAppender 147
FileAppender 147
SocketAppender 147
application deployment ways in, Tomcat 7
ANT scripts, using 65
diagram 63
TCD (Tomcat Deployer) 65
Tomcat Manager 64, 65
unpacked deployment 64
war deployment 64
application list, Tomcat 7
about 198
application details 198
application response 199
JSP 200
servlet details 199
application log 149
application slowness issue troubleshooting
about 166
database level troubleshooting 171
Tomcat 7 troubleshooting 170, 171
user end troubleshooting 166, 167
web server troubleshooting 167-169
APR 74 103
APR/APR-util
installing 104-109
APR-iconv 104
apt-get command 109

APXS 110
architecture, clustering
horizontal clustering 219, 220
vertical clustering 218
availability management, features
maintainability 250
reliability 250
security 251
awk command 159

B

benefits, clustering
high availability 217
scalability 216
bin directory 146

C

cache
tuning 260
Canonical Name(CNAME) 250
CATALINA_OPTS parameter 202
catalina.policy
about 127
Catalina Code permissions 128
System Code permissions 127
Web application permissions 129, 130
catalina.properties 126
Certificate Signing Request. *See* **CSR**
cluster 216
clustered instance
testing 237
clustered instance, testing
steps 237, 238
clustering
architecture 217
benefits 216
cloud computing 217
high performance 217
limitations 217
common databases
datasource, comparing 49
complete server status, Tomcat 7
application list 198
connections on AJP 201
connections on HTTP port (8080) 200
JVM 200

config.sh command 223, 232
configtest command 123
configuration
   troubleshooting 65-67
configuration files 39-41
configuration files, properties
   catalina.policy 40
   catalina.properties 40
   context.xml 41
   logging.properties 40
   server.xml 40
   tomcat-users.xml 40
   web.xml 40
connector types, Tomcat 7
   about 73
   APR (AJP/HTTP) Connector 74
   Java AJP Connector 74
   Java HTTP Connector 74
console log 150
Context path
   about 55
   enabling, ways 56
Context path, enabling
   command-line configuration in server.xml
      58, 59
   GUI, Tomcat Web Application Manager
      used 56-58
CSR 139

D

Database Connection Pool. *See* DBCP
database level troubleshooting
   about 171
   JVM analysis 172, 173
   Telnet DB server IP port 171, 172
database-related issues
   broken pipe exception 185, 186
   database connectivity exception 187, 188
   timeout waiting 187
database server
   setup, monitoring 193, 194
datasource
   about 44
   for MySQL 47
   for Oracle 45, 46
   for PostgreSQL 48

   in production 44
datasource comparison
   Context path 55
   MySQL 49
   Oracle 49
   PostgreSQL 50
   Tomcat Manager configuration 50
DataSource configuration, Tomcat 7 configu-
    ration
   datasource 44
   JNDI 44
DBCP 44
Demilitarized Zone (DMZ) 44, 132
deployment
   common issues 65
   staging model 62
   types 62
deployment tools
   deploy 61
   redeploy 61
   start 61
   stop 61
   undeploy 61
Deploy tab 64
development environment
   advantages 242
   need for 242
document root 59
Document Type Definition. *See* DTD
Domain Name Server (DNS) 255
DTD 46
Dynamic MBeans 210

E

environment types
   development environment 242
   diagram 241
   production environment 242
   Quality Assurance environment 242
   staging environment 242
errors, in Apache Tomcat 7 installation
   java binary permission 37
   log error 38

F

features, Apache HTTP server

clustering 92
decorator 93
modules 93
multiple website hosting 93
security 93
speed 92
static content 92

G

garbage collection collectors
  concurrent collector, features 84
  parallel collector, features 83
  serial collector, features 83
Garbage Collection (GC) 82
grep command 159

H

head command 171
heap size, Tomcat 7
  garbage collection 82
  garbage collection, facts 82
  garbage collection, types 83
  garbage collection, working 82
history, Tomcat
  support matrix 8
  version 3.0.x 8
  version 3.3.2 8
  version 4.1.40 8
  version 5.5.32 8
  version 6.0.32 8
  version 7.0.0 beta 8
  version 7.0.11 8
  version 7.0.12 8
horizontal cluster configuration, in Tomcat 7
  instance 1 230-232
  instance 2 233, 234
horizontal clustering
  about 219, 220
  advantages 220
  Apache web server, configuring 235, 236
  disadvantages 220
horizontal clustering, in Tomcat 7
  configuring, steps 230
  prerequisites 229
host manager
  pattern 152

Host name aliases 258

I

IIS integration, with Tomcat 7
  prerequisites 117
  steps 118-120
Information Technology Infrastructure
    Library. See ITIL process implemen-
    tation
installation, Apache HTTP
  about 93
  on Linux 100-103
  on Windows 94
  types 93
instance 1 configuration, horizontal cluster
  AJP port 231
  cluster attributes 231, 232
  configuration test 232
  connector port 230
  host entry 232
  shutdown port 230
  Tomcat instance startup 233
instance 1 configuration, vertical cluster
  AJP port 222
  cluster attributes 223
  configuration test 223
  connector port 222
  Shutdown port 222
  Tomcat instance startup 223
instance 2 configuration 233, 234
Internet 125
IP-based virtual hosting, virtual
    configuration
  about 255
  advantages 255
  example 256
iptables command 137
issues, web administrators
  application 164
  database 164
  network 164
  OS/Hardware 164
  user access 164
issue troubleshooting
  about 165
  application slowness 165, 166

ITIL process implementation
  about 250
  availability management 250
  capacity management 251
  Service Transition (ST) 251

J

jar files 60
Java AJP Connector 74
Java Blocking Connector. *See* BIO
Java Database Connectivity. *See* JDBC
Java Development Kit. *See* JDK
Java logging API. *See* JULI
Java Management Extension. *See* JMX
Java Monitoring and Management Console.
      See **JConsole**
Java Naming and Directory Interface. *See*
      JNDI
JavaServer Pages. *See* **JSP**
JConsole
  about 201
  tabs 205
JConsole configuration
  on Tomcat 201
JConsole configuration, on Tomcat 7
  about 201
  advantages 205
  connecting to 203, 204
  remote JMX enabling 202
JDBC 44
JDK 11
JIT 11
JMAP
  options 79
  syntax 79, 81
jmap command 81, 172
JMAP, options
  -dump 79
  -finalizerinfo 79
  -heap 79
  -histo 79
  -permstat 79
JMeter
  advantages 189
JMX 202

JNDI 44
JSP 7
jstack
  -f option 175
  -l option 175
  -m option 175
  using, for thread dump 175
JStack on 64 bit OS 176
JStack on Windows 176
JULI
  about 146
  log level 157
Just in Time. *See* JIT
JVM memory, components
  eden space 173
  from space 173
  heap configuration 173
  heap usage 173
  perm generation 173
  tenured generation 173
  to space 173
JVM (memory) issues
  about 183
  OutOfMemoryError 183, 184
  Out of memory exception 183
  Stack over flow exception 184, 185
JVM options
  about 84
  behavioral options 86
  debugging options 87
  non-standard options 85, 87
  parameter, in logs 87
  performance options 86
  standard options 84
  SurvivorRatio 87
JVM tuning 77
JVM tuning, for Tomcat
  heap size, increasing 81, 82
  JMAP 79
  JVM options 84
  need for 78

K

keytool 140
kill command
  using, for thread dump 174, 175

L

layout 148
lifecycle, Tomcat upgradation
  about 242
  steps 243
limitations, clustering
  cost 217
  monitoring 217
Linux
  Apache Tomcat 7, installing 31, 32
  Java, installing 15-18
Load testing 188
Log4j
  about 155
  advantage 155
  log level 155, 157
  log level mapping 157
  using 156, 157
log analysis
  about 159
  awk command 159
  commands 160
  grep command 159
log file 113
loggers 147
logging services
  about 145
  components, appenders 147
  components, layout 148
  components, loggers 147
  disadvantage 145
logging types, Tomcat 7
  about 148
  access log 151, 152
  application log 149
  console log 149, 150
  host manager 152
  server log 149
log level, for Log4j
  about 114, 155
  DEBUG 156
  ERROR 155
  FATAL 155
  INFO 156
  OFF 155
  TRACE 156

WARN 155
log levels types, Tomcat 7
  CONFIG 154
  FINE 154
  FINER 154
  FINEST(least) 154
  INFO 154
  SEVERE(highest) 154
  WARNING 154

M

make command 122
Managed Beans. *See* MBeans
maxKeepAlive 77
max threads 76
MBeans
  about 209
  features 209
  types 210
MD5 Message-Digest Algorithm 13
Membership service 237
Memory overview tab
  features 205
Microsoft Management Console. *See* MMC
MMC 32
Model MBeans 210
mod_jk
  about 109
  comparing, with mod_proxy 117
  configuring 110-115
  installing 110
mod_proxy
  configuring 116
Module path 113
monitoring 191
monitoring, ways
  diagram 192
  manual 193
  scripts 193
  third-party tools 192
multiple applications hosting
  on single Tomcat 7 instance 258, 259
multiple Tomcat environment
  about 259
  development 260
  production 260

quality 260
stage 260

N

name-based virtual hosting, virtual configuration
about 254
advantages 254
example 254
netsh command 136
non-standard, JVM options
behavioral options 85
debugging options 86
performance tuning options 85
non-Tomcat settings
about 135
Firewall 136, 137
password 137, 138
service, as separate user 135

O

Open MBeans 210
OpenPGP 125
Open Specification for Pretty Good Privacy.
See **OpenPGP**
OpenSTA 188
optimization, Tomcat 7
about 261
running, as non-privileged user 261
OS environment variables configuration
global path variable, setting in Windows
23, 24
JAVA_HOME 21
JAVA_HOME, setting in Linux 25-27
JAVA_HOME, setting in Windows 22, 23
PATH variable, setting in Windows 22, 23
OS tuning
about 88
files size 88
huge page size 88, 89
performance characteristics 88
Ulimits 88
Overview tab
features 207, 208

P

pattern format, access log
class name 151
directory 151
pattern 152
prefix 151
suffix 152
performance tuning, Tomcat 7
application code 70
aspects 70
database tuning 71
Infrastructure and OS 71
JVM Tuning 71
middleware services 71
need for 70
process flow 72, 73
starting with 71
PID
about 78
finding 172
prerequisites, Tomcat 7 installation
about 14
Java installation 14, 15
OS environment variables configuration 21
Process ID. *See* **PID**
ps command 224

R

Remote Method Invocation. *See* **RMI**
RMI 202
Root Cause Analysis (RCA) 73

S

Samurai
using, for thread dump analysis 177, 178
security permission, Tomcat
catalina.policy 127
catalina.properties 126, 127
server.xml 131
tomcat-users.xml 131
self-signed certificate, SSL certificate 139
server log 149
server status summary

for connections on AJP 198
for connections on HTTP port 197
for JVM 197
service setup, Apache Tomcat 7 installation
in Linux 33, 34
in Windows 32
shutdown script 35
startup script 35
Servlet 3.0, Apache Tomcat 7
about 10
Annotation-based Configuration 11
Asynchronous Support 10
Dynamic Configuration 10
software download, Tomcat 7 installation
about 12
binary package 13
integrity check, performing 13
RPM, advantages 14
source 14
SSL configuration, on Tomcat 7
need for 139
SSL certificate, types 139
SSL installation, steps 139-142
staging model, deployment
external_stage 63
nostage 62
stage 62
Standard MBeans 210
start() method 182
Statement of Work (SOW) 250

T

tabs, JConsole
about 205
MBeans 209
memory overview 205
Overview 207, 208
threads overview 206
VM Summary 207, 208
TDA
about 176
advantages 178
thread states, types 181
using, for thread dump analysis 178-180
thread dump
analyzing, for Tomcat instance 176

analyzing, Samurai used 177, 178
analyzing, Thread Dump Analyzer used
178-182
errors 182
errors, types 182
obtaining, jstack used 175
obtaining, kill command used 174, 175
Thread Dump Analyzer. *See* **TDA**
thread optimization, Tomcat 7
about 75
dedicated thread pool 76
maxKeepAlive 77
max threads 76
shared thread pool 75, 76
Threads overview tab
features 206
thread states, types
Alive but not runnable 182
blocked 182
dead 182
runnable 182
waiting 182
Tomcat
features 9
history 8
security permission 126
support matrix 8
upgrading 241
Tomcat 6 to Tomcat 7 upgradation
Tomcat 7, configuring 246
Tomcat 7, features 244, 245
Tomcat 7, installing 245, 246
Tomcat 7, prerequisites 245
ways 245
Tomcat 7
advanced configuration 253
application deployment, ways 63
complete server status 198
configuration 41
customized policies 128
DataSource configuration 42, 43
deploying 59
heap size, increasing 81, 82
horizontal clustering 229
IIS, integrating with 117
JConsole configuration 201
logging services 145

logging types 148
log levels, types 153
monitoring 191, 196
monitoring, ways 192
optimization 261
performance tuning 69
securing 132
SSL configuration 139
thread dump, obtaining 174
Tomcat Manager 194
troubleshooting 163
tuning components 73, 75
values 157
vertical clustering 220
virtual hosting 256, 257
Tomcat 7 configuration
alias configuration 250
application migration 249
application migration, steps 249
database connection settings 248
JVM configuration 247, 248
Tomcat 7 deployment
about 59
WebArchive structure 59
Tomcat 7 installation
about 12
prerequisites 14
software, downloading 12
Tomcat 7, monitoring in
Server Status 196, 197, 198
Tomcat 7, securing
non Tomcat settings 135
Tomcat settings 133
Tomcat clustering
monitoring, manual ways 238
monitoring, ways 238
Tomcat instance
installing 230
Tomcat Manager
about 125
enabling 132
enabling, steps 132
Tomcat Manager configuration
enabling 51, 52, 53
features 50
server status 54, 55
Tomcat Manager, Tomcat 7

accessing 194
advantages 194
features 196
Tomcat settings
about 133
Connector Port 133, 134
hot deployment, disabling 135
package removing, advantages 134, 135
Tomcat upgradation
environment types 241
ITIL process implementation 250
lifecycle 242
Tomcat 6 to Tomcat 7 244
tomcat-users.xml 131
**Tomcat Web Application Manager
     console 56**
troubleshooting 163
tuning components, Tomcat 7
connector types 73
thread optimization 75
types, MBeans
Attributes section, in Connector 211
Dynamic MBeans 210
Model MBeans 210
Notification section, in Connector 213
Open MBeans 210
Operation section, in Connector 212
Standard MBeans 210

U

URL mapping 113
User request flow 91, 92

V

values, Tomcat 7
%a 158
%A 158
%b 158
%B 158
%D 158
%h 158
%H 158
%I 158
%l 158
%m 158
%p 158

%q 158
%r 158
%s 158
%S 158
%t 158
%T 158
%u 158
%U 158
%v 158
vertical clustering
  about 218
  advantages 218
  disadvantages 219
vertical clustering, in Tomcat 7
  Apache web server configuration 228
  instance 1, configuring 222, 223
  instance 2, configuring 224-227
  steps 220
  Tomcat instance, installing 221
  vertical cluster, configuring 221
virtual configuration
  about 254
  IP-based virtual hosting 255
  name-based virtual hosting 254
virtual hosting, Tomcat 7
  about 256

  example 256, 257
Virtual Machine (VM) 15
VM Summary tab
  features 207, 208
VPN 194

W

web administrators
  issues 164
  middleware environment, components 164
web application
  setup, monitoring 193, 194
WebArchive
  archive directories, exploding 60
  Archive Files 60
  deployment operations 61, 62
Web server benchmarking
  about 188
  ApacheBench 188
  JMeter 189
Windows
  Apache Tomcat 7, installing 27-31
  global path variable, setting 23, 24
  Java, installing 19, 20
Worker file path 113

Thank you for buying
Apache Tomcat 7 Essentials

About Packt Publishing

Packt, pronounced 'packed', published its first book "*Mastering phpMyAdmin for Effective MySQL Management*" in April 2004 and subsequently continued to specialize in publishing highly focused books on specific technologies and solutions.

Our books and publications share the experiences of your fellow IT professionals in adapting and customizing today's systems, applications, and frameworks. Our solution based books give you the knowledge and power to customize the software and technologies you're using to get the job done. Packt books are more specific and less general than the IT books you have seen in the past. Our unique business model allows us to bring you more focused information, giving you more of what you need to know, and less of what you don't.

Packt is a modern, yet unique publishing company, which focuses on producing quality, cutting-edge books for communities of developers, administrators, and newbies alike. For more information, please visit our website: www.packtpub.com.

About Packt Open Source

In 2010, Packt launched two new brands, Packt Open Source and Packt Enterprise, in order to continue its focus on specialization. This book is part of the Packt Open Source brand, home to books published on software built around Open Source licences, and offering information to anybody from advanced developers to budding web designers. The Open Source brand also runs Packt's Open Source Royalty Scheme, by which Packt gives a royalty to each Open Source project about whose software a book is sold.

Writing for Packt

We welcome all inquiries from people who are interested in authoring. Book proposals should be sent to author@packtpub.com. If your book idea is still at an early stage and you would like to discuss it first before writing a formal book proposal, contact us; one of our commissioning editors will get in touch with you.

We're not just looking for published authors; if you have strong technical skills but no writing experience, our experienced editors can help you develop a writing career, or simply get some additional reward for your expertise.

Nginx HTTP Server

ISBN: 978-1-849510-86-8   Paperback: 348 pages

Adopt Nginx for your web applications to make the most of your infrastructure and serve pages faster than ever

1. Get started with Nginx to serve websites faster and safer

2. Learn to configure your servers and virtual hosts efficiently

3. Set up Nginx to work with PHP and other applications via FastCGI

4. Explore possible interactions between Nginx and Apache to get the best of both worlds

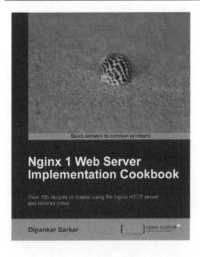

Nginx 1 Web Server Implementation Cookbook

ISBN: 978-1-84951-496-5   Paperback: 236 pages

Over 100 recipes to master using the Nginx HTTP server and reverse proxy

1. Quick recipes and practical techniques to help you maximize your experience with Nginx

2. Interesting recipes that will help you optimize your web stack and get more out of your existing setup

3. Secure your website and prevent your setup from being compromised using SSL and rate-limiting techniques

Please check **www.PacktPub.com** for information on our titles

NetBeans IDE 7
Cookbook

Over 70 highly focused practical recipes to maximize your output
with NetBeans

Rhawi Dantas

NetBeans IDE 7 Cookbook

ISBN: 978-1-84951-250-3   Paperback: 308 pages

Over 70 highly focused practical recipes to maximize
your output with NetBeans

1. Covers the full spectrum of features offered by
   the NetBeans IDE

2. Discover ready-to-implement solutions for
   developing desktop and web applications

3. Learn how to deploy, debug, and test your
   software using NetBeans IDE

4. Another title in Packt's Cookbook series giving
   clear, real-world solutions to common practical
   problems

Google App Engine Java and
GWT Application Development

Build powerful, scalable, and interactive
web applications in the cloud

Daniel Guermeur   Amy Unruh

Google App Engine Java and GWT Application Development

ISBN: 978-1-84969-044-7   Paperback: 480 pages

Build powerful, scalable, and interactive web
applications in the cloud

1. Comprehensive coverage of building scalable,
   modular, and maintainable applications with
   GWT and GAE using Java

2. Leverage the Google App Engine services
   and enhance your app functionality and
   performance

3. Integrate your application with Google
   Accounts, Facebook, and Twitter

4. Safely deploy, monitor, and maintain your GAE
   applications

Please check **www.PacktPub.com** for information on our titles

2204247R00156

Printed in Great Britain
by Amazon.co.uk, Ltd.,
Marston Gate.